T0366927

JUSTIN

II

LCL 558

JUSTIN

EPITOME OF
POMPEIUS TROGUS

BOOKS 21–44

EDITED AND TRANSLATED BY

J. C. YARDLEY

INTRODUCTION AND NOTES BY

DEXTER HOYOS

HARVARD UNIVERSITY PRESS
CAMBRIDGE, MASSACHUSETTS
LONDON, ENGLAND
2024

Library of Congress Control Number 2023051825
CIP data available from the Library of Congress

ISBN 978-0-674-99761-5

*Composed in ZephGreek and ZephText by
Technologies 'N Typography, Merrimac, Massachusetts.
Printed on acid-free paper and bound by
Maple Press, York, Pennsylvania*

CONTENTS

CONTENTS

EPITOME OF
POMPEIUS TROGUS

LIBER XXI

1. Extincto in Sicilia Dionysio tyranno in locum eius milites maximum natu ex filiis eius, nomine Dionysium, suf-
2 fecere, et naturae ius secuti, et quod firmius futurum esse
regnum, si penes unum remansisset, quam si portionibus
3 inter plures filios divideretur, arbitrantur. Sed Dionysius
inter initia regni avunculos fratrum suorum veluti aemulos
imperii sui hortatoresque puerorum ad divisionem regni
4 tollere gestiebat. Quare paulisper dissimulatum animum
prius ad favorem popularium conciliandum intendit, excusatius facturus quod statuerat, si probatus ante omnibus
5 foret. Igitur nexorum tria milia carcere dimittit, tributa
populo per triennium remittit, quibuscumque delenimen-
6 tis potest animos omnium sollicitat. Tunc ad destinatum
7 facinus conversus non cognatos tantum fratrum, sed etiam
ipsos interficit, ut, quibus consortium regni debebat, ne
spiritus quidem consortium relinqueret, tyrannidem in
suos prius quam in exteros auspicatus.

---

1 Dionysius II, who ruled for ten years from 367, was treated
by Philistus in two books down to 363/2 (Diod. Sic. 15.89.3),
though again Trogus' immediate source will have been Timaeus.
The succession occurs at Diod. Sic. 15.74, and events thereafter
are interwoven in Diodorus' account through Book 16. Though
expelled in 356, Dionysius regained the tyranny in 347, only to be
ousted again in 343, at which time he went to Corinth. Justin
omits the part played by Dion and Timoleon, both of whom enjoy

BOOK XXI

1. When the tyrant Dionysius was killed in Sicily his soldiers replaced him with the eldest of his sons, also called Dionysius,[1] thus following the natural order and also thinking the kingdom would be more stable in future if it remained with one man than if it were divided piecemeal among several sons.[2] But Dionysius at the start of his reign was eager to eliminate the uncles of his brothers as rivals for power and men who would urge their children to divide the kingdom. So temporarily veiling his intentions he first focused on winning popular support to make what he had decided on more acceptable if he first won general approval. So he released three thousand convicts from prison, granted the people a three-year tax remission, and with all manner of enticements tried to win everyone over. Then turning to the crime he had planned he killed not only the relatives of his brothers but even the brothers themselves, so that to those to whom he owed partnership in the kingdom he left not even partnership in life, inaugurating his tyranny with his own family rather than strangers.

biographies by Plutarch. See R. A. Talbert, *Timoleon and the Revival of Greek Sicily* (Cambridge, 1974).

[2] Neither Dionysius I nor his son were officially kings; they held the title of "supreme general" (*strategos autokrator*) of Syracuse, and at times *archon* (ruler).

2. Sublatis deinde aemulis in segnitiam lapsus saginam corporis ex nimia luxuria oculorumque valetudinem contraxit, adeo ut non solem, non pulverem, non denique 2 splendorem ferre lucis ipsius posset. Propter quae dum contemni se putat, saevitia grassatur nec, ut pater, carce- 3 rem nexis, sed caedibus civitatem replet; ob quae non 4 contemptior omnibus quam invisior fuit. Itaque cum bellum adversus eum Syracusani decrevissent, diu dubitavit, 5 imperium deponeret an bello resisteret. Sed a militibus praedam et urbis direptionem sperantibus descendere in 6 proelium cogitur. Victus cum iterato non felicius fortunam temptasset, legatos ad Syracusanos mittit, spondens se depositurum tyrannidem, si mitterent ad eum, quibuscum 7 sibi de pace conveniret. In quam rem missos primores in carcere retinet, atque ita incautis omnibus nec quicquam hostile metuentibus exercitum ad delendam civitatem 8 mittit. Fit igitur in ipsa urbe anceps proelium, in quo oppidanis multitudine superantibus Dionysius pellitur. Qui cum obsidionem arcis timeret, cum omni regio apparatu 9 in Italiam profugit tacitus. Exul Locrensibus sociis acceptus, velut iure regnaret, arcem occupat solitamque sibi 10 saevitiam exercet. Coniuges principum ad stuprum rapi iubebat, virgines ante nuptias abducebat stupratasque procis reddebat, locupletissimos quosque aut civitate pellebat aut occidi imperabat bonaque eorum invadebat.

---

[3] Justin's account of Dionysius II's fall is rhetorical rather than reliable; the tyrant was fairly quickly deposed by his philosophically austere uncle Dion in 356, going into exile at Locri until increasing chaos at Syracuse and in Sicily allowed him to return for a few more years in 347.

2. With his rivals then removed, he lapsed into inertia and from overindulgence developed obesity and an eye disease, one so severe that he could tolerate neither sunshine nor dust nor even daylight. Thinking he was despised because of this, he went wild with cruelty but unlike his father he did not fill the prison with debtors, but filled the city with corpses, for which he was not so much despised as hated by everyone. So when the Syracusans declared war on him, he long dithered between abandoning power and armed resistance. But he was forced into battle by his soldiers, who had hopes of plunder and sacking the city. He was defeated, and after again tempting fortune with no more success he sent ambassadors to the Syracusans promising to renounce his tyranny if they sent men to him with whom a peace treaty could be concluded. When some leading citizens were sent to him for that, he put them in prison, and with everyone off guard and fearing no hostile action sent an army to destroy their city. There was thus a critical battle within the city itself, in which Dionysius, the townspeople having superior numbers, was defeated. Since he feared being under siege in the citadel, he slipped quietly away to Italy with all his regal property.[3] Admitted as an exile by his Locrian allies, he commandeered the acropolis as if he were a legitimate ruler and continued his usual ruthlessness. Wives of leading citizens he would order seized for raping; virgins he would abduct before their marriages and return deflowered to their suitors; and all the richest people he either drove from the state or ordered them executed and confiscated their property.

2

3

4

5

6

7

8

9

10

5

3. Dein cum rapinae occasio deesset, universam civita-
2 tem callido commento circumvenit. Cum Reginorum tyranni Leophronis bello Locrenses premerentur, voverant,
si victores forent, ut die festo Veneris virgines suas pros-
3 tituerent. Quo voto intermisso cum adversa bella cum
Lucanis gererent, in contionem eos Dionysius vocat; hortatur, ut uxores filiasque suas in templum Veneris quam
4 possint ornatissimas mittant, ex quibus sorte ductae centum voto publico fungantur religionisque gratia uno stent
in lupanari mense omnibus ante iuratis viris, ne quis ullam
5 adtaminet. Quae res ne virginibus voto civitatem solventi-
bus fraudi esset, decretum facerent, ne qua virgo nuberet,
6 priusquam illae maritis traderentur. Probato consilio, quo
et superstitioni et pudicitiae virginum consulebatur, certatim omnes feminae inpensius exornatae in templum
7 Veneris conveniunt, quas omnes Dionysius inmissis militibus spoliat ornamentaque matronarum in praedam suam
8 vertit. Quarundam viros ditiores interficit, quasdam ad
9 prodendas virorum pecunias torquet. Cum his artibus per
annos sex regnasset, conspiratione Locrorum civitate pul-
10 sus in Siciliam redit. Ibi Syracusas securis omnibus post
longam intercapedinem pacis per proditionem recepit.

4. Dum haec in Sicilia geruntur, interim in Africa princeps Karthaginiensium Hanno opes suas, quibus vires rei
publicae superabat, in occupandam dominationem intendit regnumque invadere interfecto senatu conatus est.
2 Cui sceleri sollemnem nuptiarum diem filiae suae legit, ut

---

[4] For this episode Justin is the prime source.

3. Then since he lacked an opportunity for plunder, he played a crafty trick on the whole state. When the Locrians were under pressure in a war with the tyrant Leophron, they had vowed that if they were victorious, they would prostitute their virgins at the festival of Venus. The vow had remained unfulfilled and when the Locrians were unsuccessfully fighting wars with the Lucanians, Dionysius called them to a meeting; he urged them to send their wives and daughters into the temple of Venus dressed as elegantly as possible; a hundred of them, drawn by lot, would discharge their communal vow and to satisfy religion spend one month on display in a brothel, all the men earlier being sworn not to touch any of them. For this not to disadvantage any virgins who were releasing the state from its vow, they would issue a decree that no virgin should marry until these were given husbands. This plan being approved, since both religion and the virtue of the virgins were respected by it, the women all assembled at the temple of Venus decked out in expensive robes, when Dionysius sent in his soldiers, robbed them all and made the jewelry of the matrons his personal booty. The wealthier husbands of some he executed, and some he tortured into revealing their spouses' money. After he had reigned for six years using such tricks, he was driven from the city by a conspiracy of the Locrians and returned to Sicily. There, while everyone felt secure after a long interval of peace, he recovered Syracuse by treachery.

4. While this was happening in Sicily, meanwhile in Africa the leading citizen of the Carthaginians, Hanno, used his own fortune, with which he surpassed the strength of the state, to seize power and tried to gain regal power by assassinating the senate.[4] For this crime he chose the

religione votorum nefanda commenta facilius tegerentur.
3 Itaque plebi epulas in publicis porticibus, senatui in domo
sua parat, ut poculis veneno infectis secretius senatum et
sine arbitris interficeret orbamque rem publicam facilius
4 invaderet. Qua re magistratibus per ministros prodita scelus declinatum, non vindicatum est, ne in viro tam potenti
5 plus negotii faceret res cognita quam cogitata. Contenti
itaque cohibuisse decreto modum nuptiarum sumptibus
statuunt idque observari non ab uno, sed ab universis
iubent, ne persona designata, non vitia correcta viderentur.
6   Hoc consilio praeventus iterum servitia concitat statu-
taque rursus caedium die, cum denuo se proditum videret, timens iudicium munitum quoddam castellum cum
7 XX milibus servorum armatis occupat. Ibi dum Afros
regemque Maurorum concitat, capitur virgisque caesus
effossis oculis et manibus cruribusque fractis, velut a singulis membris poenae exigerentur, in conspectu populi
occiditur; corpus verberibus lacerum in crucem figitur.
8 Filii quoque cognatique omnes, etiam innoxii, supplicio
traduntur, ne quisquam aut ad imitandum scelus aut ad
mortem ulciscendam ex tam nefaria domo superesset.
   5. Interea Dionysius Syracusis receptus, cum gravior
crudeliorque in dies civitati esset, iterata conspiratione
2 obsidetur. Tunc deposito imperio arcem Syracusanis cum

---

   [5] Dionysius II was in reality forced out of Syracuse by Timoleon, the Corinthian general invited to Sicily by the distracted
Sicilian Greeks, who between 341 and 338 restored order on the
island, including a great victory over the Carthaginians at the
Crimisus River.

ceremonial day of his own daughter's wedding, so his nefarious scheming might be more easily concealed under holy vows. So for the plebeians he prepared a banquet in the public porticoes, and for the senate another in his own home, so he could murder the senators by poisoning their cups with greater secrecy and no witnesses and the more easily attack a state left without protection. When the affair was leaked to the magistrates by some servants the crime was forestalled, not punished, for fear that in the case of such a powerful man a judicial inquiry might cause more damage than the plot itself. So satisfied with restraining him, they decreed an expenditure limit on weddings and ordered it observed not only by him but by everyone, so it would seem not a case of an individual being targeted but of general wrongs corrected. 3 4 5

Thwarted by this plan he next incited a slave uprising and again fixed a day for assassinations, but when he once more found himself betrayed, fearing a trial he seized a certain fort with twenty thousand armed slaves. There while inciting the Africans and the king of the Mauretanians, he was captured, flogged, had his eyes gouged out, and his arms and legs broken, as if punishment were being inflicted on every part of his body, and then killed before the eyes of the people; his body, mutilated by the lash, was nailed to a cross. His sons, too, and all his relatives, even if innocent, were put to death, so no one from such an iniquitous family should survive either to repeat his crime or avenge his death. 6 7 8

5. Meanwhile Dionysius, reinstated in Syracuse and daily becoming more repressive and savage toward his citizens, fell prey to another conspiracy.[5] Then laying down his power he surrendered the acropolis to the Syra- 2

9

exercitu tradidit receptoque privato instrumento Corin-
3 thum in exilium proficiscitur. Ibi humillima quaeque tutis-
sima existimans in sordidissimum vitae genus descendit:
4 non contentus in publico vagari, sed potare; nec conspici
5 in popinis lupanaribusque, sed totis diebus desidere; cum
perditissimo quoque de minimis rebus disceptare; panno-
sus et squalidus incedere; risum libentius praebere quam
6 captare; in macello perstare; quod emere non poterat,
7 oculis devorare; apud aediles adversus lenones iurgare;
omniaque ista facere, ut contemnendus magis quam me-
8 tuendus videretur. Novissime ludi magistrum professus
pueros in trivio docebat, ut aut a timentibus semper in
publico videretur aut a non timentibus facilius contemne-
9 retur. Nam licet tyranni his semper vitiis abundent, tamen
simulatio haec vitiorum, non naturae erat, magisque haec
arte quam amisso regali pudore faciebat, expertus, quam
10 invisa tyrannorum forent etiam sine opibus nomina. Labo-
rabat itaque invidiam praeteritorum contemptu praesentium demere, neque honesta, sed tuta consilia cir-
11 cumspiciebat. Inter has tamen dissimulationum artes ter
insimulatus est adfectatae tyrannidis, nec aliter quam dum
contemnitur, liberatus est.

6. Inter haec Karthaginienses tanto successu rerum
Alexandri Magni exterriti, verentes, ne Persico regno et
Africum vellet adiungere, mittunt ad speculandos eius
animos Hamilcarem cognomento Rodanum, virum soller-
2 tia facundiaque ceteros insignem. Augebant enim metum

---

6 Aediles were Roman magistrates responsible for city ameni-
ties; Justin applies it, in the usual way, to similar Greek officials.
7 Cf. Arr. *Anab*. 7.15.4; Frontin. *Str.* 1.2.3 (from Trogus).

cusans together with his army and taking his personal belongings went into exile in Corinth. There, thinking the lowest levels of society the safest he lapsed into a thoroughly degrading lifestyle; not content with traipsing around town, he would even drink there; and not content with only being seen in taverns and brothels, he spent whole days in them; with any disreputable wretch he would discuss the most trivial matters; he wandered around filthy and in rags; he preferred to be laughed at than to laugh at someone else; he would hang around in the marketplace; what he could not afford to buy he devoured with his eyes; in the presence of aediles[6] he would wrangle with pimps; and all this he did so as to appear despicable rather than fearful. Eventually becoming a school master he would teach boys in the gutters so as always be seen in public by those fearing him or be more easily despised by those not fearing him. For while tyrants are always full of such vices, this was a case of simulated, not genuine, vices, and he was doing it by design rather than from loss of his regal dignity, well knowing how hated the title "tyrant" would be, even with its power removed. So he kept working to remove resentment over his past by having contempt felt for his present circumstances, and he would cast around for strategies that were not honorable but safe. Even using such artful deceptions, however, he was three times charged with aiming at tyranny, and was acquitted only because he was despised.

6. Meanwhile the Carthaginians, alarmed at Alexander the Great's success and fearing that he also wanted to add Africa to his Persian Empire, sent the Hamilcar surnamed "Rodanus," a man of outstanding ingenuity and eloquence, to probe his intentions.[7] For their fear was being height-

3   et Tyros, urbs auctorum originis suae, capta et Alexandria
4   aemula Karthaginis in terminis Africae et Aegypti condita
    et felicitas regis, apud quem nec cupiditas nec fortuna ullo
5   modo terminabantur. Igitur Hamilcar per Parmeniona
    aditu regis obtento profugisse se ad regem expulsum pa-
6   tria fingit militemque se expeditionis offert. Atque ita con-
    siliis eius exploratis in tabellis ligneis vacua desuper cera
7   inducta civibus suis omnia perscribebat. Sed Karthagini-
    enses post mortem regis reversum in patriam, quasi ur-
    bem regi venditasset, non ingrato tantum, verum etiam
    crudeli animo necaverunt.

ened both by the capture of Tyre, the city of their founders,[8] and also by the capture of Alexandria the rival of 3
Carthage on the borders of Africa and Egypt,[9] as well as 4
by the success of a king whose ambition and success knew
no bounds. So gaining an audience with the king through 5
Parmenion, Hamilcar claimed that he had fled to the king
after being expelled from his country and offered his services as soldier on the campaign. And so after probing his 6
plans in this way he gave a full account to his fellow citizens, written on wooden tablets with fresh wax poured
over them.[10] But on his return to his country after the 7
king's death, the Carthaginians, not just with ingratitude
but even cruelty, killed him for having supposedly sold out
their city to the king.

[8] See 18.3ff.

[9] Justin is surprisingly careless here: Alexandria was not captured by its founder, Alexander the Great, nor was it Carthage's
rival at any time.

[10] A trick reminiscent of Demaratus' at 2.10.13ff.

LIBER XXII

1. Agathocles, Siciliae tyrannus, qui magnitudini prioris
Dionysii successit, ad regni maiestatem ex humili et sor-
2 dido genere pervenit. Quippe in Sicilia patre figulo natus
non honestiorem pueritiam quam principia originis ha-
3 buit, siquidem forma et corporis pulchritudine egregius
4 diu vitam stupri patientia exhibuit. Annos deinde puber-
5 tatis egressus libidinem a viris ad feminas transtulit. Post
haec apud utrumque sexum famosus vitam latrociniis
6 mutavit. Interiecto tempore, cum Syracusas concessisset
7 adscitusque in civitatem inter incolas esset, diu sine fide
fuit, quoniam nec in fortunis quod amitteret, nec in vere-
8 cundia quod inquinaret habere videbatur; in summa gre-
gariam militiam sortitus non minus tunc seditiosa quam
9 antea turpi vita in omne facinus promptissimus erat; nam
et manu strenuus et in contionibus perfacundus habeba-
10 tur. Brevi itaque centurio ac deinceps tribunus militum
11 factus est. Primo bello adversus Aethnaeos magna experi-

---

1 Timaeus seems to remain Trogus' source (cf. Polyb. 12.15),
if not other writers too. There are, nonetheless, similarities with
the account of Diodorus Siculus, which begins with Book 19 in
317/6. On Agathocles see, e.g., K. Meister in *CAH* 7.1 (1984):
384–411; S. N. C. Langher, *Agatocle: Da capoparte a monarca*
(Messina, 2000).

BOOK XXII

1. Agathocles, tyrant of Sicily, who in greatness was successor to the elder Dionysius, rose to regal greatness from a modest and very lowly family.[1] For born in Sicily as the 2 son of a potter he had a boyhood no more respectable than his first beginnings, for being very physically attractive he 3 long supported himself by submitting to sexual perversion. Then on leaving his pubescent years he transferred his 4 sexual activity from men to women. After this, now having 5 a reputation among both sexes, he turned to a life of larceny. Some time later, when he came to Syracuse and was 6 accepted in the city among its resident aliens, he was long 7 without credit because he neither had property to lose nor honor to tarnish; finally enrolling as a common soldier, his 8 life being then no less turbulent than it was earlier disreputable, he was very ready for any criminal act; for he 9 was thought both a man of action and one very fluent in public assemblies. So he soon became a centurion and 10 then a military tribune. In his first campaign against the 11 people of Aetna[2] he gave a good account of himself to the

[2] Aetna, a town beside the volcano, was the home of Campanian ex-mercenary settlers; Justin wrongly separates the two here.

15

12 menta sui Syracusanis dedit. Sequenti Campanorum tantam de se spem omnibus fecit, ut in locum demortui ducis
13 Damasconis sufficeretur, cuius uxorem adulterio cognitam
14 post mortem viri in matrimonium recepit. Nec contentus,
quod ex inope repente dives factus esset, piraticam adver-
15 sus patriam exercuit. Saluti ei fuit, quod socii capti tor-
16 tique de illo negaverunt. Bis occupare imperium Syracusarum voluit, bis in exilium actus est.

2. A Murgantinis, apud quos exulabat, odio Syracusa-
2 norum primo praetor, mox dux creatur. In eo bello et urbem Leontinorum capit et patriam suam Syracusas obsi-
3 dere coepit, ad cuius auxilium Hamilcar, dux Poenorum,
inploratus depositis hostilibus odiis praesidia militum
4 mittit. Ita uno eodemque tempore Syracusae et ab hoste
civili amore defensae et a cive hostili odio inpugnatae sunt.
5 Sed Agathocles cum videret fortius defendi urbem quam
oppugnari, precibus per internuntios Hamilcarem exorat,
ut inter se et Syracusanos pacis arbitria suscipiat, peculia-
6 ria in ipsum officia sui repromittens. Qua spe inpletus
Hamilcar societatem cum eo mutuae potentiae iungit, ut
quantum virium Agathocli adversus Syracusanos dedisset,
tantum ipse ad incrementa domesticae potentiae recupe-
7 raret. Igitur non pax tantum Agathocli conciliatur, verum
8 etiam praetor Syracusis constituitur. Tunc Hamilcari expo-
sitis insignibus Cereris tactisque in obsequia Poenorum

---

3 In Diod. Sic. 19.3 Agathocles marries the widow of his lover
Damas.

4 The people of Morgantina, inland from Syracuse.

5 "Praetor" is Justin's term for the Greek office of supreme
general (*strategos autokrator*).

Syracusans. In his next against the Campanians he so   12
raised everyone's hopes in him that on the general Da-
mascon's death he was his replacement and married his   13
wife, with whom he had already been committing adul-
tery.[3] Not satisfied with suddenly going from rags to riches,   14
he engaged in piracy against his country. What saved him   15
was that when his accomplices were captured and tortured
they denied his involvement. Twice he tried to seize power   16
in Syracuse, and twice he was driven into exile.

2. By the Murgantini,[4] among whom he was exiled, he
was through their hatred of the Syracusans first made a
praetor and then their leader. In that war he captured the   2
city of Leontini and also began a siege of his own homeland of Syracuse; but the Carthaginian general Hamilcar,   3
when begged for aid, set aside his animosity and sent
military support there. Thus at one and the same time   4
Syracuse was being defended by an enemy who loved it
and also attacked by a citizen with the hatred of an enemy.
But when Agathocles could see the city being defended   5
more strongly than it was being assaulted, he entreated
Hamilcar through intermediaries to undertake peace negotiations between him and the Syracusans, promising
him private favors in return. Filled with hope by this   6
Hamilcar made a pact of reciprocal assistance with him:
whatever support he gave Agathocles against the Syracusans, he would himself receive as much from him to
increase his own power. So not only was peace settled for   7
Agathocles but he was also made praetor in Syracuse.[5]
Then laying out and touching the cult objects of Ceres   8
before Hamilcar he swore loyalty to the Carthaginians.

9 iurat. Deinde acceptis ab eo V milibus Afrorum potentis-
10 simos quosque ex principibus interficit, atque ita veluti rei
publicae statum formaturus populum in theatrum ad contionem vocari iubet contracto in gymnasio senatu, quasi
11 quaedam prius ordinaturus. Sic conpositis rebus inmissis
12 militibus populum obsidet, senatum trucidat, cuius per-
acta caede ex plebe quoque locupletissimos et promptis-
simos interficit.

3. His ita gestis militem legit exercitumque conscribit,
quo instructus finitimas civitates nihil hostile metuentes
2 ex inproviso adgreditur, Poenorum quoque socios permit-
tente Hamilcare foede vexat. Propter quod querelas Karthaginem socii non tam de Agathocle quam de Hamilcare
3 detulerunt, hunc ut dominum et tyrannum, illum ut pro-
ditorem arguentes, a quo infestissimo hosti fortunae so-
4 ciorum interposita pactione donatae sint; sicut ab initio
Syracusae in pignus societatis sint traditae, urbs semper
Poenis infesta et de imperio Siciliae Karthaginis aemula,
nunc insuper civitates sociorum eidem titulo pacis addic-
5 tas. Denuntiare igitur se haec brevi ad ipsos redundatura
ac propediem sensuros, quantum mali non Siciliae magis
quam ipsi Africae adtulerint.
6 His querelis senatus in Hamilcarem accenditur, sed
quoniam in imperio esset, tacita de eo suffragia tulerunt
et sententias, priusquam recitarentur, in urnam coniectas
obsignari iusserunt, dum alter Hamilcar, Gisgonis filius, a

---

6 In 314/3; Diod. Sic. 19.65, 70ff.

7 These allies of Carthage were the cities and peoples in western Sicily, some native Sicilian and others Phoenician.

Receiving five thousand Africans from him after that he   9
murdered all the most powerful leaders, and as if intend-   10
ing to establish a genuine constitution he had the people
called to a meeting in the theater, the senate having already been convened in the gymnasium, supposedly for
some preliminary business. With matters thus arranged   11
soldiers were sent in and he cordoned off the people and
massacred the senate, and when the slaughter ended he   12
also murdered the most wealthy and enterprising plebeians.

3. That done he raised troops and conscripted an
army,[6] equipped with which he without warning attacked
neighboring cities that had no fear of an enemy assault;
and with Hamilcar's permission he also foully persecuted   2
the Carthaginians' allies.[7] Over that the allies brought
complaints to Carthage not so much about Agathocles as
about Hamilcar, accusing one of being an overbearing ty-   3
rant and the other a traitor by whom the fortunes of their
allies had with their collusion been sacrificed to a hated
enemy; just as from the start Syracuse had been surren-   4
dered to secure an alliance, a city always hostile to the
Phoenicians and Carthage's rival for power in Sicily, now,
too, they said, their allies' states were being assigned to
the same man under a pretext of peace. They were there-   5
fore giving notice that such measures would soon recoil on
the Carthaginians, and they would soon understand how
much damage they imposed no more on Sicily than on
Africa itself.

The senate was angered with Hamilcar over these pro-   6
tests, but since he was in command they held a secret vote
on him and ordered the ballots to be put into an urn before
being read out, and sealed until the other Hamilcar, the

7 Sicilia reverteretur. Sed haec callida commenta Poenorum
et sententias inauditas mors Hamilcaris praevenit, libera-
tusque est fati munere, quem per iniuriam cives inau-
8 ditum damnaverant. Quae res Agathocli adversus Poenos
9 occasionem movendi belli dedit. Prima igitur illi cum
Hamilcare, Gisgonis filio, proelii congressio fuit, a quo
victus maiori mole reparaturus bellum Syracusas conces-
10 sit. Sed secundi certaminis eadem fortuna quae et prioris
fuit.

4. Cum igitur victores Poeni Syracusas obsidione cin-
xissent, Agathocles, quod se neque viribus parem neque
ad obsidionem ferendam instructum videret, super haec a
2 sociis crudelitate eius offensis desertus esset, statuit bellum in Africa transferre, mira prorsus audacia, ut, quibus
in solo urbis suae par non erat, eorum urbi bellum inferret,
et qui sua tueri non poterat, inpugnaret aliena victusque
3 victoribus insultaret. Huius consilii non minus admirabile
silentium quam commentum fuit. Populo hoc solum professus, invenisse se victoriae viam; animos illi tantum in
brevem obsidionis patientiam firmarent, vel cui status
praesentis fortunae displiceret, dare se ei discedendi libe-
4 ram potestatem. Cum mille sescenti discessissent, ceteros
ad obsidionis necessitatem frumento et stipendio instruit;
L tantum secum talenta ad praesentem usum aufert, ce-
5 tera ex hoste melius quam ex sociis paraturus. Omnes deinde servos militaris aetatis libertate donatos sacramento

---

8 This other Hamilcar lived in exile in Sicily but was now recalled.

9 In 312/11 and 311/10: Diod. Sic. 19.102ff., 106ff.

10 In 310/9: Diod. Sic. 20.3ff.

son of Gisgo, should return from Sicily.[8] But this clever 7
ploy of the Carthaginians and the untallied ballots was
preempted by Hamilcar's death, and thanks to a gift of fate
a man was freed whom his fellow citizens had wrongfully
condemned without a hearing. This gave Agathocles the 8
opportunity to start a war against the Carthaginians.[9] So 9
his first clash was with Hamilcar son of Gisgo, and when
defeated by him he withdrew to Syracuse to renew the
struggle with greater strength. But the outcome of the 10
second battle was the same as the first.

4. Now when the victorious Carthaginians had Syracuse under siege,[10] Agathocles could see that he was neither a match for them in strength nor sufficiently prepared
to withstand a siege, and in addition he had been deserted
by his allies, who were shocked by his inhumanity; so he 2
decided to move the war into Africa, evidently with amazing bravado in inflicting war on a city of men for whom he
had been no match on the soil of his own city, and attacking the territory of others when unable to defend his own,
a conquered man scoffing at his conquerors. The silence 3
surrounding the plan was no less astonishing than its design. This was all he told his people: he had found the way
to victory; all they need do was brace themselves to face a
brief siege, and to anyone unhappy with the present situation he granted freedom to leave. When sixteen hundred 4
left, he supplied the rest with grain and pay to face the
difficulties of a siege; and he took only fifty talents with
him for urgent needs, intending to get the rest from the
enemy rather than from his allies. Then freeing all slaves 5
of military age he swore them in and boarded them and

adegit eosque et maiorem partem ferme militum navibus inponit, ratus exaequata utriusque ordinis condicione mutuam inter eos virtutis aemulationem futuram; ceteros omnes ad tutelam patriae relinquit.

5. Septimo igitur imperii anno comitibus duobus adul-
2 tis filiis, Archagatho et Heraclida, nullo militum sciente quo veheretur, cursum in Africam dirigit, cum omnes aut in Italiam praedatum se aut in Sardiniam ituros crederent. Tunc primum, exposito in Africae litore exercitu, consi-
3 lium suum omnibus aperit. Quo in loco Syracusae positae sint ostendit, quibus aliud nullum auxilium superesset,
4 quam ut hostibus faciant, quae ipsi patiantur. Quippe aliter domi, aliter foris bella tractari. Domi ea sola auxilia esse, quae patriae vires subministrent; foris hostem etiam suis viribus vinci, deficientibus sociis et odio diuturni
5 imperii externa auxilia circumspicientibus. Huc accedere, quod urbes castellaque Africae non muris cinctae, non in montibus positae sint, sed in planis campis sine ullis munimentis iaceant, quas omnes metu excidii facile ad
6 belli societatem perlici posse. Maius igitur Karthaginiensibus ab ipsa Africa quam ex Sicilia exarsurum bellum, coituraque auxilia omnium adversus unam urbem nomine quam opibus ampliorem, et quas non adtulerit vires, inde
7 sumpturum. Nec in repentino Poenorum metu modicum momentum victoriae fore, qui tanta audacia hostium perculsi trepidaturi sint. Accessura et villarum incendia,
8 castellorum urbiumque contumacium direptionem, tum
9 ipsius Karthaginis obsidionem, quibus omnibus non sibi

most of the soldiers on ships, thinking that with a level-
ing of social classes there would be competition in brav-
ery among them; the others he left behind to protect the
country.

5. So in the seventh year of his reign he accompanied
by his two grown sons, Archagathus and Heraclides, set a 2
course for Africa, with none of his soldiers knowing where
they were bound, since they all thought they were either
off to plunder Italy or heading for Sardinia. Only when the
army was put ashore on the coast of Africa did he reveal
his strategy to everyone. He explained how Syracuse was 3
placed, how they had no other option than to inflicting on
the enemy what they were suffering themselves. For wars 4
are handled one way at home, he said, and another abroad.
At home one's only help was what their country's strength
could provide; abroad, an enemy could also be defeated
by his own strength should its allies defect and from hatred of long subjugation cast about for external aid. There 5
was the further advantage, he said, that cities and strong-
holds of Africa were not walled and not set on mountains
but lay on open plains with no fortifications, and from fear
of being destroyed they could all easily be induced to join
their war. So a greater war would flare up for the Cartha- 6
ginians from Africa itself than from Sicily, and everyone's
forces would rally against one city whose reputation was
greater than its resources, and from that he would draw
the strength he had not brought with him. Nor would the 7
sudden alarm among the Carthaginians add only little to
their victory, for they would panic, alarmed by their foe's
audacity. Added to that would also be the burning of 8
farms, pillaging of defiant cities and fortresses, and finally
the siege of Carthage itself, from all of which they would 9

23

10 tantum in alios, sed et aliis in se sentient patere bella. His
non solum Poenos vinci, sed et Siciliam liberari posse; nec
enim moraturos in eius obsidione hostes, cum sua urgean-
11 tur. Nusquam igitur alibi facilius bellum, sed nec praedam
uberiorem inveniri posse; nam capta Karthagine omnem
12 Africam Siciliamque praemium victorum fore. Gloriam
certe tam honestae militiae tantam in omne aevum futuram, ut terminari nullo tempore oblivionis possit, ut dicatur eos solos mortalium esse, qui bella, quae domi ferre
non poterant, ad hostes transtulerint ultroque victores
13 insecuti sint et obsessores urbis suae obsederint. Omnibus
igitur forti ac laeto animo bellum ineundum, quo nullum
aliud possit aut praemium victoribus uberius aut victis
monumentum inlustrius dare.

6. His quidem adhortationibus animi militum erige-
bantur, sed terrebat eos portenti religio, quod navigatant-
2 bus sol defecerat. Cuius rei rationem non minore cura rex
quam belli reddebat, adfirmans, si prius quam proficisce-
rentur factum esset, crediturum adversum profecturis
prodigium esse; nunc, quia egressis acciderit, illis, ad quos
3 eatur, portendere. Porro defectus naturalium siderum
semper praesentem rerum statum mutare, certumque
esse et florentibus Karthaginiensium opibus et laboribus
4 adversisque rebus suis commutationem significari. Sic
consolatis militibus universas naves consentiente exercitu

---

11 The eclipse occurred on August 15, 310. Agathocles was not
yet a king—he took on that title five years later, imitating the new
eastern monarchs.   12 The Latin expression here, *naturalium siderum* (natural stars), seems to be unique to Justin and
probably refers to the planets, including the sun and the moon,
which can be said to govern nature (so Gronovius).

understand that they could not only make war on others
but also face war from others themselves. By these means   10
not only could the Carthaginians be defeated, but Sicily
could also be liberated; for their enemies would not spend
time there besieging it when their own land was under
attack. Nowhere else then could an easier campaign or   11
richer plunder be found; for with Carthage captured all
Africa and Sicily would become the prize of the victors.
The glory of such an honorable campaign would certainly   12
last into every age, being so great that it could never end
in oblivion, so great that it would be said that they alone
of mortal men took into enemy territory a war they could
not support at home, and that they actually attacked their
victors and put under siege the men besieging *their* city.
So they must all go into war with a confident and cheerful   13
spirit, for no other war could give them either a richer
prize in victory or a more glorious memorial in defeat.

6. The morale of the soldiers was raised by such encouragement, but they were also alarmed by a religious
portent, because a solar eclipse had occurred while they
were at sea.[11] The king explained the event no less care-   2
fully than he did his war strategy, assuring them that had
it happened before they left he would have considered it
an evil portent for those departing, but that now, coming
after their departure, it was a portent for those against
whom they were sailing. In fact, he said, an eclipse of the   3
planets[12] always indicated a change in the present circumstances, and this must indicate change both in the prosperity of the Carthaginians and in their own trials and
tribulations. With his soldiers thus reassured, he then with   4
the army's agreement ordered all the ships to be burned

incendi iubet, ut omnes scirent auxilio fugae adempto aut
5 vincendum aut moriendum esse. Dein cum omnia, qua-
cumque ingrederentur, prosternerent, castella villasque
incenderent, obvius ei fuit cum XXX milibus paganorum
6 Hanno, sed proelio commisso duo de Siculis, tria milia de
7 Poenis cum ipso duce cecidere. Hac victoria et Siculorum
animi eriguntur et Poenorum franguntur.

8   Agathocles victis hostibus urbes castellaque expugnat,
9 praedas ingentes agit, hostium multa milia trucidat. Castra
deinde in quinto lapide a Karthagine statuit, ut damna
carissimarum rerum vastitatemque agrorum et incendia
10 villarum de muris ipsius urbis specularentur. Interea ingens tota Africa deleti Poenorum exercitus fama occupa-
11 tarumque urbium divulgatur. Stupor itaque omnes et admiratio incessit, unde tanto imperio tam subitum bellum,
praesertim ab hoste iam victo; admiratio deinde paulatim
12 in contemptum Poenorum vertitur. Nec multo post non
Afri tantum, verum etiam urbes nobilissimae novitatem
secutae ad Agathoclem defecere frumentoque et stipendio victorem instruxere.

7. His Poenorum malis etiam deletus in Sicilia cum
imperatore exercitus velut quidam aerumnarum cumulus
2 accessit. Nam post profectionem a Sicilia Agathoclis in
obsidione Syracusarum Poeni segniores redditi ab Antan-

---

[13] An interesting case of variation in numbers: according to
Diod. Sic. 20.13.1, two hundred Greeks fell and a thousand Carthaginians (noting that some put the latter figure as high as three
thousand), while Oros. 4.6.25 puts the figure at two thousand
Carthaginians and two Sicilians! That Hanno led "peasants" is a
sneer but not a fact.

for everyone to know that with all opportunity for escape
removed they must either conquer or die. Then after lay- 5
ing waste everything wherever they went, and burning
fortresses and country houses, he was confronted by
Hanno with thirty thousand peasants, but at the start of 6
the battle two thousand Sicilians and three thousand Carthaginians were killed together with their leader himself.[13]
With this victory the Sicilians' spirits were raised and 7
those of the Carthaginians broken.

   After defeating his enemies, Agathocles stormed cities 8
and fortresses, carried off huge amounts of plunder, and
slaughtered many thousands of the enemy. He then estab- 9
lished camp five miles from Carthage so its inhabitants
could view the loss of their dearest possessions, the destruction of their land, and the burning of their farms from
the walls of the city itself. Meanwhile word spread far and 10
wide throughout Africa of the destruction of the Carthaginian army and the capture of their cities. Shock and 11
amazement thus struck everybody that so great a power
could be so suddenly attacked, especially by an already
defeated enemy; and admiration for the Carthaginians
then gradually turned to contempt. And not much later 12
not only the Africans but even the most famous cities accepted the new situation, defected to Agathocles, and supplied the victor with grain and money.

   7. After these Carthaginian failures the loss of an army
in Sicily together with its commander[14] also came to crown
their misfortunes. For after Agathocles' departure from 2
Sicily reports were arriving that the Carthaginians had
become more lethargic in the siege of Syracuse and been

---

14 In 309/8: Diod. Sic. 20.29ff.

EPITOME OF POMPEIUS TROGUS

dro, fratre regis Agathoclis, occidione caesi nuntiabantur.
3 Itaque cum domi forisque eadem fortuna Karthaginiensium esset, iam non tributariae tantum ab his urbes,
verum etiam socii reges deficiebant, amicitiarum iura non
fide, sed successu ponderantes.
4   Erat inter ceteros rex Cyrenarum Ophellas, qui spe
inproba regnum totius Africae amplexus societatem cum
Agathocle per legatos iunxerat pactusque cum eo fuerat,
ut Siciliae illi, sibi Africae imperium victis Karthagini-
5 ensibus cederet. Itaque cum ad belli societatem cum ingenti exercitu ipse venisset, Agathocles blando adloquio et
humili adulatione, cum saepius simul cenassent adoptatus-
6 que filius eius ab Ophella esset, incautum interficit occu-
patoque exercitu eius iterato Karthaginienses omnibus
viribus bellum cientes magno utriusque exercitus san-
7 guine gravi proelio superat. Hoc certaminis discrimine
tanta desperatio inlata Poenis est, ut, nisi in exercitu Agathoclis orta seditio fuisset, transiturus ad eum Bomilcar,
8 rex Poenorum, cum exercitu fuerit. Ob quam noxam in
medio foro a Poenis patibulo suffixus est, ut idem locus
monumentum suppliciorum eius esset, qui ante fuerat
9 ornamentum honorum. Sed Bomilcar magno animo crudelitatem civium tulit, adeo ut de summa cruce veluti de
10 tribunali in Poenorum scelera contionaretur, obiectans
illis nunc Hannonem falsa adfectati regni invidia circum-

---

15 In 308/7: Diod. Sic. 20.38ff. Ophellas was the Macedonian
governor, not king, of Cyrene.
16 Bomilcar, the general defending Carthage, attempted a
coup in the city in 308—apparently with Agathocles' secret encouragement—but was defeated and captured.

massacred by Antandrus, brother of King Agathocles. So 3
since Carthaginian fortunes were the same both at home
and abroad, not only were their tribute-paying cities defecting, but so also were allied princes, who based friendship obligations not on loyalty but success.

There was among them the king of Cyrene Ophellas, 4
who in the outrageous hope of ruling all of Africa[15] had
made an alliance with Agathocles through delegates, and
had negotiated with him that command of Sicily should go
to him and Africa to himself if the Carthaginians were
defeated. Now when he himself came to join the war with 5
a huge army, Agathocles plied him with unctuous remarks
and abject flattery (for they had often dined together, and
his son had been adopted by Ophellas), then killed him 6
while he was off his guard, commandeered his army, and
in a momentous battle defeated the Carthaginians as they
were renewing the war in full force, with much blood
spilled in both armies. After this decisive battle such de- 7
spair descended on the Carthaginians that, had there not
been a mutiny in the army of Agathocles, Bomilcar, king
of the Phoenicians, would have deserted to him with his
army.[16] For that mistake he was crucified in the center of 8
the forum by the Carthaginians, so that the same place
should witness his torment that had earlier served to
crown his honors. Bomilcar, however, accepted the cruelty 9
of his fellow citizens with magnanimity, even addressing
the Carthaginians on their wrongs from the height of his
cross as if from a court bench, accusing them first of trap- 10
ping Hanno on a false and malicious charge of aspiring to

ventum, nunc Gisgonis innocentis exilium, nunc in Hamilcarem, patruum suum, tacita suffragia, quod Agathoclem
socium illis facere quam hostem maluerit. Haec cum in
maxima populi contione vociferatus esset, expiravit.

8. Interea Agathocles profligatis in Africa rebus, tradito
Archagatho filio exercitu in Siciliam recurrit, nihil actum
in Africa existimans, si amplius Syracusae obsiderentur.
2 Nam post occisum Hamilcarem, Gisgonis filium, novus
3 eo a Poenis missus exercitus fuerat. Statim igitur primo
adventu eius omnes Siciliae urbes auditis rebus, quas in
Africa gesserat, certatim se ei tradunt, atque ita pulsis e
4 Sicilia Poenis totius insulae imperium occupavit. In Africam deinde reversus seditione militum excipitur, nam sti-
pendiorum solutio in adventum patris dilata a filio fuerat.
5 Igitur in contionem vocatos blandis verbis permulsit:
stipendia illis non a se flagitanda esse, sed ab hoste quae-
renda; communem victoriam, communem praedam fu-
6 turam. Paulum modo adniterentur, dum belli reliquiae
peraguntur, cum sciant Karthaginem captam spes omnium
7 expleturam. Sedato militari tumultu interiectis diebus ad
castra hostium exercitum ducit, ibi inconsultius proelium
8 committendo maiorem partem exercitus perdidit. Cum
itaque in castra fugisset versamque in se invidiam temere
commissi belli videret pristinamque offensam non depensi
stipendii metueret, concubia nocte solus a castris cum
Archagatho filio profugit.
9 Quod ubi milites cognovere, haud secus quam si ab
hoste capti essent, trepidavere, bis se a rege suo in mediis

---

17 In 307/6. Cf. Diod. Sic. 20.54ff., which does not quite
square in detail.

kingship, then of exiling the innocent Gisgo, and then of
secretly voting against his uncle Hamilcar for preferring
to make Agathocles their ally rather than their enemy.
After loudly proclaiming such charges before a huge gathering of the people, he breathed his last.

8. Meanwhile Agathocles, his duties in Africa now
mostly over, passed the army on to his son Archagathus
and returned to Sicily, thinking nothing achieved in Africa
if Syracuse remained under siege.[17] For after Hamilcar, 2
son of Gisgo, was killed, a new army had been sent there
by the Carthaginians. So immediately on his arrival all the 3
Sicilian cities, having heard of his achievements in Africa,
rushed to surrender to him, and so with the Carthaginians
driven from Sicily he took over the whole island. Then on 4
returning to Africa he faced a mutiny of his troops, for
their pay had been withheld by his son until his father's
return. So summoning the men to an assembly he soothed 5
them with conciliatory words; their pay should be demanded not from him but from the enemy, he said; victory
would be shared, and the spoils shared. Only a little effort 6
was needed while the war was being finished off, since
they knew that capturing Carthage would fulfill the hopes
of them all. The soldiers' disorder was calmed and some 7
days later he led his army to the enemy camp, but there
by incautiously committing to battle he lost most of the
army. So when he fled back to camp and saw the indigna- 8
tion facing him for recklessly joining battle and also feared
the men's earlier rancor over not being paid, he fled from
the camp early in the evening with only his son Archagathus.

When the soldiers discovered it, they panicked no less 9
than if they had been taken by their enemy, crying out that

31

hostibus relictos esse proclamantes, salutemque suam desertam ab eo esse, quorum ne sepultura quidem re-
10 linquenda fuerit. Cum persequi regem vellent, a Numidis excepti in castra revertuntur, conprehenso tamen reductoque Archagatho, qui a patre noctis errore discesserat.
11 Agathocles autem navibus, quibus reversus a Sicilia fuerat, cum custodibus earundem Syracusas defertur, exemplum
12 flagitii singulare, rex exercitus sui desertor filiorumque
13 pater proditor. Interim in Africa post fugam regis milites pactione cum hostibus facta, interfectis Agathoclis liberis
14 Karthaginiensibus se tradidere. Archagathus cum occideretur ab Arcesilao, amico antea patris, rogavit eum, quidnam liberis eius facturum Agathoclem putet, per quem ipse liberis careat. Tunc respondit satis habere se, quod
15 superstites eos esse Agathoclis liberis sciat. Post haec Poeni ad persequendas belli reliquias duces in Siciliam miserunt, cum quibus Agathocles pacem aequis condicionibus fecit.

they had now been twice left amid enemies by their own king and their lives forfeited, men even whose burial should not have been neglected. Although they wished to follow the king, they were overtaken by the Numidians and returned to camp, but Archagathus was caught and brought back—he had become separated from his father after losing his way in the dark. Agathocles was taken back to Syracuse in the ships with which he had returned from Sicily, together with the men who had been guarding them, an outstanding example of disgraceful conduct, a king deserting his own army, a father betraying his sons. Meanwhile in Africa after the flight of their king the Sicilian soldiers came to terms with the enemy, and after killing the children of Agathocles surrendered to the Carthaginians. When Archagathus was being put to death by Arcesilaus, the former friend of his father, he asked him what he thought Agathocles would do to the children of the man by whom he was now being left childless. He then replied that he was quite satisfied knowing that they had outlived the children of Agathocles. After this the Carthaginians sent generals to Sicily to finish off what remained of the war, and Agathocles made peace with them on equable terms.[18]

10

11

12

13

14

15

[18] In 306/5: Diod. Sic. 20.77ff.

LIBER XXIII

1. Agathocles, rex Siciliae, pacificatus cum Karthaginiensibus partem civitatium a se fiducia virium dissidentem
2 armis subegit. Dein quasi angustis insulae terminis clauderetur, cuius imperii partem primis incrementis ne speraverat quidem, in Italiam transcendit, exemplum Diony-
3 sii secutus, qui multas Italiae civitates subegerat. Primi igitur hostes illi Bruttii fuere, quia et fortissimi tum et opulentissimi videbantur, simul et ad iniurias vicinorum
4 prompti. Nam multas civitates Graeci nominis Italia expu-
5 lerant; auctores quoque suos Lucanos bello vicerant et
6 pacem cum his aequis legibus fecerant. Tanta feritas animorum erat, ut nec origini suae parcerent.
7   Namque Lucani isdem legibus liberos suos quibus et
8 Spartani instituere soliti erant. Quippe ab initio pubertatis in silvis inter pastores habebantur sine ministerio servili, sine veste, quam induerent vel cui incuberent, ut a primis annis duritiae parsimoniaeque sine ullo usu urbis adsues-
9 cerent. Cibus his praeda venatica, potus aut lactis aut fontium liquor erat. Sic ad labores bellicos indurabantur.
10 Horum igitur ex numero L primo ex agris finitimorum

---

[1] For Agathocles' crossing to Italy in the 290s, see Diod. Sic. 21.3f., 8, then 16 for his death in 289. For Dionysius see 20.1.1ff., 5.1ff.

BOOK XXIII

1. Agathocles, king of Sicily, after making peace with the Carthaginians, subdued by armed force some city-states that were rising against him through confidence in their strength.[1] Then as if he were confined by the narrow 2 bounds of an island over which in earlier early days he had not even hoped for partial rule, he crossed into Italy, following the example of Dionysius, who had subdued numerous Italian states. So his first enemies were the Bruttii, 3 because they seemed both the strongest and richest, while also being people ready to inflict harm on their neighbors. For they had driven many communities of Greek origin 4 from Italy; and they had also defeated their founders the 5 Lucanians in battle and made peace with them on even terms. Such was their aggressiveness that they would spare 6 not even their own race.

For the Lucanians had been using the same system as 7 the Spartans in educating their children. In fact these 8 were from early puberty kept in the woods among shepherds, having no slaves serving them and no clothes to wear or sleep on, so that from their early years they would become accustomed to hardship and deprivation, having no contact with city life. Their food was hunted animals, 9 their drink either milk or spring water. This was how they were toughened for the hardships of war. Now, fifty of 10 their number started regularly plundering their neigh-

praedare soliti, confluente deinde multitudine sollicitati
praeda cum plures facti essent, infestas regiones red-
11 debant. Itaque fatigatus querelis sociorum Dionysius,
Siciliae tyrannus, sexcentos Afros ad conpescendos eos
12 miserat; quorum castellum proditum sibi per Bruttiam
mulierem expugnaverunt ibique civitatem concurrentibus
ad opinionem novae urbis pastoribus statuerunt Brut-
13 tiosque se ex nomine mulieris vocaverunt. Primum illis
14 cum Lucanis, originis suae auctoribus, bellum fuit, qua
victoria erecti cum pacem aequo iure fecissent, ceteros
finitimos armis subegerunt tantasque opes brevi consecuti
15 sunt, ut perniciosi etiam regibus haberentur. Denique
Alexander, rex Epiri, cum in auxilium Graecarum civitatium cum magno exercitu in Italiam venisset, cum omni-
16 bus copiis ab his deletus est. Quare feritas eorum successu
17 felicitatis incensa diu terribilis finitimis fuit. Ad postremum inploratus Agathocles spe ampliandi regni a Sicilia
in Italiam traiecit.

2. Principio adventus opinione eius concussi legatos ad
2 eum societatem amicitiamque petentes miserunt. Quos
Agathocles ad cenam invitatos, ne exercitum traici viderent, et in posterum statuta his die conscensa navi frus-
3 tratus est. Sed fraudis haud laetus eventus fuit, siquidem
reverti eum in Siciliam interiectis paucis diebus vis morbi
4 coegit, quo toto corpore conprehensus per omnes nervos
articulosque umore pestifero grassante velut intestino sin-
5 gulorum membrorum bello inpugnabatur. Ex qua despera-

---

[2] Their name was the Lucanian word for "slaves" or "rebels"
(so Diod. Sic. 16.15.1–2; Strabo 6.255C).

[3] See 12.2.1ff., 18.1.2.

bors' fields, and when many others flooded to join them
and their numbers grew, attracted by the spoils, they
started creating havoc throughout the area. So, wearied by   11
complaints from his allies, Dionysius, the Sicilian tyrant,
had sent six hundred Africans to suppress them; and after   12
their stronghold was betrayed by a woman called Bruttia
they overwhelmed it, and when shepherds came quickly
to join them there on hearing of the city's reputation they
called themselves "Bruttii" after the woman's name.[2]
Their first war was with the Lucanians, the founders of   13
their race; and gaining confidence from a victory they   14
made peace on even terms, crushed all their neighbors in
war, and soon gained such power as to be thought a threat
even to kings. Finally when Alexander, king of Epirus,   15
came into Italy with a large army to assist the Greek city-
states, he was destroyed by them with all his troops.[3] So   16
their ferocity, inflamed by their success, long made them
fearful to their neighbors. Finally receiving an appeal   17
for help and hoping to enlarge his kingdom Agathocles
crossed from Sicily to Italy.

2. Shocked at the report of his coming the Bruttii first
sent ambassadors to him seeking an alliance and friendship. Agathocles invited them to dinner so they should not   2
see his army being ferried over, and after fixing an audience for them for the next day he boarded a ship and
eluded them. But the deception had no happy outcome,   3
for he was forced to return to Sicily within a few days by
a violent disease with which he was seized throughout his   4
body in all its sinews and joints, and as the noxious fluid
advanced it was as if he were being attacked in every limb.
From this desperate situation war broke out between his   5

tione bellum inter filium nepotemque eius regnum iam
quasi mortui vindicantibus oritur; occiso filio regnum nepos occupavit.

6   Igitur Agathocles, cum morbi cura et aegritudo gra-
viores essent et inter se alterum alterius malo cresceret,
desperatis rebus uxorem suam Theoxenam genitosque ex
ea duos parvulos cum omni pecunia et familia regalique
instrumento, quo praeter illum nemo regum ditior fuit,
navibus inpositos Aegyptum, unde uxorem acceperat, remittit, timens, ne praedonem regni sui hostem paterentur.

7 Quamquam uxor diu ne ab aegro divelleretur deprecata
est, ne discessus suus adiungi nepotis parricidio posset et
tam cruente haec deseruisse virum quam ille inpugnasse

8 avum videretur. Nubendo se non prosperae tantum, sed
omnis fortunae inisse societatem, nec invitam periculo
spiritus sui empturam, ut extremos viri spiritus exciperet
et exsequiarum officium, in quod profecta se nemo sit

9 successurus, obsequio debitae pietatis inpleret. Disce-
dentes parvuli flebili ululatu amplexi patrem tenebant; ex
altera parte uxor maritum non amplius visura osculis fati-

10 gabat. Nec minus senis lacrimae miserabiles erant. Fle-
bant hi morientem patrem, ille exules liberos, hi discessu
suo solitudinem patris, aegri senis, ille in spem regni sus-

11 ceptos relinqui in egestate lugebat. Inter haec regia omnis
adsistentium fletibus tam crudelis discidii inpleta resona-

12 bat. Tandem finem lacrimis necessitas profectionis in-

---

[4] A daughter of Ptolemy I Soter.

son and his grandson who were both already claiming the kingdom as though he were dead; and when the son was killed the grandson seized the kingdom.

So when his anxiety over the disease and the malady 6 itself were both increasing and each was exacerbating the other, Agathocles in despair put his wife Theoxena and his two young children by her aboard ships, together with all his money, slaves and royal appurtenances (in which there was no king richer than he), and sent them back to Egypt, from where he had received his wife,[4] fearing they would have the usurper of his throne as their enemy. His wife 7 long begged not to be torn from her sick husband so her leaving should not compound the wrong of the grandson's parricide and make her seem as heartless in abandoning her husband as the grandson had been in attacking his grandfather. In marrying him she had bound herself not 8 only to his good fortunes but to all of them, she said, and even at the risk of her own life she would not be unwilling to buy the opportunity to catch her husband's last breaths and fulfill her duty to bury him, discharging the solemn duty owed a spouse which, if she left, no other would undertake. Departing the little children kept clinging to 9 their father's embrace with tearful laments; on the other side of him a wife who was never again to see her husband smothered him with kisses. Nor were the old man's tears any less pitiful. They wept for their dying father, he for 10 his children's exile; they lamented the loneliness of their father, a sick old man, after their departure, he for the children born to the prospect of a throne but now left destitute. Meanwhile the whole palace rang with the lam- 11 entations of people witnessing such a cruel separation. Finally the need to leave put an end to their tears and the 12

13 posuit et mors regis proficiscentes filios insecuta est. Dum
haec aguntur, Karthaginienses cognitis quae in Sicilia age-
bantur, occasionem totius insulae occupandae datam sibi
existimantes magnis viribus eo traiciunt multasque civitates subigunt.

3. Eo tempore et Pyrrus adversus Romanos bellum
2 gerebat, qui inploratus a Sicilia in auxilium, sicuti dictum
est, cum Syracusas venisset, rex Siciliae sicut Epiri appel-
3 latur. Quarum rerum felicitate laetus Heleno filio Siciliae
velut avitum (nam susceptus ex filia Agathoclis regis erat),
4 Alexandro autem Italiae regnum destinat. Post haec multa
5 secunda proelia cum Karthaginiensibus facit. Interiecto
deinde tempore legati ab Italicis sociis venere nuntiantes,
resisti Romanis non posse deditionemque futuram, nisi
6 subveniat. Anxius tam ambiguo periculo incertusque quid
ageret vel quibus primum subveniret, in utrumque pronus
7 consultabat; quippe instantibus hinc Karthaginiensibus,
inde Romanis periculosum videbatur exercitum in Italiam
non traicere, periculosius a Sicilia deducere, ne aut illi non
8 lata ope aut hi deserti amitterentur. In hoc aestu periculorum tutissimus portus consiliorum visus est omnibus
viribus decernere in Sicilia et profligatis Karthaginiensi-
9 bus victorem exercitum transponere in Italiam. Itaque
conserto proelio cum superior fuisset, quoniam tamen a
10 Sicilia abiret pro victo fugere visus est; ac propterea socii
ab eo defecerunt et imperium Siciliae tam cito amisit,

---

5 Cf. Diod. Sic. 21.18.
6 Continued from 18.2; sources are indicated at 18.1. The
continuing account is at Plut. *Vit. Pyrrh.* 22ff. But Justin compresses events: Agathocles died in 289, Pyrrhus' war with Rome
began in 280, and he went to Sicily in 278.

death of the king followed his children's departure. While   13
this was taking place, the Carthaginians, having heard
what was happening in Sicily[5] and thinking they were
granted an opportunity to seize the whole island, crossed
in great strength and subdued many city-states.

3. At that time Pyrrhus was also fighting a war with the
Romans:[6] his aid had been sought by Sicily, as noted   2
above, and when he reached Syracuse he was hailed as
king of Sicily as well as Epirus. Cheered by such good   3
fortune he earmarked Sicily as his son Helenus' ancestral
kingdom (for he was the son of King Agathocles' daughter)
and Italy as Alexander's. After this he fought many suc-   4
cessful battles with the Carthaginians. Some time later,   5
delegates came to him from his Italian allies reporting that
resisting the Romans was impossible and that they faced
surrender unless he brought help. Worried by such a dan-   6
gerous predicament and uncertain what to do or whom to
help first, he was leaning in both directions; for with Car-   7
thaginians threatening him here and Romans there it
seemed dangerous not to take his army into Italy and more
dangerous still to take it out of Sicily: on the one hand it
could lost to him by failure to bring help, on the other by
being abandoned by him. In this sea of troubles the safest   8
harbor for his plans seemed to be to decide the issue in
Sicily with all his troops and once the Carthaginians were
defeated to take his victorious army over to Italy. He   9
therefore committed to battle, and although he prevailed,
in leaving Sicily he nevertheless appeared to be fleeing in
defeat; and because of that his allies defected from him   10
and he lost his Sicilian empire as swiftly as he had acquired

11 quam facile quaesierat. Sed nec in Italia meliore felicitate
usus in Epirum revertitur. Admirabilis utriusque res casus
12 in exemplum fuit. Nam sicut ante secunda fortuna rebus
supra vota fluentibus Italiae Siciliaeque imperium et tot
de Romanis victorias adtraxerat, ita nunc adversa velut in
ostentationem fragilitatis humanae destruens, quae cumu-
laverat, Siciliensi ruinae naufragium maris et foedam adversus Romanos pugnam turpemque ab Italia discessum
adiecit.

4. Post profectionem a Sicilia Pyrri magistratus Hiero
2 creatur, cuius tanta moderatio fuit, ut consentiente omnium civitatium favore dux adversus Karthaginienses pri-
3 mum, mox rex crearetur. Huius futurae maiestatis ipsa
4 infantis educatio quasi praenuntia fuit. Quippe genitus
erat patre Hieroclito, nobili viro, cuius origo a Gelone,
5 antiquo Siciliae tyranno, manabat, sed maternum illi ge-
6 nus sordidum atque adeo pudibundum fuit. Nam ex an-
cilla natus ac propterea a patre velut dehonestamentum
7 generis expositus fuerat. Sed parvulum et humanae opis
egentem apes congesto circa iacentem melle multis die-
8 bus aluere. Ob quam rem responso aruspicum admonitus
pater, qui regnum infanti portendi canebant, parvulum
recolligit omnique studio ad spem maiestatis, quae pro-
9 mittebatur, instituit. Eidem in ludo inter coaequales dis-
centi lupus tabulam in turba puerorum repente con-
10 spectus eripuit. Adulescenti quoque prima bella ineunti
11 aquila in clipeo, noctua in hasta consedit. Quod ostentum

---

[7] Cf. Polyb. 1.8f.; Diod. Sic. 22.13. Hiero became leader of
Syracuse in the later 270s, made peace with the Carthaginians,
and was acclaimed king in the mid-260s. His father was Hierocles
(not Hieroclitus); the story of his birth is fiction.

it. But having no greater success in Italy either he re-   11
turned to Epirus. The outcome of both campaigns served
as an exemplary warning. For just as he had earlier, while   12
fortune favored him, enjoyed success beyond his prayers
and won dominion in Italy and Sicily and so many victories
over the Romans, so now, with misfortune destroying all
that he had achieved as though to demonstrate the frailty
of the human condition, it added to his Sicilian debacle a
shipwreck at sea, an ignominious battle against the Romans, and a disgraceful withdrawal from Italy.

4. After Pyrrhus' departure from Sicily, Hiero became
chief magistrate,[7] a man of such moderation that with the   2
full support of all the city-states he was first made general
in the war against the Carthaginians, and shortly afterward
king. His forthcoming sovereignty was virtually foretold   3
by his childhood upbringing. In fact his father was Hiero-   4
clitus, a nobleman, who was descended from Gelon, former tyrant of Sicily, but his mother's family was lowly and   5
even embarrassingly so. For he had been born of a slave   6
girl and for that reason exposed by his father as a disgrace
to his family. But the baby, even though lacking human   7
assistance, was fed for many days by bees that heaped
honey around him where he lay. Because of that his father,   8
advised by soothsayers, who predicted that a throne lay
ahead for the child, took back the infant and made every
effort to train him for the sovereignty that he was promised. When the same child was at lessons in school among   9
his peers a wolf that was suddenly spotted among a crowd
of boys seized his writing tablet. In his youth, too, when   10
he was entering his first military campaigns, an eagle settled on his shield and an owl on his spear. This portent was   11

et consilio cautum et manu promptum regemque futurum
12 significabat. Denique adversus provocatores saepe pugna-
13 vit semperque victoriam reportavit. A Pyrro rege multis
14 militaribus donis donatus est. Pulchritudo ei corporis in-
15 signis, vires quoque in homine admirabiles fuere. In adloquio blandus, in negotio iustus, in imperio moderatus,
prorsus ut nihil ei regium deesse praeter regnum videretur.

indicating that he was to be a prudent politician, a courageous fighter, and a king. Indeed he often fought against 12
people who challenged him and always prevailed. From 13
King Pyrrhus he received many military awards. He had 14
extremely good looks, and also strength amazing in a man.
In conversation he was charming, in business dealings 15
principled, and in exercise of authority fair-minded, so
that he clearly lacked no regal attribute except a kingdom.

LIBER XXIV

1. Dum haec in Sicilia geruntur, interim in Graecia dissi-
dentibus inter se bello Ptolomeo Cerauno et Antiocho et
2 Antigono regibus omnes ferme Graeciae civitates ducibus
Spartanis, velut occasione data ad spem libertatis erectae,
missis invicem legatis, per quos in societatis foedera alli-
3 garentur, in bellum prorumpunt et, ne cum Antigono, sub
cuius regno erant, bellum coepisse viderentur, socios eius
4 Aetolos adgrediuntur, causas belli praetendentes, quod
consensu Graeciae sacratum Apollini Cirraeum campum
5 per vim occupassent. Huic bello ducem deligunt Area, qui
adunato exercitu urbes sataque in his campis posita depo-
6 pulatur, quae auferri non poterant incendit. Quod cum e
montibus conspicati pastores Aetolorum essent, congre-
gati admodum quingenti sparsos hostes ignorantesque,
quanta manus esset, quoniam conspectum illis metus et
incendiorum fumus abstulerat, consectantur trucidatis-
que admodum novem milibus praedones in fugam ver-
7 terunt. Reparantibus deinde Spartanis bellum auxilium
multae civitates negaverunt, existimantes eos domina-
8 tionem, non libertatem Graeciae quaerere. Interea inter
reges bellum finitur; nam Ptolomeus pulso Antigono cum

---

[1] For the sacred plain cf. 8.1.4n.

BOOK XXIV

1. While this was taking place in Sicily, meanwhile the kings Ptolemy Ceraunus, Antiochus and Antigonus were at war with each other in Greece; nearly all the Greek 2 city-states, led by the Spartans, were encouraged to hopes of liberty by the opportunity they seemed to be given, and after sending each other embassies to cement alliances they plunged into war; and not to appear to have opened 3 war with Antigonus, under whose rule they were, they attacked his allies the Aetolians, their pretext for war being 4 that they had seized the plain of Cirrha which by panhellenic accord was sacred to Apollo.[1] For this war they chose 5 as their general Areus, who united their forces, raided the Aetolian cities and the crops sown in their fields, and burned what could not be carried off. When this was spot- 6 ted from the hills by some Aetolian shepherds, some five hundred of them gathered together and pursued their enemies, who were dispersed and unaware of the number they faced since panic and smoking fires had blocked their vision, and after killing about nine thousand they put them to flight. When the Spartans then restarted the war many 7 states refused to help them, believing their aim the domination of Greece and not its liberation. Meanwhile the war 8 between the kings came to an end; for Ptolemy, defeating

47

regnum totius Macedoniae occupasset, pacem cum Antiocho facit adfinitatemque cum Pyrro rege data ei in matrimonium filia sua iungit.

2. Exinde externo metu deposito inpium et facinorosum animum ad domesticae scelera convertit insidiasque Arsinoae, sorori suae, instruit, quibus et filios eius vita et

2 ipsam Cassandreae urbis possessione privaret. Primus ei dolus fuit simulato amore sororis matrimonium petere; aliter enim ad sororis filios, quorum regnum occupaverat,

3 quam concordiae fraude pervenire non poterat. Sed nota

4 scelerata Ptolomei voluntas sorori erat. Itaque non credenti mandat velle se cum filiis eius regni consortium iungere; cum quibus non ideo se armis contendisse, quoniam eripere his regnum, sed quod id facere sui muneris vellet.

5 In hoc mitteret arbitrum iuris iurandi, quo praesente apud deos patrios quibus vellet obsecrationibus se obligaret.

6 Incerta Arsinoe quid ageret; si mitteret, decipi periurio, si non mitteret, provocare rabiem fraternae crudelitatis ti-

7 mebat. Itaque plus liberis quam sibi timens, quos matrimonio suo protecturam se arbitrabatur, mittit ex amicis

8 suis Dionem; quo perducto in sanctissimum Iovis templum veterrimae Macedonum religionis Ptolomeus sumptis in manus altaribus, contingens ipsa simulacra et pulvinaria deorum inauditis ultimisque execrationibus adiurat,

9 se sincera fide sororis matrimonium petere nuncupatu-

---

[2] See 17.2.15.   [3] See 17.2.4ff.   [4] Or, perhaps, "Ptolemy's criminal intent was recognized by his sister."

[5] This ought to refer to the temple of Zeus at Dium, which, since its Greek form is *Dion*, casts suspicion on the reality of Arsinoë's friend.

Antigonus and seizing the whole of all Macedonia, made peace with Antiochus and cemented a family alliance with Pyrrhus by giving him his daughter in marriage.[2]

2. Then with external threats removed he also turned his impious and villainous mind to domestic crimes and set a trap for his own sister Arsinoë[3] with which to deprive her sons of their lives and Arsinoë herself of possession of the city of Cassandrea. His first scheme was to feign love 2 for his sister and ask her to marry him; for he had no way of reaching the sister's sons, whose kingdom he had seized, other than by contrived friendship. But Ptolemy's nefari- 3 ous intention became known to his sister.[4] So when she 4 would not believe him he reported to her that he wished to share the kingdom with her sons, that he had gone to war with them not because he wanted to wrest the king- dom from them but because he wished to make it his personal gift to them. On this matter, she should send a 5 man to witness his oath, and in his presence he would before their ancestral gods bind himself with any pledges she wished. Arsinoë was unsure how to react; if she did 6 send someone, she feared being duped by perjury; if she did not, she feared provoking her brother's insane cruelty. So fearing more for her children than herself, and thinking 7 that she would protect them by marrying him, she sent one of her friends, Dion. When he was taken to Jupiter's most 8 holy temple, venerated from days of old by the Macedo- nians,[5] Ptolemy grasped the altar with his hands and, touching the very statues and cushioned seats of the gods, swore with bizarre and extravagant oaths that it was in all 9 sincerity that he sought marriage with his sister, that he

rumque se eam reginam, neque in contumeliam eius se
aliam uxorem aliosve quam filios eius liberos habiturum.

10 Arsinoe postquam et spe inpleta est et metu soluta, ipsa
cum fratre conloquitur, cuius vultus et blandientes oculi
cum fidem non minorem quam ius iurandum promit-
terent, reclamante Ptolomeo filio fraudem subesse, in
matrimonium fratris concedit.

3. Nuptiae magno apparatu laetitiaque omnium ce-
2 lebrantur. Ad contionem quoque vocato exercitu capiti
3 sororis diadema inponit reginamque eam appellat. Quo
nomine in laetitiam effusa Arsinoe, quia quod morte Lysimachi, prioris mariti, amiserat recepisset, ultro virum in
urbem suam Cassandream invitat, cuius urbis cupiditate
4 fraus struebatur. Praegressa igitur virum diem festum urbi
in adventum eius indicit, domos, templa ceteraque omnia
5 exornari iubet, aras ubique hostiasque disponi; filios quoque suos, Lysimachum sedecim annos natum, Philippum
triennio minorem, utrumque forma insignem, coronatos
6 occurrere iubet. Quos Ptolomeus ad celandam fraudem
cupide et ultra modum verae adfectionis amplexus osculis
7 diu fatigat. Vbi ad portam ventum est, occupari arcem
iubet, pueros interfici. Qui cum ad matrem confugissent,
in gremio eius inter ipsa oscula trucidantur, proclamante
8 Arsinoe, quid tantum nefas aut nubendo aut post nuptias
contraxisset. Pro filiis saepe se percussoribus obtulit, frequenter corpore suo puerorum corpora amplexata protexit

---

6 We are left to conclude that the third son, Ptolemy, refused
to go (see above, 24.2.10).

would declare her his queen and not shame her by taking
any other wife or having children other than hers as sons.
Now that she was both filled with hope and freed from   10
fear, Arsinoe herself talked with her brother, and his expression and melting eyes promised no less integrity than
his oath, whereupon, despite her son Ptolemy's protests
that treachery was afoot, she agreed to marriage with her
brother.

3. The wedding was celebrated with great pomp and
universal rejoicing. The army also called to the gathering,   2
he set a diadem on his sister's head and addressed her as
queen. At the title Arsinoë was beside herself with joy   3
because she had recovered what she had lost on the death
of Lysimachus, her former husband, and she even invited
the man to her own city of Cassandrea, a city in which,
through his lust for it, a trap was being prepared. So pre-   4
ceding her husband, she declared a city holiday in honor
of his arrival and ordered houses, temples, and everything
else to be decorated, and altars and sacrificial victims to
be set in place everywhere; and she also ordered her   5
sons—Lysimachus, sixteen years old, and Philip, three
years younger, both strikingly good looking boys—to meet
him, wearing garlands.[6] These, in order to conceal his   6
treachery, Ptolemy eagerly embraced and in a manner ex-
ceeding real affection, and he long showered them with
kisses. When they came to the gate he ordered the citadel   7
seized and the boys killed. When they fled to their mother
they were butchered in her arms as she kissed them, while   8
Arsinoe cried out asking what terrible crime she had committed in marrying him or after their marriage. In place
of her sons, she time and again offered herself to the assassins; often with her own body she shielded her boys'

51

vulneraque excipere, quae liberis intendebantur, voluit.
9   Ad postremum etiam spoliata funeribus filiorum scissa
veste et crinibus sparsis cum duobus servulis ex urbe pro-
tracta Samothraciam in exilium abiit, eo miserior, quod
10 mori ei cum filiis non licuit. Sed nec Ptolomeo inulta scelera fuerunt; quippe diis inmortalibus tot periuria et tam
cruenta parricidia vindicantibus brevi post a Gallis spoliatus regno captusque vitam ferro, ut meruerat, amisit.

4. Namque Galli abundante multitudine, cum eos non
caperent terrae, quae genuerant, CCC milia hominum ad
2   sedes novas quaerendas velut ver sacrum miserunt. Ex his
portio in Italia consedit, quae et urbem Romanam captam
3   incendit et portio Illyricos sinus ducibus avibus (nam au-
gurandi studio Galli praeter ceteros callent) per strages
4   barbarorum penetravit et in Pannonia consedit; gens as-
pera, audax, bellicosa, quae prima post Herculem, cui ea
res virtutis admirationem et inmortalitatis fidem dedit,
Alpium invicta iuga et frigore intractabilia loca transcen-
5   dit. Ibi domitis Pannoniis per multos annos cum finitimis
6   varia bella gesserunt. Hortante deinde successu divisis
agminibus alii Graeciam, alii Macedoniam omnia ferro
7   prosternentes petivere, tantusque terror Gallici nominis
erat, ut etiam reges non lacessiti ultro pacem ingenti pecunia mercarentur.
8   Solus rex Macedoniae Ptolomeus adventum Gallorum
intrepidus audivit eisque cum paucis et incompositis,

---

7 The "sacred spring" (Latin *ver sacrum*) was an Italic practice
of marking out children born at a certain time to be sent to form
a new settlement when they reached adulthood.

8 Roughly modern Hungary (*Barr.* 20 C3).

bodies in her embrace and tried to take the wounds that
were aimed at her children. Finally even denied burial of   9
her sons, she was dragged from the city with two slaves,
clothes torn and hair disheveled, and she went into exile
in Samothrace, her misery all the greater for not being
allowed to die with her sons. But Ptolemy's crimes did not   10
go unpunished, either; for with the immortal gods exacting
vengeance for so many treacherous acts and such bloody
murders, he was soon robbed of his throne by the Gauls,
captured and, as he deserved, lost his life to the sword.

4. Now since the Gauls were becoming overpopulated,
when the lands that had produced them were incapable of
sustaining them, they sent three hundred thousand in
quest of new homes as a "sacred spring."[7] Some of them   2
settled in Italy and captured and burned the city of Rome,
and some led by birds (for in the practice of augury the   3
Gauls are unsurpassed) massacred barbarians, penetrated
the recesses of Illyria and settled in Pannonia;[8] a violent,   4
reckless, bellicose race, they were the first after Hercules
to cross the impassable heights of the Alps—a feat that
earned him renown for valor and belief in his immortal-
ity—and areas uninhabitable from the cold. There after   5
subduing the Pannonians they spent many years fighting
various wars against their neighbors. Then, encouraged by   6
their success, they divided their armies and some headed
for Greece and others for Macedonia, laying waste everything with the sword; and such was the terror inspired by   7
the Gallic name that even kings not under attack would
readily buy peace with huge amounts of money.

Only the king of Macedonia Ptolemy heard of the   8
Gauls' approach undaunted, and with a few disorganized

quasi bella non difficilius quam scelera patrarentur, parri-
9 cidiorum furiis agitatus occurrit. Dardanorum quoque
legationem XX milia armatorum in auxilium offerentem
sprevit, addita insuper contumelia, actum de Macedonia
dicens, si, cum totum Orientem soli domuerint, nunc in
10 vindictam finium Dardanis egeant; milites se habere filios
eorum, qui sub Alexandro rege stipendia toto orbe terra-
11 rum victores fecerint. Quae ubi Dardano regi nuntiata
sunt, inclitum illud Macedoniae regnum brevi inmaturi
iuvenis temeritate casurum dixit.

5. Igitur Galli duce Belgio ad temptandos Macedonum
animos legatos ad Ptolomeum mittunt, offerentes pacem,
2 si emere velit; sed Ptolomeus inter suos belli metu pacem
3 Gallos petere gloriatus est. Nec minus ferociter se legatis
quam inter amicos iactavit, aliter se pacem daturum ne-
gando, nisi principes suos obsides dederint et arma tradi-
4 derint; non enim fidem se nisi inermibus habiturum. Re-
nuntiata legatione risere Galli, undique adclamantes brevi
5 sensurum, sibi an illi consulentes pacem obtulerint. Inter-
6 iectis diebus proelium conseritur; victi Macedones cae-
duntur; Ptolomeus multis vulneribus saucius capitur; caput eius amputatum et lancea fixum tota acie ad terrorem
7 hostium circumfertur. Paucos ex Macedonibus fuga serva-
vit; ceteri aut capti aut occisi.
8 Haec cum nuntiata per omnem Macedoniam essent,
portae urbium clauduntur, luctu omnia replentur:

---

9 The Dardanians dwelt in what is now North Macedonia.
10 This occurred in 279, after he had reigned one year and five
months (Porphyry of Tyre *FGrH* 260 F 3.9).

troops he went out to face them, as though wars could be fought as easily as crimes committed, driven by the Furies that punish parricide. He even spurned a deputation of Dardanians[9] that offered twenty thousand armed men to aid him, adding the insult that Macedon was finished if its people now needed Dardanians to defend its borders after it had single-handedly conquered the entire East; he had soldiers that were sons of men who had under King Alexander served victoriously throughout the world, he said. When this was reported to the Dardanian king, he said the famed kingdom of Macedonia would soon fall through the recklessness of an immature youth.

5. So under the leadership of Belgius the Gauls sent delegates to Ptolemy to sound out the Macedonians, offering peace if he wished to buy it; but Ptolemy boasted among his people that the Gauls were seeking peace because they feared a war. Nor was he any less arrogant in bragging to the legates than he was among his friends, saying he would grant no peace unless they gave their leaders as hostages and surrendered their weapons—for he would not trust them if they were not disarmed. When the legation reported back the Gauls laughed, everywhere exclaiming that he would soon understand whether their peace offer was better for him or for them. After a few days there was a battle; the Macedonians were defeated and cut down; Ptolemy was captured with many wounds; his head was severed, fixed on a lance and paraded throughout the battlefield to strike terror in the enemy.[10] A few of the Macedonians were saved by flight; the rest were either captured or killed.

When this was reported throughout Macedonia, city gates were closed and everywhere was full of lamentation;

9   nunc orbitatem amissorum filiorum dolebant, nunc exci-
dia urbium metuebant, nunc Alexandri Philippique, regum suorum, nomina sicuti numina in auxilium vocabant;

10   sub illis se non solum tutos, verum etiam victores orbis
11   terrarum extitisse; ut tuerentur patriam suam, quam gloria
rerum gestarum caelo proximam reddidissent, ut opem
adflictis ferrent, quos furor et temeritas Ptolomei regis

12   perdidisset, orabant. Desperantibus omnibus non votis
agendum Sosthenes, unus de principibus Macedonum,
ratus contracta iuventute et Gallos victoria exultantes
conpescuit et Macedoniam ab hostili populatione defen-

13   dit. Ob quae virtutis beneficia multis nobilibus regnum
14   Macedoniae adfectantibus ignobilis ipse praeponitur, et
cum rex ab exercitu appellatus esset, ipse non in regis, sed
in ducis nomen iurare milites conpulit.

      6. Interea Brennus, quo duce portio Gallorum in Grae-
ciam se effuderat, audita victoria suorum, qui Belgio duce
Macedonas vicerant, indignatus parta victoria opimam
praedam et Orientis spoliis onustam tam facile relictam
esse, ipse adunatis CL milibus peditum et XV milibus

2   equitum in Macedoniam inrumpit. Cum agros villasque
popularetur, occurrit ei cum instructo exercitu Macedonum Sosthenes; sed pauci a pluribus, trepidi a valentibus

3   facile vincuntur. Itaque cum victi se Macedones intra

---

11 From Porphyry *FGrH* 260 F 3.10f., we learn that between
Ptolemy Ceraunus and Sosthenes Macedon was ruled for two
months by Ceraunus' brother Meleager and for forty-five days by
Antipater, son of Philip and grandson of Cassander; there were
also periods of anarchy, but Sosthenes was in power from 278/7
to 276/5.

now they were grieving for the loss of sons, now fearing 9
the destruction of their cities, now calling out the names
of their kings Alexander and Philip as gods to help them;
under them they had not only been secure but even con- 10
querors of the world, they said; and they were now beg- 11
ging them to protect their fatherland, which by their glorious achievements they had raised close to heaven, and to
bring aid to a shattered people that King Ptolemy's madness and recklessness had destroyed. When they were all 12
in despair Sosthenes, one of the Macedonian generals,[11]
thinking they should not be resorting to prayers, gathered
the young men together, brought the Gauls to halt while
they were elated their victory, and defended Macedonia
against the enemy's pillaging. For such courageous ser- 13
vices he, although himself lowborn, was chosen over many
noblemen aspiring to the Macedonian Kingdom, and al- 14
though he was hailed as king by the army, he made the
soldiers take their oath to him not as "king" but as "commander."

6. Meanwhile Brennus, under whose leadership some
Gauls had flooded into Greece, had now heard his countrymen's victory over the Macedonians under Belgius'
leadership; and angry that after the victory was won a rich
plunder that was also swollen with the spoils of the East
had been so easily abandoned he personally brought a
hundred and fifty thousand infantry and fifteen thousand
cavalry together and invaded Macedonia. While pillaging 2
fields and farms he was confronted by Sosthenes with a
Macedonian army ready for battle; but few against many
and nervous men facing stalwart men they were easily
defeated. So, when the defeated Macedonians then se- 3

muros urbium condidissent, victor Brennus nemine pro-
4 hibente totius Macedoniae agros depraedatur. Inde quasi
terrena iam spolia sorderent, animum ad deorum inmortalium templa convertit, scurriliter iocatus locupletes deos
5 largiri hominibus oportere. Statim igitur Delphos iter vertit, praedam religioni, aurum offensae deorum inmortalium praeferens; quos nullis opibus egere, ut qui eas largiri
6 hominibus solent, adfirmabat. Templum autem Apollinis
Delphis positum est in monte Parnasso, in rupe undique
inpendente; ibi civitatem frequentia hominum fecit, qui
admiratione maiestatis undique concurrentes in eo saxo
7 consedere. Atque ita templum et civitatem non muri, sed
praecipitia, nec manu facta, sed naturalia praesidia de-
fendunt, prorsus ut incertum sit, utrum munimentum loci
8 an maiestas dei plus hic admirationis habeat. Media saxi
rupes in formam theatri recessit. Quamobrem et hominum clamor et si quando accedit tubarum sonus, perso-
nantibus et resonantibus inter se rupibus multiplex audiri
ampliorque quam editur resonare solet. Quae res maiorem maiestatis terrorem ignaris rei et admirationem
9 stupentibus plerumque adfert. In hoc rupis amfractu
media ferme montis altitudine planities exigua est, atque
in ea profundum terrae foramen, quod in oracula patet, ex
quo frigidus spiritus vi quadam velut vento in sublime
expulsus mentes vatum in vecordiam vertit inpletasque
10 deo responsa consulentibus dare cogit. Multa igitur ibi et
opulenta regum ac populorum visuntur munera quaeque

creted themselves within the walls of their cities, the victorious Brennus, with no one hindering him, pillaged all
the Macedonian countryside. Then, as if earthly spoils   4
were now paltry, he turned his attention to the temples of
the immortal gods, offensively quipping that gods, being
rich, should, be generous to men. So he immediately   5
veered toward Delphi, setting plunder above religion and
gold above offending the immortal gods; these, he insisted, needed no riches since they kept showering them
on men. Now the temple of Apollo at Delphi is set on Mt.   6
Parnassus, on a cliff sheer on every side; there a community was formed by large numbers of people who converg-
ing there from all parts through admiration for its gran-
deur settled on that rock. Thus the temple and community   7
are protected not by walls but precipices, and have not
man-made but natural fortifications, so strong that it is
uncertain whether the defenses of the place or the majesty
of the god earn it the greater admiration. The center of   8
the cliff recedes into the shape of a theater. Because of
that both people's shouts and any noise from trumpets are
usually heard many times over as the rocks resound and
echo among themselves, multiplied and magnified beyond
normal volume. The phenomenon heightens fear of its
majesty for those unaware of it and admiration in those
bewildered by it. In this curvature of the rock is a narrow   9
plateau about halfway up the hill, and on it is a deep hole
in the ground that lies open for delivering oracles; and
from it a chilly puff of air expelled by a wind-like force
deranges the priests' minds and forces them when inspired by the god to give responses to those consulting
him. Thus many rich gifts from kings and peoples may be   10
seen there, and by their magnificence they clearly demon-

59

magnificentia sui reddentium vota gratam voluntatem et deorum responsa manifestant.

7. Igitur Brennus cum in conspectu haberet templum, diu deliberavit, an confestim rem adgrederetur an vero fessis via militibus noctis spatium ad resumendas vires
2 daret. Aenianum et Thessalorum duces, qui se ad praedae societatem iunxerant, amputari moras iubebant, dum
3 inparati hostes et recens adventus sui terror esset; interiecta nocte et animos hostibus, forsitan et auxilia acces-
4 sura, et, vias, quae tunc pateant, obstructum iri. Sed Gallorum vulgus ex longa inopia, ubi primum vino ceterisque commeatibus referta rura invenit, non minus abundantia
5 quam victoria laetum per agros se sparserat, desertisque signis ad occupanda omnia pro victoribus vagabantur.
6 Quae res dilationem Delphis dedit. Prima namque opinione adventus Gallorum prohibiti agrestes oraculis fe-
7 runtur messes vinaque villis efferre. Cuius rei salutare praeceptum non prius intellectum est, quam vini ceterarumque copiarum abundantia velut mora Gallis obiecta
8 auxilia finitimorum convenere. Prius itaque urbem suam Delphi aucti viribus sociorum permunivere, quam Galli vino velut praedae incubantes ad signa revocarentur.
9 Habebat Brennus lecta ex omni exercitu peditum sexaginta quinque milia; Delphorum sociorumque non nisi
10 quattuor milia milites erant, quorum contemptu Brennus ad acuendos suorum animos praedae ubertatem omnibus ostendebat statuasque cum quadrigis, quarum ingens co-

---

12 The Aeneanes: a people living in the upper Spercheios valley (*OCD* s.v.).

strate the gratitude of people fulfilling their vows and the reliability of the gods' responses.

7. Now when Brennus had the temple in view, he long debated whether to set to work immediately or give his travel-weary troops a night's respite to recoup their strength. The Aenian[12] and Thessalian leaders, who had joined him to share the plunder, kept urging him to shorten delays while the enemy was unprepared and the panic inspired by his arrival still fresh; overnight their enemies could gain both courage and perhaps even reinforcements, they said, and the roads then open would be blocked. But when the Gallic horde after long deprivation discovered the countryside replete with wine and other provisions, they, no less pleased with such bounty than they might have been with victory, had dispersed throughout the fields, and leaving their standards were wandering around like victors to seize everything. This gave Delphi a respite. For at the first word of the arrival of the Gauls peasants were forbidden by the oracles to remove harvested crops and wine from their farms. The precautionary nature of this was not understood until the Gauls were delayed by their large quantities of wine and other provisions and help arrived from neighboring people. Thus the people of Delphi, reinforced with allied troops, fortified their city before the Gauls, hovering over wine as their plunder, could be brought back to their standards. Brennus had a force of sixty-five thousand infantry selected from his whole army; the Delphians and their allies had no more than four thousand soldiers. Contemptuous of these and to sharpen his own men's spirits Brennus would point out to everyone the abundance of their booty, and the statues and chariots, large numbers of which could be

pia procul visebatur, solido auro fusas esse plusque in pondere quam in specie habere praedae adfirmabat.

8. Hac adseveratione incitati Galli, simul et hesterno
mero saucii, sine respectu periculorum in bellum ruebant.
2 Contra Delphi plus in deo quam in viribus deputantes
cum contemptu hostium resistebant scandentesque Gallos e summo montis vertice partim saxo, partim armis
3 obruebant. In hoc partium certamine repente universorum templorum antistites, simul et ipsae vates sparsis crinibus cum insignibus atque infulis pavidi vecordesque in
4 primam pugnantium aciem procurrunt. Advenisse deum
clamant, eumque se vidisse desilientem in templum per
5 culminis aperta fastigia, dum omnes opem dei suppliciter
inplorant, iuvenem supra humanum modum insignis pulchritudinis; comitesque ei duas armatas virgines ex pro-
pinquis duabus Dianae Minervaeque aedibus occurrisse;
6 nec oculis tantum haec se perspexisse, audisse etiam stri-
7 dorem arcus ac strepitum armorum. Proinde ne cunc-
tarentur diis antesignanis hostem caedere et victoriae
deorum socios se adiungere summis obsecrationibus mo-
nebant.

8 Quibus vocibus incensi omnes certatim in proelium
9 prosiliunt. Praesentiam dei et ipsi statim sensere, nam et
terrae motu portio montis abrupta Gallorum stravit exercitum et confertissimi cunei non sine vulneribus hostium
10 dissipati ruebant. Insecuta deinde tempestas est, quae

seen in the distance; and he kept emphasizing that these were cast in solid gold and that the weight in the plunder was greater than appeared.

8. Stirred by this claim, and also tipsy with the previous day's wine, the Gauls charged into battle heedless of danger. The Delphians, however, relying more on the god 2 than their strength, contemptuously resisted their enemy, and as the Gauls climbed up they would overwhelm them from the mountaintop, some with stones, some with weapons. In this struggle between the two the priests from all 3 the temples, and at the same time even the prophetesses themselves, hair disheveled and wearing their insignia and fillets, suddenly rushed forward trembling and frenzied into the front line of fighters. The god had come, they 4 shouted, and they had seen him leaping down into his temple through an opening in the roof, while everyone 5 was humbly begging for divine aid—a young superhuman figure of remarkable beauty; and as his companions two virgins in armor had come to meet him from the two nearby temples of Diana and Minerva; and they had not 6 only seen these things with their eyes but had also heard the twang of a bow and the clash of weapons! So they 7 should not hesitate to massacre their enemy as the gods were standing by their frontline troops and warning them with the most earnest entreaties.

Fired by such cries they all charged into battle compet- 8 ing with each other. The presence of the god they also 9 immediately felt themselves, for part of the mountain was sheared off by an earthquake and crushed the army of the Gauls; and their dense phalanxes scattered, not without wounds from their enemy and were destroyed. A storm 10 then followed that finished off the wounded with hail and

11 grandine et frigore saucios ex vulneribus absumpsit. Dux
ipse Brennus cum dolorem vulnerum ferre non posset,
12 pugione vitam finivit. Alter ex ducibus punitis belli auctoribus cum decem milibus sauciorum citato agmine Grae-
13 cia excedit. Sed nec fugientibus fortuna commodior fuit,
siquidem pavidis nulla sub tectis acta nox, nullus sine la-
14 bore et periculo dies; adsidui imbres et gelu nix concreta
et fames et lassitudo et super haec maximum pervigiliae
15 malum miseras infelicis belli reliquias obterebant. Gentes
quoque nationesque, per quas iter habebant, palantes
16 velut praedam sectabantur. Quo pacto evenit, ut nemo ex
tanto exercitu, qui paulo ante fiducia virium etiam deos
contemnebat, vel ad memoriam tantae cladis superesset.

freezing temperatures. Their own leader Brennus, unable 11
to bear the pain of his wounds, ended his life with a dagger.
His second in command punished those who had started 12
the war and swiftly left Greece with ten thousand wounded
men. But not even to the fugitives was Fortune any kinder, 13
for in their terror they spent no night under shelter and
not a day free of hardship and danger; incessant rain, frost- 14
hardened snow, hunger, exhaustion and, worst of all, lack
of sleep kept grinding down the sad remnants of the ill-
starred campaign. Peoples and tribes through which they 15
had to journey would hound the straggling force as their
prey. So it turned out that from such a huge army, which 16
shortly before from confidence in its strength had felt contempt even for the gods, none survived even to record
such a massive defeat.

LIBER XXV

1. Inter duos reges, Antigonum et Antiochum statuta pace cum in Macedoniam Antigonus reverteretur, novus eidem
2 repente hostis exortus est Quippe Galli, qui a Brenno duce, cum in Graeciam proficisceretur, ad terminos gentis tuendos relicti fuerant, ne soli desides viderentur, pedi-
3 tum XV milia, equitum tria milia armaverunt fugatisque Getarum Triballorumque copiis Macedoniae inminentes legatos ad regem miserunt, qui pacem ei venalem offer-
4 rent, simul et regis castra specularentur. Quos Antigonus pro regali munificentia ingenti apparatu epularum ad ce-
5 nam invitavit. Sed Galli expositum grande auri argentique pondus admirantes atque praedae ubertate sollicitati in-
6 festiores quam venerant revertuntur. Quibus et elephan-tos ad terrorem velut invisitatas barbaris formas rex os-
7 tendi iusserat, naves onustas copiis demonstrari, ignarus, quod, quibus ostentatione virium metum se inicere existi-mabat, eorum animos ut ad opimam praedam sollicitabat.
8 Itaque legati reversi ad suos omnia in maius extollentes
9 opes pariter et neglegentiam regis ostendunt; referta auro et argento castra, sed neque vallo fossave munita; et quasi satis munimenti in divitiis haberent, ita eos omnia officia

---

[1] The year is 276; cf. Diod. Sic. 22.4.

BOOK XXV

1. After peace had been settled between the two kings Antigonus and Antiochus, Antigonus was returning to Macedonia when a new enemy suddenly arose before him. For the Gauls who had been left by Brennus to defend 2 their nation's boundaries when he was leaving for Greece,[1] in order not to appear indolent put fifteen thousand infantry and three thousand cavalry under arms, routed the 3 forces of the Getae and Triballi, and threatening Macedonia sent delegates to the king to offer him peace at a price and also investigate the king's camp. With regal generosity 4 Antigonus invited them to dinner, giving them with magnificent feast. But the Gauls, amazed at the large amount 5 of gold and silver on display and tempted by the rich plunder, returned more aggressive than when they came. To 6 intimidate them the king had even ordered them to be shown his elephants, creatures unknown to barbarians, and put ships on display laden with troops, unaware that 7 men he thought he was intimidating by flaunting his strength he was only enticing to rich plunder. So on re- 8 turning to their people and exaggerating everything, the delegates advertised the wealth of the king as well as his carelessness; the camp was full of gold and silver, they said, 9 but defended neither by ditch nor rampart; and as if they had protection enough in their wealth they had suspended

10 militaria intermisisse, prorsus quasi ferri auxilio non indi-
gerent, quoniam auro abundarent.

2. Hac relatione avidae gentis animi satis ad praedam
2 incitabantur; accedebat tamen et exemplum Belgi, qui
non magno ante tempore Macedonum exercitum cum
3 rege trucidaverat. Itaque consentientibus omnibus nocte
castra regis adgrediuntur, qui praesentiens tantam tem-
pestatem signum pridie dederat, ut omnibus ablatis in
proxima silva taciti se occultarent. Neque aliter servata
4 castra quam quod deserta sunt, siquidem Galli, ubi omnia
vacantia nec sine defensoribus modo, verum etiam sine
custodibus vident, non fugam hostium, sed dolum arbi-
5 trantes, diu intrare portas timuerunt. Ad postremum inte-
gris et intactis munimentis scrutantes potius quam diri-
6 pientes castra occupaverunt. Nunc ablatis quae invenerant
ad litus convertuntur. Ibi dum naves incautius diripiunt, a
remigibus et ab exercitus parte, quae eo cum coniugibus
et liberis confugerant, nihil tale metuentes trucidantur,
7 tantaque caedes Gallorum fuit, ut Antigono pacem opinio
huius victoriae non a Gallis tantum, verum etiam a finiti-
8 morum feritate praestiterit. Quamquam Gallorum ea
tempestate tantae fecunditatis iuventus fuit, ut Asiam
9 omnem velut examine aliquo inplerent. Denique neque
reges Orientis sine mercennario Gallorum exercitu ulla
bella gesserunt, neque pulsi regno ad alios quam ad Gallos
10 confugerunt. Tantus terror Gallici nominis et armorum
invicta felicitas erat, ut aliter neque maiestatem suam tutam neque amissam recuperare se posse sine Gallica vir-
11 tute arbitrarentur. Itaque in auxilium a Bithyniae rege

---

2 That is, weapons made of it.

all military duties, not of course needing the help of iron[2] 10
since they were awash with gold!

2. By this report the spirits of an avaricious race were
being well enough primed for plunder; but there was also
the example of Belgius, who not much earlier had mas- 2
sacred a Macedonian army together with its king. So with 3
all in agreement they made a night attack on the camp of
the king who, anticipating such a storm, had the previous
day given the signal for his men to remove everything and
quietly conceal themselves in the nearest wood. And by
nothing other was the camp saved than that it was deserted
for the Gauls, when they saw it completely unoccupied 4
and lacking not only defenders but even guards, suspected
it was not flight but trickery on their enemy's part and for
a long time long feared to enter the gates. Finally leaving 5
its defenses whole and intact they took over the camp,
rummaging rather than pillaging it. Carrying off what they 6
found they now converged on the seashore. There while
they were carelessly ransacking ships and fearing no such
thing they were massacred by the oarsmen and some of
the army that had fled there with their wives and children,
and so great was the slaughter of the Gauls that word of 7
this victory brought peace for Antigonus not just with the
Gauls but even his ferocious neighbors. However the 8
young Gauls at the time were so fertile that they were filling all Asia like a swarm. In fact not even eastern kings 9
would fight any wars without a Gallic mercenary army, and
if driven from their kingdoms they sought refuge with
none but the Gauls. Such was the fear inspired by the 10
Gallic name and such its military success that they thought
they could neither safeguard their sovereignty nor recover
it if lost without Gallic prowess. So when asked for aid 11

EPITOME OF POMPEIUS TROGUS

invocati regnum cum eo parta victoria diviserunt eamque
regionem Gallograeciam cognominaverunt.

3. Dum haec in Asia geruntur, interim in Sicilia Pyrrus
a Poenis navali proelio victus ab Antigono, Macedoniae
rege, supplementum militum per legatos petit, denun-
2 tians, ni mittat, redire se in regnum necesse habere, incrementa rerum, quae de Romanis voluerit, de ipso quaesi-
3 turum. Quod ubi negatum legati retulerunt, dissimulatis
4 causis repentinam fingit profectionem. Socios interim
parare bellum iubet, arcis Tarentinae custodiam Heleno
5 filio et amico Miloni tradit. Reversus in Epirum statim
fines Macedoniae invadit; cui Antigonus cum exercitu
6 occurrit victusque proelio in fugam vertitur. Atque ita Pyrrus Macedoniam in deditionem accepit et veluti damna
amissae Siciliae Italiaeque adquisito Macedoniae regno
pensasset, relictum Tarenti filium et amicum arcessit.
7 Antigonus autem cum paucis equitibus, fugae comitibus,
repente fortunae ornamentis destitutus amissi regni spe-
culaturus eventus Thessalonicam se recepit, ut inde cum
conducta Gallorum mercennaria manu bellum repararet.
8 Rursus ab Ptolomeo, Pyrri filio, funditus victus; cum septem comitibus fugiens non iam reciperandi regni spem,
sed salutis latebras ac fugae solitudines captat.

4. Igitur Pyrrus in tanto fastigio regni conlocatus iam
nec eo, ad quod votis perveniendum fuerat, contentus

---

3 See 18.1.3.

70

by the king of Bithynia they shared his kingdom with
him when victory was won and named that region Gallograecia.

3. While this was happening in Asia, meanwhile in Sicily Pyrrhus, defeated by the Carthaginians in a sea battle,
through delegates asked for reinforcements from Antigonus, king of Macedonia, warning him that if he did not 2
send them he would have to withdraw into his own kingdom and ask of him the territorial expansion he had sought
from the Romans. When the delegates returned with a 3
refusal, Pyrrhus, concealing his reasons, feigned a sudden
departure. Meanwhile he ordered his allies to prepare for 4
war, and he passed defense of the citadel of Tarentum to
his son Helenus and his friend Milo. Returning to Epirus 5
he immediately invaded Macedonian territory; Antigonus
confronted him with an army and defeated in battle turned
to flight. And so Pyrrhus accepted the surrender of Mace- 6
don and as if he had compensated for the loss of Sicily and
Italy by the acquisition of the kingdom of Macedonia, he
sent for the son left at Tarentum and his friend. Antigonus, 7
with a few cavalrymen accompanying him in flight and
suddenly stripped of his prestigious position, withdrew to
Thessalonica to observe such events as would follow his
loss of the throne, so that from there he might renew the
war with a band of hired Gallic mercenaries. He was once 8
again decisively beaten by Ptolemy, Pyrrhus' son;[3] and
fleeing with seven companions he was no longer grasping
at hope of recovering his kingdom, but of a safe hiding
place and an escape in the wilderness.

4. Now despite being placed in such a great position of
power Pyrrhus, still not satisfied with what he could hardly
have wished for earlier, had his eyes on the kingdoms of

2   Graeciae Asiaeque regna meditatur. Neque illi maior ex
imperio quam ex bello voluptas erat, nec quicquam Pyr-
3   rum, qua tulisset imperium, sustinere valuit. Sed ut ad
devincenda regna invictus habebatur, ita devictis adquisi-
tisque celeriter carebat. Tanto melius studebat adquirere
4   imperia quam retinere. Itaque cum copias Chersoneso
transposuisset, legationibus Atheniensium et Achaeorum
5   Messeniorumque excipitur. Sed et Graecia omnis admiratione nominis eius, simul et rerum adversus Romanos
Poenosque gestarum adtonita adventum eius expectabat.
6   Primum illi bellum adversus Spartanos fuit; maiore mulie-
rum quam virorum virtute exceptus et Ptolomeum filium
7   et exercitus partem robustissimam amisit; quippe op-
pugnanti urbem ad tutelam patriae tanta multitudo femi-
narum concurrit, ut non fortius victus quam verecundius
recederet.

8   Porro Ptolomeum filium eius adeo strenuum et manu
fortem fuisse tradunt, ut urbem Corcyram cum sexage-
simo ceperit, idem proelio navali quinqueremem ex sca-
9   pha cum septimo insiluerit captamque tenuerit, in op-
pugnatione quoque Spartanorum usque in mediam urbem
equo procucurrerit ibique concursu multitudinis interfec-
10   tus sit. Cuius corpus ut relatum patri est, dixisse Pyrrum
ferunt, aliquanto tardius eum, quam timuerit ipse vel temeritas eius meruerit, occisum esse.

     5. Repulsus ab Spartanis Pyrrus Argos petit; ibi dum
Antigonum in urbe clausum expugnare conatur, inter confertissimos violentissime dimicans saxo de muris ictus
2   occiditur. Caput eius Antigono refertur, qui victoria mitius

Greece and Asia. He had no greater pleasure from ruling   2
than he did from war, and nothing could resist Pyrrhus
wherever he directed his power. But although he was con-   3
sidered unbeatable in conquering kingdoms, he would
also quickly lose what he had conquered and acquired. So
much more eager was he to gain power than to hold on to
it. Now when he had moved his troops to the Chersonese,   4
he was welcomed by deputations from the Athenians,
Achaeans and Messenians. But from admiration for his   5
reputation as well as his exploits against the Romans and
Carthaginians, all Greece was also awaiting his arrival. His   6
first war was against the Spartans; facing greater courage
from their women than their men he lost both his son
Ptolemy and the strongest part of his army; for when he   7
attacked the city such a great crowd of women rushed to
defend their fatherland that he withdrew, overcome less
by their strength than by shame.

Now Ptolemy his son was, they say, such a strong and   8
powerful fighter that he captured the city of Corcyra with
sixty men, and in a naval battle also jumped aboard a quin-
quireme from a small boat with seven men, took it and
held on to it; and that in the attack on Sparta he also rode   9
his horse right into the city center and was there killed
when surrounded by a crowd. When his body was brought   10
to his father, they say that Pyrrhus observed he had been
killed later than he himself feared or the boy's recklessness
deserved.

5. When driven back by the Spartans Pyrrhus made for
Argos; and there while trying to capture Antigonus, who
had shut himself up in the city, he was killed by a stone
hurled from the walls while he fought furiously in the thick
of the fray. His head was brought to Antigonus, who show-   2

usus filium eius Helenum cum Epirotis sibi deditum in
regnum remisit eique insepulti patris ossa in patriam refe-
renda tradidit.

3   Satis constans inter omnes auctores fama est, nullum
nec eius nec superioris aetatis regem conparandum Pyrro
fuisse, raroque non inter reges tantum, verum etiam inter
inlustres viros aut vitae sanctioris aut iustitiae probatioris

4   visum fuisse, scientiam certe rei militaris in illo viro tantam fuisse, ut cum Lysimacho, Demetrio, Antigono, tantis

5   regibus, bella gesserit, invictus semper fuerit, Illyriorum
quoque, Siculorum Romanorumque et Karthaginiensibus
bellis numquam inferior, plerumque etiam victor extiterit;

6   qui patriam certe suam angustam ignobilemque fama rerum gestarum et claritate nominis sui toto orbe inlustrem
reddiderit.

ing mercy in victory, sent his son Helenus back to his kingdom after he surrendered with the Epirots, and he gave him the remains of his still unburied father to be taken home.

It is generally agreed among all authors that no king of 3 that or any earlier period could be compared with Pyrrhus, and that rarely, not only among kings but even among illustrious men, had anyone appeared of purer life or more transparent honesty, and that certainly in that man lay 4 such a grasp of military science that in his campaigns against the mighty kings Lysimachus, Demetrius, and Antigonus he always remained undefeated, while in those 5 against Illyrians, Sicilians, Romans and Carthaginians he was never the loser and very often emerged the victor; and 6 his small, insignificant country he by the fame of his achievements and the glory of his name certainly made famous throughout the world.

LIBER XXVI

1. Post mortem Pyrri non in Macedonia tantum, verum
etiam in Asia Graeciaque magni bellorum motus fuere.
2 Nam et Peloponnensii per proditionem Antigono traditi;
3 et variante hominum partim dolore, partim gaudio, prout
singulae civitates aut auxilium de Pyrro speraverant aut
metus sustinuerant, ita aut cum Antigono societatem iun-
gebant aut mutuis inter se odiis in bellum ruebant.
4   Inter hunc turbatarum provinciarum motum Epiorum
quoque urbs ab Aristotimo principe per tyrannidem occu-
5 patur. A quo cum multi ex primoribus occisi, plures in
exilium acti essent, Aetolis per legatos postulantibus, con-
6 iuges liberosque exulum redderet, primo negavit, postea,
quasi paeniteret, proficiscendi ad suos potestatem omni-
7 bus matronis dedit diemque profectionis statuit. Illae,
quasi in perpetuum cum viris exulaturae, pretiosissima
quaeque auferentes, cum ad portam quasi uno agmine

---

1 Reading *Epiorum* (Seel: *Meti-* or *Epir-* or *Eli-* MSS). But
although the Epeii lived in Elis in the western Peloponnese, other
evidence (see next note) shows that Aristotimus tyrannized over
the city of Elis itself, capital of the region. Justin perhaps wrote
Eliorum (of the Eleans), for the group name *Elii* is found in other
authors, including Cicero (*Div.* 2.28).

2 The text is problematic, but Elis is historically correct. Justin

BOOK XXVI

1. After the death of Pyrrhus there were important out-
breaks of war not only in Macedonia, but also in Asia and
Greece. For the Peloponnesians were also treacherously   2
delivered up to Antigonus; and with people's hopes waver-   3
ing between dismay and joy as various states had been
either hoping for aid from Pyrrhus or living in fear of him,
they were either forming alliances with Antigonus or from
hatred of each other rushing into war.

   Amid this upheaval in the turbulent provinces the city   4
of the Epeii[1] was also seized with a tyranny by Aristotimus,
its foremost citizen.[2] When many of their leading people   5
had been killed by him and more driven into exile, and the
Aetolians demanded through delegates that he return
their wives and children, he at first refused but later, seem-   6
ingly relenting, he gave all married women permission to
rejoin their husbands and fixed a day for their departure.
They, thinking they faced permanent exile with their hus-   7
bands, took all their most prized possessions and assembled at the gate to set off in a single column, but then,

is the major source; cf. Plut. *Mor.* 249f, 250f, 253b; Paus. 5.5.1.
Justin fails to make clear that the exiles fled across the Gulf of
Corinth to Aetolia. The time is around 271/0. The anachronistic
use of the word "provinces" reveals the later Roman perspective.

profecturae convenissent, omnibus rebus spoliatae in carcerem recluduntur, occisis prius in gremio matrum parvulis liberis, virginibus ad stuprum direptis.

8 Hac tam saeva dominatione stupentibus omnibus princeps eorum Hellanicus, senex et liberis orbus, ut qui nec aetatis nec pigneris respectu timeret, contractos domum
9 fidissimos amicorum in vindictam patriae hortatur. Cunctantibus privato periculo publicum finire et deliberandi spatium postulantibus arcessitis servis iubet obserari fores tyrannoque nuntiare, mitteret qui coniuratos apud se conprehenderet; obiectans singulis se, quia liberandae patriae
10 auctor esse non possit, desertae ultorem futurum. Tunc illi ancipiti periculo circumventi honestiorem viam eligentes coniurant in tyranni necem, atque ita Aristotimus quinto quam tyrannidem occupaverat mense opprimitur.

2. Interea Antigonus cum multiplici bello et Ptolomei regis et Spartanorum premeretur novusque illi hostis Gallograeciae exercitus adfluxisset, in speciem castrorum parva manu adversus ceteros relicta adversus Gallos totis
2 viribus proficiscitur. Quibus cognitis Galli, cum et ipsi se proelio pararent, in auspicia pugnae hostias caedunt, quarum extis cum magna caedes interitusque omnium prasediceretur, non in timorem, sed in furorem versi sperantesque deorum minas expiari caede suorum posse,

---

3 That is, Antigonus II Gonatas (276–239) and Ptolemy II Philadelphus (282–246). We enter the obscurities of what is known as the Chremonidean War (after the mover of an Athenian decree), which probably began in 268 and for which the other main source is Paus. 3.6.4ff.; cf. Diod. Sic. 20.29; Plut. *Vit. Agis* 3.7. The Gauls were Antigonus' mercenaries, who revolted at Megara in 266.

stripped of everything, they were thrown in prison, little
children first being murdered in the laps of their mothers
and young girls dragged off to be raped.

With everyone stunned by such cruel, tyrannical con-   8
duct, their leading citizen Hellanicus, an old and childless
man and so one with no fear about age and family ties,
brought home his most loyal friends and urged them to
vindicate the liberty of their fatherland. Seeing them hes-   9
itate to face personal danger to end a communal one and
demanding time to reflect, he called his slaves, ordered
the doors locked, and had the tyrant sent a message that
he should send men to arrest conspirators in his house;
and berating his friends one by one he said that since he
could not be the champion of their country's liberation he
would be the avenger of its desertion. Then, caught be-   10
tween two hazards and choosing the more honorable
course, they swore to kill the tyrant, and so Aristotimus
was brought down in the fifth month after he seized the
tyranny.

2. Meanwhile Antigonus was under pressure with numerous wars with both King Ptolemy and the Spartans,
and as a new enemy for him an army from Gallograecia[3]
had also flooded in; so, leaving a small contingent to face
the others, he set out against the Gauls in full force. When   2
the Gauls heard of it while they were also preparing for
battle, they killed sacrificial animals to have auspices for
the engagement; and when by the entrails great carnage
and complete destruction was foretold, they became not
fearful but furious, and hoping the gods' portents could be
averted by killing their own people they butchered their

coniuges et liberos suos trucidant, auspicia belli a parrici-
3 dio incipientes. Tanta rabies feros animos invaserat, ut non
parcerent aetati, cui etiam hostes pepercissent, bellumque
internecivum cum liberis liberorumque matribus gere-
4 rent, pro quibus bella suscipi solent. Itaque quasi scelere
vitam victoriamque redemissent, sicut erant cruenti ex
recenti suorum caede, in proelium non meliore eventu
5 quam omine proficiscuntur; siquidem pugnantes prius
parricidiorum furiae quam hostes circumvenere, obver-
santibusque ante oculos manibus interemptorum omnes
6 occidione caesi. Tanta strages fuit, ut pariter cum hominibus dii consensisse in exitium parricidarum viderentur.

7   Post huius pugnae eventum Ptolomeus et Spartani
victorem hostium exercitum declinantes in tutiora se re-
8 cipiunt. Antigonus quoque ubi eorum discessum videt,
recenti adhuc ex priore victoria militum ardore bellum
9 Atheniensibus infert. In quo cum occupatus esset, interim
Alexander, rex Epiri, ulcisci mortem patris Pyrri cupiens
10 fines Macedoniae depopulatur. Adversus quem cum reversus a Graecia Antigonus esset, transitione militum des-
11 titutus regnum Macedoniae cum exercitu amittit. Huius
filius Demetrius, puer admodum, absente patre reparato
exercitu non solum amissam Macedoniam recepit, verum
12 etiam Epiri regno Alexandrum spoliat. Tanta vel mobilitas
militum vel fortunae varietas erat, ut vicissim reges nunc
exules, ⟨exules⟩ nunc reges viderentur.

---

4 Probably in 262/1. Alexander II had succeeded Pyrrhus
some ten years earlier. The details of Justin's account are suspect
as to Antigonus' defeat and Demetrius' role, though the latter
became co-regent with Antigonus in 257.

wives and children, inaugurating the auspices for the war with murder. Such was the fury that gripped their savage 3 minds that they would not spare even those of an age their enemies would have spared, and they waged murderous war on their children and their children's mothers, for whom wars are usually undertaken. Thus as if they had by 4 their crime redeemed their lives and the victory, they went into battle still bloody from the recent murder of their families to a result no better than the omen; for in battle 5 they were surrounded by the avenging Furies of parricide before they were by their enemy, and with their victims' spirits dancing before their eyes they were all completely wiped out. So great was the carnage that the gods seemed 6 to have agreed with men to destroy the parricides.

Following the outcome of this battle, Ptolemy and the 7 Spartans, avoiding their enemy's victorious army, withdrew into safer areas. Antigonus, on seeing them retreat 8 and his men still full of spirit after their earlier victory, also made war on the Athenians. While he was preoccupied 9 with that, Alexander, king of Epirus, being eager to avenge the death of his father Pyrrhus, meanwhile raided Macedonian territory.[4] When Antigonus returned from Greece 10 to confront him, he was deserted by his soldiers and lost the kingdom of Macedonia together with his army. His son 11 Demetrius, still just a boy, rebuilt the army in his father's absence and not only recovered the lost Macedonia but even robbed Alexander of the kingdom of Epirus. Such 12 was either soldiers' unreliability or fortune's fickleness that kings could now find themselves exiles and exiles now kings.

3. Igitur Alexander, cum exul ad Acarnanas confugisset, non minore Epirotarum desiderio quam sociorum auxilio in regnum restituitur.

2 Per idem tempus rex Cyrenarum Magas decedit, qui ante infirmitatem Beronicen, unicam filiam, ad finienda
3 cum Ptolomeo fratre certamina filio eius desponderat. Sed post mortem regis mater virginis Arsinoe, ut invita se contractum matrimonium solveretur, misit qui ad nuptias virginis regnumque Cyrenarum Demetrium, fratrem regis Antigoni, a Macedonia arcesserent, qui et ipse ex filia Pto
4 lomei procreatus erat. Sed nec Demetrius moram fecit. Itaque cum secundante vento celeriter Cyrenas advolasset, fiducia pulchritudinis, qua animis placere socrus coeperat, statim a principio superbus regiae familiae militibusque inpotens erat studiumque placendi a virgine in
5 matrem contulerat. Quae res suspecta primo virgini, dein
6 popularibus militibusque invisa fuit. Itaque versis omnium animis in Ptolomei filium insidiae Demetrio conparantur, cui, cum in lectum socrus concessisset, percussores inmit
7 tuntur. Sed Arsinoe audita voce filiae ad fores stantis et praecipientis, ut matri parceretur, adulterum paulisper
8 corpore suo protexit. Quo interfecto Beronice et stupra matris salva pietate ulta est et in matrimonio sortiendo iudicium patris secuta.

---

[5] This abrupt reversal of Alexander of Epirus' fortunes suggests that Justin, or a later copyist, left out a mention of how he was restored.　　[6] He was, in fact, Ptolemy II's half brother. Demetrius the Fair died in 250.　　[7] Justin's "Beronice" has been normalized to the conventional "Berenice." The widowed queen was named Apama, not Arsinoë; she was the daughter of King Antiochus I and granddaughter of Seleucus.

3. So Alexander, after he had fled to the Acarnanians as an exile, was restored to his throne no less by the Epirots' wishes than aid from his allies.[5]

At this same time King Magas of Cyrene[6] died, but 2 before his illness he to end his quarrels with him, had engaged his only daughter Berenice to the son of his brother Ptolemy. But after the king's death the girl's 3 mother Arsinoë,[7] in order to have annulment of a marriage contracted against her will, sent a deputation to summon Demetrius, brother of King Antigonus, from Macedonia to marry the young woman and assume the throne of Cyrene, he himself being born of a daughter of Ptolemy. But Demetrius did not delay, either. So, after coming 4 swiftly to Cyrene with a favoring wind, he, being confident in his good looks, with which his mother-in-law had already become enamored, was from the start arrogant toward the royal family and overbearing with the soldiers and he had also turned his eagerness to please from the girl to the mother. This first raised the girl's suspicions, 5 then the people's and soldiers' hatred. And so after every- 6 body's support turned to Ptolemy's son, there was a plot hatched against Demetrius, and when his mother-in-law admitted him to her bed assassins were brought in. But 7 when Arsinoë heard the voice of her daughter who stood at the door giving orders for her mother to be spared, she for a short time shielded the adulterer with her own body. By his killing Berenice had her revenge for her mother's 8 dishonor and also followed her father's judgment in choice of husband.

LIBER XXVII

1. Mortuo Syriae rege Antiocho, cum in locum eius filius
Seleucus successisset, hortante matre Laodice, quae pro-
2 hibere debuerat, auspicia regni a parricidio coepit; quippe
Beronicen, novercam suam, sororem Ptolomei, regis Ae-
3 gypti, cum parvulo fratre ex ea suscepto interfecit. Quo
facinore perpetrato et infamiae maculam subiit et Pto-
4 lomei se bello inplicuit. Porro Beronice, cum ad se inter-
5 ficiendam missos didicisset, Daphinae se claudit. Vbi cum
obsideri eam cum parvulo filio nuntiatum Asiae civitatibus
esset, recordatione paternae maiorumque eius dignitatis
casum tam indignae fortunae miserantes auxilia ei omnes
6 misere. Frater quoque Ptolomeus periculo sororis exter-
7 ritus relicto regno cum omnibus viribus advolat. Sed Beronice ante adventum auxiliorum, cum vi expugnari non
posset, dolo circumventa trucidatur. Indigna res omnibus
8 visa. Itaque [cum] universae civitates [quae defecerant,
ingentem classem conparassent, repente] exemplo crude-

---

1 Antiochus II Theos had ruled from 261 to 246; his son Seleucus II Callinicus then reigned until 225. Laodice was Antiochus' sister and wife. Berenice was sister to Ptolemy III Euergetes, who also came to the throne in 246. The conflict is the
so-called Laodicean War. This Berenice was not the one men-

4

BOOK XXVII

1. When King Antiochus of Syria died his son Seleucus[1] succeeded him, and with the encouragement of his mother Laodice, who ought to have restrained him, he inaugurated his reign with parricide; for he killed his stepmother 2 Berenice, sister of Ptolemy, king of Egypt, together with her son, his little half brother by her. Perpetrating that 3 crime he both tainted himself with ignominy and also involved himself in a war with Ptolemy. Now Berenice, 4 learning that men had been sent to murder her, barricaded herself at Daphina.[2] When it was reported in the cities of 5 Asia that she was under siege with her little son, everyone, remembering her father's and forefather's station and feeling pity for such an undeserved fate, sent her aid. Her 6 brother Ptolemy, too, alarmed at his sister's danger, left his kingdom and rushed to her with all his forces. But Ber- 7 enice, before help could arrive and although she could not be taken by attack, was treacherously betrayed and murdered.[3] This seemed despicable to everyone. So all the 8 cities, appalled by such extraordinary cruelty and at the

tioned in the previous book, but both met violent deaths as Egyptian royals, a dangerous status.

[2] Daphne, a suburb of Antioch.

[3] Cf. Val. Max. 9.10 ext. 1; Polyaenus, *Strat.* 8.50.

litatis exterritae simul et in ultionem eius, quam defensuri

9 fuerant, Ptolomeo se tradunt, qui nisi in Aegyptum domestica seditione revocatus esset, totum regnum Seleuci

10 occupasset. Tantum vel illi odium parricidale scelus vel huic favorem indigne peremptae mors sororis adtulerat.

2. Post discessum Ptolomei Seleucus cum adversus civitates, quae defecerant, ingentem classem conparasset, repente velut diis ipsis parricidium vindicantibus orta

2 tempestate classem naufragio amittit; nec quicquam illi ex tanto adparatu praeter nudum corpus et spiritum et pau-

3 cos naufragii comites residuos fortuna fecit. Misera quidem res, optanda Seleuco fuit; siquidem civitates, quae odio eius ad Ptolomeum transierant, velut diis arbitris satisfactum sibi esset, repentina animorum mutatione in naufragi misericordiam versae imperio se eius restituunt.

4 Laetus igitur malis suis et damnis ditior redditus veluti par

5 viribus bellum Ptolomeo infert, sed quasi ad ludibrium tantum Fortunae natus esset nec propter aliud opes regni recepisset, quam ut amitteret, victus proelio non multo quam post naufragium comitatior trepidus Antiochiam confugit.

6 Inde ad Antiochum fratrem litteras facit, quibus auxilium eius inplorat oblata ei Asia intra finem Tauri montis

7 in praemium latae opis. Antiochus autem cum esset annos XIV natus, supra aetatem regni avidus occasionem non tam pio animo, quam offerebatur, adripuit, sed latronis more fratri totum eripere cupiens puer sceleratam viri-

---

[4] This Antiochus, Seleucus II's younger brother, ruled the empire's territories in Asia Minor, while the king held those to the east (many of which he lost as years passed).

same time to avenge the woman they had been going to
defend, defected to Ptolemy, and had he not been recalled 9
to Egypt by a local rebellion he would have seized the
entire kingdom of Seleucus. So much hatred had a parri- 10
cidal crime brought for one, so much support a sister's
undeserved death for the other.

2. After Ptolemy's departure Seleucus had assembled a
huge fleet to counter cities that had defected, when suddenly, with the gods themselves seemingly avenging the
murder, a storm arose and he lost the fleet in a shipwreck;
and from so great armada fortune left him nothing more 2
than his naked body, his life, and a few companions who
survived the wreck. Though a sad affair, it should have 3
been welcomed by Seleucus; for those states that from
hatred of him had defected to Ptolemy suddenly, as if in
the gods' eyes sufficient atonement had been made, had a
change of heart and from pity over the shipwreck returned
to his authority. So, pleased with his misfortunes and en- 4
riched by his losses, he as if his equal in strength made war
on Ptolemy, but as if he had been born only to be Fortune's 5
plaything and had recovered his royal power only to lose
it, he was defeated in battle and with little more of a retinue than after his shipwreck, fled in panic to Antioch.

From there he wrote a letter to his brother Antiochus, 6
in which he begged for his aid, offering him Asia within
the bounds of the Taurus range as reward for his help.[4]
Antiochus, however, although he was only fourteen years 7
old had a lust for power beyond his age and he seized the
opportunity not with the integrity with which it was being
offered but wishing like a thief to take everything from his
brother, and though a boy he had the malevolence of a

8 lemque sumit audaciam. Vnde Hierax est cognominatus,
quia non hominis, sed accipitris ritu in alienis eripiendis
9 vitam sectaretur. Interea Ptolomeus cum Antiochum in
auxilium Seleuco venire cognovisset, ne cum duobus uno
tempore dimicaret, in annos X cum Seleuco pacem facit;
10 sed pax ab hoste data interpellatur a fratre, qui conducto
Gallorum mercennario exercitu pro auxilio bellum, pro
11 fratre hostem imploratus exhibuit. In eo proelio virtute
Gallorum victor quidem Antiochus fuit, sed Galli arbi-
trantes Seleucum in proelio cecidisse in ipsum Antiochum
arma vertere, liberius depopulaturi Asiam, si omnem stir-
12 pem regiam extinxissent. Quod ubi sensit Antiochus, velut
a praedonibus auro se redemit societatemque cum mer-
cennariis suis iungit.

3. Interea rex Bithyniae Eumenes sparsis consump-
tisque fratribus bello intestinae discordiae quasi vacantem
Asiae possessionem invasurus victorem Antiochum Gal-
2 losque adgreditur. Nec difficile saucios adhuc ex superiore
3 congressione integer ipse viribus superat. Ea namque
tempestate omnia bella in exitium Asiae gerebantur: uti
quisque fortior fuisset, Asiam velut praedam occupabat.
4 Seleucus et Antiochus fratres bellum propter Asiam gerebant, Ptolomeus, rex Aegypti, sub specie sororiae ultionis

---

5 *Hierax* is Greek for "hawk."

6 These Gauls, and other mercenary armies so termed, had
settled in central Asia Minor; their territory was from then on
called Galatia (Greek for "Gaul").

7 Trogus' *Prologue* tells us the battle was fought near Ancyra.

8 Eumenes I was not king of Bithynia but of Pergamum, the
region around Sardis in western Asia Minor. He was king of Per-

man. So he was nicknamed "Hierax," because he would, 8
not like a man but a bird of prey spend his life filching the
possessions of others.[5] Meanwhile when Ptolemy learned 9
that Antiochus was coming to help Seleucus he, in order
not to be fighting both at the same time, made a ten-year
peace with Seleucus; but the peace granted by his enemy 10
was broken by his brother, who hired a Gallic mercenary
army[6] and when asked for his help revealed himself as his
enemy not his brother. In that battle Antiochus emerged 11
victor through the courage of the Gauls,[7] but the Gauls
thinking Seleucus had fallen in the battle turned their
weapons on Antiochus himself, feeling freer to pillage Asia
if they wiped out the whole royal line. When Antiochus 12
realized that he ransomed himself with gold though from
bandits and made an alliance with his own mercenaries.

3. Meanwhile with the brothers estranged and exhausted from their violent feuding, King Eumenes of
Bithynia decided to invade Asia, which was now virtually
left open,[8] and he attacked the victorious Antiochus and
the Gauls. Nor did he have difficulty overcoming them, 2
still weak as they were from their earlier campaign while
his own strength was intact. For at that time all wars were 3
focused on destroying Asia; the stronger either one was,
he saw Asia as his prize. The brothers Seleucus and Antio- 4
chus were fighting a war over Asia, and Ptolemy, king of
Egypt, ostensibly to avenge his sister, also had his eyes on

gamum from 263 to 241; the ruler here, as Trogus correctly has
it in his *Prologue*, was his successor, Attalus I (241–197). The
battle took place soon after that at Ancyra, around 235, near
Pergamum.

5 Asiae inhiabat. Hinc Bithynus Eumenes, inde Galli, humi-
liorum semper mercennaria manus, Asiam depopulaban-
tur, cum interea nemo defensor Asiae inter tot praedones
inveniebatur.

6 Victo Antiocho cum Eumenes maiorem partem Asiae
occupasset, ne tunc quidem fratres perdito praemio, propter quod bellum gerebant, concordare potuerunt, sed
omisso externo hoste in mutuum exitium bellum reparant.

7 In eo Antiochus denuo victus multorum dierum fuga fatigatus tandem ad socerum suum Ariamenem, regem Cap-
8 padociae, pervehitur. A quo cum benigne primum exceptus esset, interiectis diebus cognito quod insidiae sibi
9 pararentur, salutem fuga quaesivit. Igitur cum profugo
nusquam tutus locus esset, ad Ptolomeum hostem, cuius
fidem tutiorem quam fratris existimabat, decurrit, memor
vel quae facturus fratri esset vel quae meruisset a fratre.

10 Sed Ptolomeus non amicior dedito quam hosti factus ad-
11 servari eum artissima custodia iubet. Hinc quoque Antiochus opera cuiusdam meretricis adiutus, quam familiarius
noverat, deceptis custodibus elabitur fugiensque a latro-
12 nibus interficitur. Seleucus quoque iisdem ferme diebus
amisso regno equo praecipitatus finitur. Sic fratres quasi
et germanis casibus exules ambo post regna scelerum suorum poenas luerunt.

Asia. Here the Bithynian Eumenes and there the Gauls,   5
ever the mercenary force of the weaker, were both pillaging Asia, and meanwhile among so many brigands no de-
fender of Asia could be found.

After Antiochus was defeated and when Eumenes had   6
seized most of Asia, not even then, despite the prize for
which they were fighting being lost, could the brothers be
reconciled, but forgetting external enemies they restarted
a war of mutual destruction. In that war Antiochus was   7
again defeated, and exhausted after fleeing for many days
he finally reached his father-in-law Ariamenes, king of
Cappadocia.[9] From him he at first received a kind wel-   8
come, but on discovering some days later that a plot was
being engineered against him, he sought safety in flight.
Then when he found no safe haven as a fugitive, he turned   9
to his enemy Ptolemy, whose integrity he trusted more
than his brother's, remembering either what he had intended doing to his brother or had deserved from his
brother. But Ptolemy, feeling no more friendly toward on   10
his surrender than when he was his enemy, ordered him
placed under very close arrest. From here, too, Antiochus,   11
helped by a courtesan with whom he had become quite
intimate, slipped away and while fleeing was killed by bandits. Seleucus also lost his kingdom at about that time and   12
died after being thrown off his horse. Thus the brothers
as if also exiled through twin fates both paid the penalty
for their crimes after being kings.[10]

[9] Ariamenes of Cappadocia was the father-in-law of Antiochus' sister Stratonice.
[10] These deaths occurred in 226/5. Antiochus Hierax was
killed in Thrace (Polyb. 5.74).

LIBER XXVIII

1. Olympias, Pyrri Epirotae regis filia, amisso marito eodemque germano fratre Alexandro cum tutelam filiorum
ex eo susceptorum, Pyrri et Ptolomei, regnique administrationem in se recepisset, Aetolis partem Acarnaniae, quam
in portionem belli pater pupillorum acceperat, eripere
2 volentibus ad regem Macedoniae Demetrium decurrit
eique habenti uxorem Antiochi, regis Syriae, sororem filiam suam Phthiam in matrimonium tradit, ut auxilium,
quod misericordia non poterat, iure cognationis obtineret.
3 Fiunt igitur nuptiae, quibus et novi matrimonii gratia ad-
4 quiritur et veteris offensa contrahitur. Nam prior uxor,
velut matrimonio pulsa, sponte sua ad fratrem Antiochum
discedit eumque in mariti bellum inpellit.
5 Acarnanes quoque diffisi Epirotis adversus Aetolos
auxilium Romanorum inplorantes obtinuerunt a Romano
6 senatu, ut legati mitterentur, qui denuntiarent Aetolis,
praesidia ab urbibus Acarnaniae deducerent pateren-

---

[1] From this point a parallel account is Polyb. 2.2ff.; the time
is the late 230s. As Trogus' source, Timagenes is suggested. One
can, however, detect in section 2 the overblown arrogance of the
Aetolians, which is so much a part of Polybius' portrayal. Demetrius II, son of Antigonus II Gonatas, was king of Macedonia from
239 to 229. His first wife was named Stratonice.

BOOK XXVIII

1. Olympias, daughter of King Pyrrhus of Epirus, after losing her husband Alexander, who was also her brother, assumed guardianship of Pyrrhus and Ptolemy, her sons by him, as well as government of the kingdom. When the Aetolians wished to take from her the part of Acarnania that the father of her boys had received for contributing to their war, she turned to King Demetrius of Macedonia;[1] and although he already had as a wife the sister of Antiochus, king of Syria, she gave him her daughter Phthia in marriage so that any help she could not gain from his sympathy she might from a family connection. A wedding accordingly followed, by which he gained influence from the new marriage and hatred from the old. For his earlier wife, feeling driven from her marriage, spontaneously went off to her brother Antiochus and pushed him into war with her husband.

The Acarnanians, distrusting the Epirots and seeking Roman aid against the Aetolians, also gained a commitment from the Roman senate for delegates to be sent to order the Aetolians to remove their garrisons from the cities of Acarnania and leave free the only people that had

turque liberos esse, qui soli quondam adversus Troianos,
auctores originis suae, auxilia Graecis non miserint.

2. Sed Aetoli legationem Romanorum superbe audi-
vere, Poenos illis et Gallos, a quibus tot bellis occidione
2 caesi sint exprobrantes dicentesque prius illis portas adversus Karthaginienses aperiendas, quas clauserit metus
3 Punici belli, quam in Graeciam arma transferenda. Memi-
4 nisse deinde iubent, qui quibus minentur. Adversus Gallos
urbem eos suam tueri non potuisse captamque non ferro
5 defendisse, sed auro redemisse; quam gentem se aliquanto maiore manu Graeciam ingressam non solum nullis externis viribus, sed ne domesticis quidem totis adiutos
universam delesse, sedemque sepulcris eorum praebuisse,
6 quam illi urbibus imperioque suo proposuerant; contra
Italiam trepidis ex recenti urbis suae incendio Romanis
7 universam ferme a Gallis occupatam. Prius igitur Gallos
Italia pellendos quam minentur Aetolis, priusque sua de-
8 fendenda quam aliena appetenda. Quos autem homines
Romanos esse? Nempe pastores, qui latrocinio iustis do-
9 minis ademptum solum teneant, qui uxores cum propter
10 originis dehonestamenta non invenirent, vi publica rapue-
rint, qui denique urbem ipsam parricidio condiderint
murorumque fundamenta fraterno sanguine adsperserint.
11 Aetolos autem principes Graeciae semper fuisse et sicut

---

2 There is no other evidence for such an embassy from the
Acarnanians to Rome, and it looks like a rhetorical fiction.
3 See 6.6.5, 20.5.4, 43.5.9; the sentiment is repeated in Mith-
ridates' speech at 38.4.8. For the Gallic invasion of Greece, see
Books 24 and 25.   4 The taking of Sabine women; see Livy
Book 1 and below, 43.3.2.

not in the past sent the Greeks help against the Trojans, the founders of their race.[2]

2. But the Aetolians listened to the Roman delegation with scorn, taunting them with the Carthaginians and Gauls by whom they were massacred in so many wars and saying they must first open up the gates now closed through fear of a Punic war and face the Carthaginians, before taking their weapons into Greece. Then they told them to remember who was threatening whom. Facing the Gauls they had been unable to protect their own city and when it was captured they had not defended it with iron but ransomed it with gold;[3] and when that race of people entered Greece with a larger force they had completely destroyed them not only unaided by foreign troops but not even using all of their own, and had offered them a burial site where they had intended to found cities and their empire; Italy however, while the Romans were still panicking after the recent burning of the city, had been almost completely overrun by the Gauls. So the Gauls should be driven from Italy before they threatened the Aetolians, and they should first defend their own land before attacking that of other people. What were these Romans anyway? Shepherds, of course, who were merely occupying land stolen from its rightful owners, who when unable to find wives because of their shameful origins seized them with state-authorized force,[4] and even founded their very city with a murder and smeared its walls' foundations with a brother's blood.[5] The Aetolians, however, were always leaders of Greece, and just as they

[5] Romulus' elimination of Remus.

12 dignitate, ita et virtute ceteris praestitisse; solos denique
    esse, qui Macedonas imperio terrarum semper florentes
    contempserint, qui Philippum regem non timuerint, qui
    Alexandri Magni post Persas Indosque devictos, cum
13 omnes nomen eius horrerent, edicta spreverint. Monere
    igitur se Romanos, contenti sint fortuna praesenti nec
    provocent arma, quibus et Gallos caesos et Macedonas
14 contemptos videant. Sic dimissa legatione Romanorum,
    ne fortius locuti quam fecisse viderentur, fines Epiri regni
    et Acarnaniae depopulantur.

    3. Iam Olympias filiis regna tradiderat, et in locum
2   Pyrri, fratris defuncti, Ptolomeus successerat, qui cum ho-
    stibus instructo exercitu obvius processisset, infirmitate
3   correptus in itinere decedit. Olympias quoque gemino
    funerum vulnere adflicta, aegre spiritum trahens non diu
4   filiis supervixit. Cum ex gente regia sola Nereis virgo cum
5   Laodamia sorore superesset, Nereis nubit Geloni, Siciliae
    tyranni filio, Laudamia autem cum in aram Dianae confu-
6   gisset, concursu populi interficitur. Quod facinus dii in-
    mortales adsiduis cladibus gentis et prope interitu totius
7   populi vindicaverunt. Nam et sterilitatem famemque passi
    et intestina discordia vexati externis ad postremum bellis
8   paene consumpti sunt. Milo quoque, Laodamiae percus-
    sor, in furorem versus nunc ferro, nunc saxo, in summa
    dentibus laceratis visceribus duodecima die interiit.
9   His in Epiro gestis interim in Macedonia Deme-
    trius rex relicto filio Philippo, parvulo admodum, decedit,

had surpassed everyone else in status so had they also in
courage; in fact only they had shown contempt for the   12
Macedonians and their ever flourishing power, who had
no fear of King Philip, and who disregarded Alexander the
Great's edicts when Persians and Indians were defeated
and everyone shuddered at the mention of his name. So   13
they were warning the Romans to be satisfied with their
present success, they said, and not challenge the weapons
by which they could see Gauls had been killed and Macedonians despised. Dismissing the Roman delegation with   14
that and not to appear braver in words than action, they
plundered the frontiers of the Epirot Kingdom and Acarnania.

3. By now Olympias had transferred her kingdom to
her sons, and Ptolemy had succeeded his deceased brother
Pyrrhus, who, after he set out against his enemy with an   2
army in array, fell ill and died en route. Olympias, too,   3
grief-stricken by the two deaths and barely able to draw
breath, did not long survive her sons. When from the royal   4
line only a young girl Nereis and her sister Laodamia remained, Nereis married Gelon, the son of the tyrant of   5
Sicily, but when Laodamia sought refuge at the altar of
Diana she was killed in a riot of the people. That crime   6
the immortal gods punished by visiting perpetual disasters
on their line and almost total destruction on their people.
For after suffering crop failure and famine and also being   7
riven with civil discord, they were finally almost destroyed
by foreign wars. Milo, Laodamia's assassin, also went in-   8
sane, and after mutilating his own vital organs, now with
a sword, then with a stone, and finally with his teeth he
died eleven days later.

After these events in Epirus King Demetrius died in   9
Macedonia, leaving his son Philip, who was still only a

10 cui Antigonus tutor datus acccpta in matrimonium matre
11 pupilli regem se constitui laborat. Interiecto deinde tempore cum seditione minaci Macedonum clausus in regia
12 teneretur, in publicum sine satellitibus procedit, pro-
iectoque in vulgus diademate ac purpura dare haec eos
alteri iubet, qui aut imperare illis nesciat aut cui parere
13 ipsi sciant; se adhuc invidiosum illud regnum non volup-
14 tatibus, sed laboribus ac periculis sentire. Commemorat
deinde beneficia sua: ut defectionem sociorum vindicave-
rit, ut Dardanos Thessalosque exultantes morte Demetrii
regis conpescuerit, ut denique dignitatem Macedonum
15 non solum defenderit, verum et auxerit. Quorum si illos
paeniteat, deponere imperium et reddere illis munus
16 suum, quia regem quaerant, cui imperent. Cum populus
pudore motus recipere eum regnum iuberet, tam diu re-
cusavit, quoad seditionis auctores supplicio traderentur.

4. Post haec bellum Spartanis infert, qui soli Philippi
Alexandrique bellis et imperium Macedonum et omnibus
2 metuenda arma contempserant. Inter duas nobilissimas
gentes bellum summis utrimque viribus fuit, cum hi pro
vetere Macedonum gloria, illi non solum pro inlibata
3 libertate, sed etiam pro salute certarent. Victi Lacedaemonii non ipsi tantum, verum etiam coniuges liberique

---

6 Demetrius died in 229, defeated by Dardanians. Antigonus
III Doson ruled until 221. He was a nephew of Antigonus II. We
are at Polyb. 2.44ff.; his castigation of Phylarchus at 2.56 makes
the latter a possible source for Trogus, directly or not. We also
have Plut. *Vit. Arat.* (Aratus himself wrote of the period); *Vit.
Cleom.* 7ff., esp. 16ff.; *Vit. Phil.* 5ff.

7 The author's opinion, with some justification, is, in the word
"alone," at odds with the claims of the Aetolians at 28.3.12. King

boy,[6] and when Antigonus who had been appointed his   10
guardian married his ward's mother he worked hard to
have himself made king. Then a little later when he was   11
shut in the palace during a dangerous insurrection of the
Macedonians, he ventured out into the streets without
bodyguards, and throwing into the crowd his diadem and   12
purple robe he told them to give them to someone who
would either not know how to rule them or they themselves would know how to obey; so disagreeable did he   13
find that rule, with no pleasures but only hardship and
dangers. He then recalled his benefits to them: how he   14
punished the defection of their allies, how he subdued the
Dardanians and Thessalians when they were gloating over
the death of King Demetrius, and finally how he not only
defended the prestige of the Macedonians but even raised
it. If they had regrets about these things, he said, he was 15
laying down his power and returning his office to them
because they wanted a king they could command. When   16
the people were moved to shame and told him to take back
his rule, he refused for a long time, until the sedition's
leaders were surrendered for execution.

4. After this he attacked the Spartans, who alone in the
wars with Philip and Alexander had been contemptuous
of both the empire of the Macedonians and their arms that
were fearful to everyone.[7] Between the two truly out-   2
standing peoples there was a full scale war to which they
both committed all their strength, the one for Macedon's
glory of old, the other not just for its intact freedom but
even for its survival. In defeat not only the Lacedaemoni-   3
ans themselves but also their women and children stout-

Cleomenes II of Sparta was defeated at the battle of Sellasia, near
Sparta, in 223.

4 magno animo fortunam tulcre. Nemo quippe in acie saluti
   pepercit, nulla amissum coniugem flevit, filiorum mortem
   senes laudabant, patribus in acie caesis filii gratulabantur,
   suam vicem omnes dolebant, quod non et ipsi pro patriae
5 libertate cecidissent. Patentibus omnes domibus saucios
6 excipiebant, vulnera curabant, lassos reficiebant; inter
   haec nullus in urbe strepitus, nulla trepidatio, magisque
   omnes publicam quam privatam fortunam lugebant.
7   Inter haec Cleomenes rex post multas hostium caedes
   toto corpore suo pariter et hostium cruore madens super-
8 venit ingressusque in urbem non humi consedit, non cibum aut potum poposcit, non denique armorum onus
9 deposuit, sed adclinis parieti, cum IV milia sola ex pugna
   superfuisse conspexisset, hortatus, ut se ad meliora rei
10 publicae tempora reservarent, tum cum coniuge et liberis
   Aegyptum ad Ptolomeum proficiscitur, a quo honorifice
11 exceptus diu in summa dignatione regis vixit. Postremo
   post Ptolomei mortem a filio eius cum omni familia interficitur.
12   Antigonus autem caesis occidione Spartanis fortunam
   tantae urbis miseratus a direptione milites prohibuit veniamque his, qui superfuerunt, dedit, praefatus bellum se
13 cum Cleomene, non cum Spartanis habuisse, cuius fuga
14 omnis ira eius finita sit; nec minori sibi gloriae fore, si ab
   eo servata Lacedaemon, a quo solo capta sit, proderetur.
15 Parcere igitur solo urbis ac tectis, quoniam homines, qui-
16 bus parceret, non superfuissent. Nec multo post ipse decedit regnumque Philippo pupillo, annos quattuordecim
   nato, tradidit.

heartedly accepted their fate. For no man begrudged his   4
life in the battle, no woman wept for a lost spouse, old men
lauded sons' deaths, sons rejoiced over fathers killed in
action, and all lamented their lot in not having themselves
fallen for their country's freedom. Opening their doors   5
they were all taking in the injured, tending wounds, and
reviving the fatigued; and meanwhile there was no tur-   6
moil, no panic in the city, and all were lamenting their
shared plight rather than their own.

Meanwhile after killing large number of the foe King   7
Cleomenes arrived, his entire body soaked with both his
own and the enemy's blood, and entering the city he did   8
not sit on the ground, ask for food or drink, or even lay
down the burden of his arms, but leaning against a wall
and seeing that a mere four thousand had survived the   9
battle, he encouraged the men to save themselves for better times that their state would see. Then together with his   10
wife and children he left for the court of Ptolemy in Egypt,
and given a dignitary's welcome by him he lived a long
time in the king's highest regard. Finally, after Ptolemy's   11
death, he was killed by his son together with all his family.

Now after his complete slaughter of the Spartans An-   12
tigonus, feeling pity for the misfortunes of so great a city,
forbade his men to plunder and pardoned all those who
survived, saying that his war had been with Cleomenes not   13
the Spartans, and that with his flight all his anger was over;
nor would he have any less glory if it were recorded that   14
Sparta had been saved by him, the only man by whom it
had been captured. So he was sparing the city's land and   15
buildings, he said, since the men he would have spared
had not survived. Not much later he died himself and   16
passed the kingdom on to his fourteen-year-old ward,
Philip.

LIBER XXIX

1. Isdem ferme temporibus prope universi orbis imperia
2 nova regum successione mutata sunt. Nam et in Macedonia Philippus mortuo Antigono, tutore eodemque vitrico,
3 annorum XIV regnum suscepit; et in Asia interfecto Se-
4 leuco inpubes adhuc rex Antiochus constitutus est; Cappadociae quoque regnum Ariarathi, puero admodum,
5 pater ipse tradiderat; Aegyptum patre ac matre interfectis
occupaverat Ptolomeus, cui ex facinoris crimine cogno-
6 mentum Philopator fuit. Sed et Spartani in locum Cleo-
7 menis suffecerant Lycurgum. Et ne qua temporibus mutatio deesset, apud Karthaginienses quoque aetate inmatura
dux Hannibal constituitur, non penuria seniorum, sed
odio Romanorum, quo inbutum eum a pueritia sciebant,
8 fatale non tam Romanis quam ipsi Africae malum. His
regibus pueris tametsi nulli senioris aetatis rectores erant,
tamen in suorum quisque maiorum vestigia intentis magna
9 indoles virtutis enituit. Solus Ptolomeus, sicut scelestus in

---

[1] Cf. Polyb. 2.71. The successors are Philip V (221–179), Antiochus III ("the Great"; 223–187), Ariarathes IV Eusebes (220–
ca. 162), Ptolemy IV Philopator (222–205). Lycurgus was king of
Sparta from 219 to circa 212. On Hannibal see Polyb. 3.8ff.

[2] "Father-lover": a rare example of Justin's, or Trogus', sense
of humor.

BOOK XXIX

1. At about this same time, virtually worldwide, empires were changing with new successions of kings.[1] For in 2 Macedonia Philip, on the death of Antigonus, his guardian as well as his stepfather, also started his reign at the age of fourteen; in Asia when Seleucus was killed Antiochus 3 was also made king before even reaching puberty; the 4 kingdom of Cappadocia had also been personally transferred to Ariarathes by his father when he was still a boy; and Ptolemy had seized Egypt, after murdering his 5 mother and father, a heinous crime for which he earned the name "Philopator."[2] But the Spartans had also re- 6 placed Cleomenes with Lycurgus. And for there to be no 7 shortage of changes, Hannibal was at that time also made general among the Carthaginians at an early age, not from a shortage of older men but from hatred of the Romans that the Carthaginians knew had been imbued in him since boyhood, but which would prove deadly not so much for the Romans as for Africa itself. Although these boy- 8 kings had no men of riper years guiding them, they in their eagerness to follow in their forefathers' footsteps nevertheless revealed great natural abilities. Only Ptolemy was 9

10 occupando, ita et segnis in administrando regno fuit. Philippum Dardani ceterique omnes finitimi populi, quibus velut inmortale odium cum Macedonum regibus erat,
11 contemptu aetatis adsidue lacessebant. Contra ille submotis hostibus non contentus sua defendisse ultro Aetolis bellum inferre gestiebat.

2. Quae agitantem illum Demetrius, rex Illyriorum, nuper a Paulo, Romano consule, victus supplicibus precibus
2 adgreditur, iniuriam Romanorum querens, qui non contenti Italiae terminis, imperium spe inproba totius
3 orbis amplexi, bellum cum omnibus regibus gerant. Sic illos Siciliae, sic Sardiniae Hispaniaeque, sic denique totius Africae imperium adfectantes bellum cum Poenis et
4 Hannibale suscepisse; sibi quoque non aliam ob causam, quam quod Italiae finitimus videbatur, bellum inlatum, quasi nefas esset aliquem regem iuxta imperii eorum ter-
5 minos esse. Sed et ipsi cavendum exemplum esse, cuius quanto promptius nobiliusque sit regnum, tanto sit Roma-
6 nos acriores hostes habiturus. Super haec cedere se illi regno, quod Romani occupaverint, profitetur, gratius habiturus, si in possessione imperii sui socium potius quam
7 hostes videret. Huiuscemodi oratione inpulit Philippum, ut omissis Aetolis bellum Romanis inferret, minus negotii

---

3 See Polyb. 5.34ff., 79ff., and below, Book 30.
4 The defeat was by L. Aemilius Paullus in 219; Polyb. 3.16, 18f.; *MRR* 1.236. Demetrius of Pharos was not in fact a king but a tyrant (in the Greek sense), put in power by the Romans in 228, then ejected when he fell out with them. Events in this book were covered in Polyb. 4–5, 7–11; Livy treats the period of the war with Hannibal in Books 21–30. Polybius was Livy's main source for Greek affairs.

both villainous in seizing his kingdom and idle in admin-
istering it.³ In the case of Philip, the Dardanians and all   10
the other neighboring peoples felt perpetual hatred for
the Macedonian kings, and from contempt for him be-
cause of his age they were constantly harassing him. He in   11
return, after warding off his enemies but then still not
content with having defended his own territory, was itch-
ing to make war on the Aetolians.

2. While he was considering this he was approached
with abject entreaties by Demetrius, king of the Illyrians,
who, recently defeated by the Roman consul Paullus,⁴ was
complaining about his ill-treatment by the Romans; these,   2
he said, not content with the boundaries of Italy and hav-
ing outrageous hopes of world domination, would make
war on all kings. So in aiming for domination of Sicily, of   3
Sardinia and Spain and finally, indeed, of all Africa, they
had started a war with the Carthaginians and Hannibal, he
said; and he himself had also been attacked for no other   4
reason than that he seemed to be close to Italy—as if it
were a crime for any king to be on the border of their
empire. But Philip should himself also beware of his ex-   5
ample, for since his kingdom was more accessible and
famous, he would have the Romans as even fiercer ene-
mies. In addition, he said, he ceded to him his kingdom,   6
which the Romans had seized, and he would find it more
agreeable seeing an ally in possession of his empire rather
than his enemies. By this sort of talk he pushed Philip into   7
overlooking the Aetolians and attacking the Romans,

existimantem, quod iam victos eos ab Hannibale apud Tra-
8 simenum lacum audierat. Itaque ne eodem tempore multis bellis detineretur, pacem cum Aetolis facit, non quasi
alio bellum translaturus, sed ut Graeciae quieti con-
sulturus, quam numquam in maiore periculo fuisse ad-
9 firmabat, siquidem consurgentibus ab Occidente novis
Poenorum ac Romanorum imperiis, quibus una haec a
Graecia atque Asia sit mora, dum inter se bello discrimen
imperii faciunt; ceterum statim victoribus transitum in
Orientem fore.

3. Videre se itaque, ait, consurgentem in Italia nubem
illam trucis et cruenti belli; videre tonantem ac fulmi-
nantem ab occasu procellam, quam in quascumque terrarum partes victoriae tempestas detulerit, magno cruoris
2 imbre omnia foedaturam. Frequenter Graeciam ingentes
motus passam, nunc Persarum, nunc Gallorum, nunc
Macedonum bellis, sed omnia illa levia fuisse existimatu-
ros, si ea, quae nunc in Italia concurrat manus, extra ter-
3 ram illam se effuderit. Cernere se, quam cruenta et san-
guinaria inter se bella utrique populi et viribus copiarum
et ducum artibus gerant, quae rabies finiri solo partis al-
4 terius interitu sine ruina finitimorum non possit. Feros
igitur victorum animos minus quidem Macedoniae quam
Graeciae timendos, quia et remotior et in vindictam sui
5 robustior sit; scire tamen se eos, qui tantis viribus concur-
rant, non contentos hoc fine victoriae fore, metuendum-
que sibi quoque certamen eorum, qui superiores extite-
rint.

---

⁵ In 217.   ⁶ This speech, including the storm image that
follows, echoes that which Polyb. 5.104 attributes to Agelaus of
Naupactus.

which he thought would be less difficult since he had now heard of their defeat by Hannibal at Lake Trasimene.[5] So not to be preoccupied with many wars at the same time, he made peace with the Aetolians, ostensibly not to move the war elsewhere but to maintain the tranquility of Greece, which, he insisted, had never been in greater danger; for with the rise of the new empires of Carthage and Rome in the west, all that held these back from attacking Greece and Asia was their struggle for supremacy among themselves; but the victors would immediately have a crossing to the East.[6]

3. So, he said, he saw rising in Italy the cloud of a fierce and bloody war; he saw a blast of thunder and lightning coming from the west that would, wherever in the world the squall of victory took it, foul everything with a torrential rain of blood. Greece had often experienced violent upheavals in wars fought now with the Persians, now with the Gauls, now with the Macedonians, but all of them they will think trivial if the forces now clashing in Italy should pour out beyond that country. He could see what bloody, murderous wars the two peoples were fighting against each other with their mighty forces and their generals' stratagems, a madness not to be ended by one side's destruction without it ruining its neighbors. So the ferocity of the victors was less to be feared by Macedonia than by Greece, because it was both farther off and also more capable of defending itself; but he knew that men who clashed with such might would not be ready to stop at victory, and he must fear having to fight the side that came off better.

6   Hoc praetexto finito cum Aetolis bello nihil aliud quam
Poenorum Romanorumque bella respiciens singulorum
7 vires perpendebat. Sed nec Romani, tametsi Poeni et
Hannibal in cervicibus erant, soluti metu Macedonico vi-
8 debantur; quippe terrebat eos et vetus Macedonum de-
victi Orientis gloria et Philippus studio Alexandri aemulationis incensus, quem promptum in bella industriumque
cognoverant.

4. Igitur Philippus, cum iterato victos a Poenis Romanos didicisset, aperte hostem se his professus naves, qui-
2 bus in Italiam exercitum traiceret, fabricare coepit. Legatum deinde ad Hannibalem iungendae societatis gratia
3 cum epistulis mittit, qui conprehensus et ad senatum perductus incolumis dimissus est, non in honorem regis, sed
4 ne dubius adhuc indubitatus hostis redderetur. Postea
vero, cum Romanis nuntiatum esset in Italiam Philippum
copias traiecturum, Laevinum praetorem cum instructis
5 navibus ad prohibendum transitum mittunt. Qui cum in
Graeciam traiecisset, multis promissis inpellit Aetolos
bellum adversus Philippum suscipere. Philippus quoque
Achaeos in Romanorum bella sollicitat.

6   Interea et Dardani Macedoniae fines vastare coeperunt, abductisque XX milibus captivorum Philippum a
7 Romano bello ad tuendum regnum revocaverunt. Dum
haec aguntur, Laevinus praetor iuncta cum Attalo rege
societate Graeciam populatur. Quibus cladibus perculsae

---

7 At Cannae in 216.   8 Livy 23.33. M. Valerius Laevinus
was praetor in 215 and was concerned with Greece until 211.

9 And the Aetolian League, in 212 or 211: Livy 26.24ff.; Sherk
no. 2 (part of the treaty's text on a damaged inscription). Attalus
I was king of Pergamum from 241 to 197.

Ending his war with the Aetolians with this pretext and focusing on nothing other than the Carthaginian and Roman wars, he started assessing the strength of each side. But despite having the Carthaginians and Hannibal at their throats, the Romans still did not seem free of fear of Macedon; for they were intimidated both by the Macedonians' longstanding reputation as conquerors of the East and by Philip's burning desire to emulate Alexander, for they knew him as someone ready for war and a man of action.

4. So on learning that Romans had again been defeated by the Carthaginians,[7] Philip openly declared himself their enemy and started building ships with which to transport his army to Italy. He then sent a delegate to Hannibal with letters for forming an alliance, but when the man was captured and brought before the senate he was released unharmed, not from regard for the king but so a still hesitant enemy should not become a committed one.[8] Then later, when it was reported to the Romans that Philip would be sending his troops over to Italy, they sent the praetor Laevinus with a fleet of ships to block his crossing. He, on crossing to Greece, with many promises pushed the Aetolians into war against Philip. Philip also induced the Achaeans into wars against the Romans.

In the meantime the Dardanians also started raiding Macedonian territory, and after taking twenty thousand captives they brought Philip away from the Roman campaign to defend his kingdom. While this was in progress, the praetor Laevinus had made an alliance with King Attalus and was raiding Greece.[9] Shaken by such blows the

EPITOME OF POMPEIUS TROGUS

civitates auxilium petentes Philippum legationibus fati-
8   gant; nec non et Illyriorum reges lateri eius haerentes
adsiduis precibus promissa exigebant. Super haec vastati
9   Macedones ultionem flagitabant. Quibus tot tantisque
rebus obsessus, cui rei primum occurreret, ambigebat;
omnibus tamen propediem auxilia se missurum pollicetur,
non quia facere posset quae promittebat, sed ut spe inple-
10 tos in societatis iure retineret. Prima tamen illi expeditio
adversus Dardanos fuit, qui absentiam eius aucupantes
11 maiore belli mole Macedoniae inminebant. Cum Romanis
quoque pacem facit, contentis interim bellum Macedonicum distulisse. Philopoemeni, Achaeorum duci, quem ad
Romanos sociorum animos sollicitare didicerat, insidias
praetendit. Quibus ille cognitis vitatisque discedere ab eo
Achaeos auctoritate sua coegit.

city-states kept harassing Philip with delegations seeking his aid; and in addition Illyrian kings were also sticking to 8 his side and with persistent entreaties demanding he fulfill his promises. In addition, the devastated Macedonians were demanding revenge. Beset so many and such urgent 9 problems, Philip was at a loss which issue to address first; but he promised everyone that he would promptly send help, not because he could do what he promised but so that by filling them with hope he might keep them loyal to their alliance. His first campaign, however, was against the 10 Dardanians, who after waiting for him to leave his kingdom then threatened Macedonia with a force greater than his. He also made peace with the Romans, who were 11 happy enough to have meanwhile put off a war with Macedon.[10] For Philopoemen, the Achaean leader who, he had learned, was trying to win the support of Macedon's allies over to the Romans he set a trap. On discovering it and avoiding it, Philopoemen through his authority forced the Achaeans to abandon Philip.

[10] The Peace of Phoenice in 205; Livy 29.12. For Philopoemen see Plut. *Vit. Phil.* 12.

LIBER XXX

1. Philippo in Macedonia magnis rebus intento in Aegypto
2 Ptolomei diversi mores erant; quippe regno parricidio
parto et ad necem utriusque parentis caede etiam fratris
adstructa, veluti rebus feliciter gestis luxuriae se tradide-
3 rat, regisque mores omnis secuta regia erat. Itaque non
amici tantum praefectique, verum etiam omnis exercitus
depositis militiae studiis otio ac desidia corrupti marce-
4 bant. Quibus rebus cognitis Antiochus, rex Syriae, vetere
inter se regnorum odio stimulante repentino bello multas
5 urbes eius oppressit ipsamque Aegyptum adgreditur. Tre-
pidare igitur Ptolomeus, legationibus missis, quoad vires
6 pararet morari Antiochum. Magno deinde exercitu in
Graecia conducto secundum proelium facit, spoliassetque
7 regno Antiochum, si fortunam virtute iuvisset. Sed contentus reciperatione urbium, quas amiserat, facta pace
avide materiam quietis adripuit revolutusque in luxuriam

---

1 See Book 29 n. 2. Cf. Polyb. 14.11 for Agathoclia.
2 Ptolemy IV did not murder his father (Ptolemy III), but to
eliminate any threat to his and his chief ministers' power these,
Sosibius and Agathocles, arranged for the killings of his mother
(Berenice), his uncle, and his three brothers. He married the
surviving sister, another Arsinoë (Justin wrongly calls her Eurydice).

BOOK XXX

1. While Philip was busy with weighty matters in Macedonia Ptolemy's character in Egypt was quite different;[1] for 2 after gaining the throne by murder and also adding the killing of both parents to the assassination of his brother,[2] he had after what he considered great success surrendered himself to a life of luxury, and the king's conduct had been followed by the whole palace. So not only were his friends 3 and prefects becoming corrupt and indolent, but so also was the whole army, which lost all interest in military service. On hearing of such conduct Antiochus, king of Syria, 4 prompted by the long-standing hatred between their kingdoms, overran many of his cities and attacked Egypt itself. So Ptolemy panicked, and sending off delegations tried to 5 delay Antiochus until he could marshal troops. Then after 6 raising a great army in Greece he fought a successful battle,[3] and he would have robbed Antiochus of his kingdom had he aided fortune with courage. But content with re- 7 covering the cities he had lost, he made peace and eagerly seized the opportunity for idleness: then relapsing into prodigality he killed his wife, Eurydice, who was also his

[3] The battle of Raphia, near Gaza, in 217, one of the largest battles in Hellenistic history, with reportedly seventy-five thousand Ptolemaic troops versus sixty-eight thousand Seleucids.

occisa Eurydice, uxore eademque sorore sua, Agathocliae
8 meretricis inlecebris capitur, atque ita omissa magnitudine nominis ac maiestatis oblitus noctes in stupris, dies
9 in conviviis consumit. Adduntur instrumenta luxuriae,
tympana et crepundia; nec iam spectator rex, sed magister
10 nequitiae nervorum oblectamenta modulatur. Haec primo
laborantis regiae tacita pestis et occulta mala fuere.

2. Dehinc crescente licentia iam nec parietibus regiae
2 domus contineri meretricis audacia potest, quam proter-
viorem sociata cum Agathocle fratre, ambitiosae pulchri-
3 tudinis scorto, cotidiana regis stupra faciebant. Accedebat
et mater Oenanthe, quae geminae subolis inlecebris de-
4 vinctum regem tenebat. Itaque non contenti rege iam
etiam regnum possident, iam in publico visuntur, iam
5 salutantur, iam comitantur. Agathocles regis lateri iunctus
civitatem regebat, tribunatus et praefecturas et ducatus
mulieres ordinabant; nec quisquam in regno suo minus
6 poterat quam rex ipse, cum interim relicto quinquenni ex
Eurydice sorore filio moritur. Sed mors eius, dum pecu-
niam regiam mulieres rapiunt et imperium inita cum per-
ditissimis societate occupare conantur, diu occultata fuit.
7 Re tamen cognita concursu multitudinis et Agathocles
occiditur et mulieres in ultionem Eurydices patibulis suf-
8 figuntur. Morte regis, supplicio meretricum velut expiata
regni infamia legatos Alexandrini ad Romanos misere,

---

4 In 205. His successor was Ptolemy V Epiphanes (204–180);
see Polyb. 15.20, 25ff., and below, the beginning of Book 31. For
the Roman involvement see Sherk no. 3.

sister, and became captivated by the allurements of the courtesan Agathoclia; and so with no thought for the greatness of his name and forgetting his royal dignity, he spent his nights whoring and his days feasting. Added to these were instruments of dissipation, drums and tambourines; and now no longer a spectator king but master of the depravity he was providing amusement on stringed instruments. This was the start of the tottering palace's silent plague and hidden maladies.

2. After that the license increased and the whore's effrontery could no longer be confined within the palace walls, as she became all the more shameless with the king's daily debaucheries that were shared with her brother Agathocles, a good-looking boy prostituting himself for advancement. There was also their mother Oenanthe, who by the allure of her two children had the king under her thumb. So not content with just having the king under them they were also now appropriating the kingdom, now appearing in public, now being saluted, now being attended by a retinue. Agathocles, always at the king's side, would be the one ruling the state, while tribunates, governorships and military commands were dispensed by the women, and in his kingdom no one had less power than the king himself, when he meanwhile died and left a five-year-old son whom he had had by his sister Eurydice.[4] But while the women were looting the royal treasury and attempting to seize power with the very worst people, his death was for a long time kept secret. But when the matter became known Agathocles was killed in a mob riot and the women were also crucified as vengeance for Eurydice. With the king dead, and the whores punished, the Alexandrians, feeling their kingdom's disgrace now expiated, sent

8

9

10

2

3

4

5

6

7

8

orantes ut tutelam pupilli susciperent tuerenturque regnum Aegypti, quod iam Philippum et Antiochum facta inter se pactione divisisse dicebant.

3. Grata legatio Romanis fuit causas belli adversus Philippum quaerentibus, qui insidiatus temporibus belli Punici fuerat. Huc accedebat, quod Poenis et Hannibale superatis nullius magis arma metuebant, reputantibus quantum motum Pyrrus parva Macedonum manu in Italia fecisset, quantasque res Macedones in Oriente gessissent.

3 Mittuntur itaque legati, qui Philippo et Antiocho denun-
4 tient, regno Aegypti abstineant. Mittitur et M. Lepidus in Aegyptum, qui tutorio nomine regnum pupilli administret.

5 Dum haec aguntur, interim legationes Attali regis et Rhodiorum iniurias Philippi querentes Romam venerunt. Quae res omnem cunctationem Macedonici belli senatui
6 eximit. Statim igitur titulo ferendi sociis auxiliis bellum adversus Philippum decernitur, legionesque cum consule
7 in Macedoniam mittuntur. Nec multo post tempore fiducia Romanorum tota Graecia adversus Philippum spe pristinae libertatis erecta bellum ei intulit; atque ita cum undi-
8 que rex urgeretur, pacem petere conpellitur. Dehinc cum expositae condiciones pacis a Romanis essent, repetere
9 sua et Attalus et Rhodii et Achaei et Aetoli coepere. Contra Philippus adduci se posse, ut Romanis pareat, con-

---

5 This supposed role for Lepidus was a later Aemilian family legend; Lepidus was one of three envoys sent to the East in 201 in diplomatic preparations for the new war with Macedonia; if he visited Egypt, it was only a brief stay.

6 In 201. For the following, see Polyb. 16 and 18; Diod. Sic. 28.5ff.; Livy 31–33; Plut. *Vit. Flam.*

delegates to the Romans to plead with them to assume protection of their ward and guard the kingdom of Egypt, because already, they said, Philip and Antiochus had by a mutual agreement divided it between them.

3. The legation pleased the Romans as they were seeking reasons for war with Philip, who had plotted against them at the time of the Punic War. A further consideration 2 was that with the Carthaginians and Hannibal now defeated there was no one whose forces they feared more when they reflected on the upheaval that Pyrrhus had caused in Italy with a small force of Macedonians and on how great Macedonian exploits in the East had been. So 3 delegates were sent to warn Philip and Antiochus to keep out of the kingdom of Egypt. Marcus Lepidus was also 4 sent to Egypt to administer the orphan's kingdom as his legal guardian.[5]

During these events, embassies from King Attalus and 5 the Rhodians meanwhile came to Rome complaining of wrongs suffered at Philip's hands.[6] This removed from the senate any hesitation about war with Macedon. So immediately, with a pretext of bringing aid to their allies, war 6 was declared on Philip and legions were sent into Macedonia with a consul. And not much later, through confidence in the Romans, all Greece went to war against 7 Philip hoping to regain its earlier freedom; and so since the king was under pressure everywhere he was forced to sue for peace. Then when the terms of the peace had been 8 laid out by the Romans, Attalus, the Rhodians, Achaeans and Aetolians all began reclaiming what was theirs. Philip 9 for his part agreed he could be brought to accept the Ro-

cedebat; ceterum indignum esse Graecos a Philippo et
Alexandro, maioribus suis, victos et sub iugum Macedonici imperii subactos veluti victores leges pacis sibi dicere,
quibus prius sit servitutis ratio reddenda quam libertas
10 vindicanda. Ad postremum tamen petente eo indutiae
duorum mensium datae, ut pax, quae in Macedonia non
conveniebat, Romae a senatu peteretur.

4. Eodem anno inter insulas Theram et Therasiam me-
2 dio utriusque ripae maris spatio terrae motus fuit, in quo
cum admiratione navigantium repente ex profundo cum
3 calidis aquis insula emersit. In Asia quoque eadem die
idem motus terrae Rhodum multasque alias civitates gra-
vis ruinarum labe concussit, quasdam solidas absorbuit.
4 Quo prodigio territis omnibus vates cecinere, oriens Romanorum imperium vetus Graecorum ac Macedonum
voraturum.

5 Interim a senatu repudiata pace Philippus in societa-
6 tem belli Nabim tyrannum sollicitat. Atque ita cum in
aciem exercitum instructis e diverso hostibus produxisset,
hortari suos coepit referendo Persas, Bactros Indosque et
omnem Asiam Orientis fine a Macedonibus perdomitam;
7 tantoque hoc bellum fortius quam illa sustinendum,
8 quanto sit imperio libertas carior. Sed et Flamininus, Romanus consul, relatione rerum gestarum recentissime

---

7 These events took place in late 198/early 197. Philip was now
facing the young consul T. Quinctius Flamininus and had lost
most of his allies.   8 Of Sparta. Nabis in fact gave Philip no
help and soon sided with Rome. T. Quinctius Flamininus was sent
to Greece as consul in 198, continued as proconsul (197–194),
and arranged the peace treaty with Philip in 196, after defeating
him at Cynoscephalae in June 197. Cf. Sherk nos. 4–6.

mans' conditions; but he said it was demeaning to have Greeks, men defeated by his ancestors Philip and Alexander and brought under the yoke of the Macedonian Empire, dictating peace terms to him like victors—they should be explaining how they became his subjects before trying to assert their independence. Finally however he   10 was at his request granted a two-month truce so that a peace that could not be settled in Macedonia, could be sought in Rome from the senate.[7]

4. That same year an earthquake occurred between the islands of Thera and Therasia, halfway between the coasts of the two, and during it to the astonishment of sailors an   2 island suddenly emerged from the ocean depths amid boiling waters. In Asia, too, on that same day the same   3 earthquake shook Rhodes and many other cities, causing catastrophic damage as it leveled buildings and swallowed some cities whole. Everyone was terrified by the prodi-   4 gious event and the soothsayers predicted that the rising Roman Empire would devour the old one of the Greeks and Macedonians.

Meanwhile after being denied a peace treaty by the   5 senate Philip enticed the tyrant Nabis[8] into joining him in the war. Then when he had brought his army out into the   6 battle line facing the enemy, he proceeded to exhort his men by reminding them of the Persians, Bactrians, Indians and all Asia to the far East that had been overcome by the Macedonians; this war must be faced with much   7 greater resolve than those others, he said, freedom being so much precious than empire. But Flamininus, the Roman consul, was also stimulating his troops to battle, re-   8

suos stimulabat in proelium, ostendendo hinc Karthaginem cum Sicilia, inde Italiam et Hispaniam Romana
9 virtute perdomitas. Ne Hannibalem quidem Alexandro
Magno postponendum, quo Italia pulso Africam ipsam,
10 tertiam partem mundi, superaverint. Sed nec Macedonas
11 veteri fama, sed praesentibus viribus aestimandos, quia
non cum Alexandro Magno, quem invictum audiant, nec
cum exercitu eius, qui totum Orientem devicerit, bellum
12 gerant, sed cum Philippo, puero inmaturae aetatis, qui
regni terminos adversus finitimos aegre defendat, et cum
his Macedonibus, qui non ita pridem praedae Dardanis
13 fuerint. Illos maiorum decora, se suorum militum comme-
14 morare. Non enim alio exercitu Hannibalem et Poenos et
totum ferme Occidentem, sed his ipsis, quos in acie habeat, militibus subactos.

15 His adhortationibus utrimque concitati milites proelio
concurrunt, alteri Orientis, alteri Occidentis imperio glo-
riantes, ferentesque in bellum alii maiorum suorum antiquam et obsoletam gloriam, alii virentem recentibus
16 experimentis virtutis florem. Sed Macedonas Romana
17 Fortuna vicit. Fractus itaque bello Philippus pace a Flaminino consule petita nomen quidem regium retinuit, sed
omnibus Graeciae urbibus, velut regni membris extra terminos antiquae possessionis, amissis solam Macedoniam
18 retinuit. Offensi tamen Aetoli, quia non arbitrio eorum
Macedonia quoque adempta regi et data sibi in praemium
belli esset, legatos ad Antiochum mittunt, qui eum adulatione magnitudinis in Romana bella spe societatis universae Graeciae inpellerent.

---

9 That is, Alexander the Great and his army.

120

minding them of their most recent achievements and
pointing out Carthage and Sicily on one side and Italy and
Spain on the other, lands crushed by Roman courage. Not   9
even Hannibal could be thought inferior to Alexander the
Great, he said, but after driving him from Italy they had
conquered Africa itself, one-third of the world. But the   10
Macedonians must be judged not by their reputation of
old but by their present strength, since it was not with   11
Alexander the Great, who they were told was invincible,
that they were at war, and not with his army that had conquered the entire East, but with Philip, an immature boy
who had difficulty protecting his frontiers against his   12
neighbors, and with these Macedonians who not so long
ago had been the prey of the Dardanians. Those men[9]   13
commemorated the glorious feats of their forefathers, he
those of his own men. For by no other army had Hannibal,   14
the Carthaginians and almost all the West been overcome
but by these very soldiers he now had in the battle line.

With both sides galvanized by such exhortations they   15
clashed in battle, one side priding itself on its eastern
empire, the other on its western, one taking into war its
ancestors' faded glory, the other its freshly blossoming
renown from recent experience in battle. But the Mace-   16
donians were defeated by Roman Fortune. So defeated in   17
battle Philip sued for peace from Flamininus, and although he retained the title of king he lost all the cities of
Greece (the portions of his realm outside his ancient do-
main) and retained only Macedonia. The Aetolians, how-   18
ever, were displeased that Macedonia had not also been
taken from the king as they suggested and given to them
as their prize of war, so they sent delegates to Antiochus
to flatter him on his greatness and push him into wars with
the Romans in the hope of a pan-Greek alliance.

LIBER XXXI

1. Mortuo Ptolomeo Philopatore, rege Aegypti, contemptaque parvuli filii eius aetate, qui in spem regni relictus praeda etiam domesticis erat, Antiochus, rex Syriae, occupare Aegyptum statuit. Itaque Phoenicen ceterasque Syriae quidem, sed iuris Aegypti civitates cum invasisset, legatos ad eum senatus mittit, qui denuntiarent ei, abstineret regno pupilli postremis patris precibus fidei suae traditi. Quibus spretis interiecto tempore alia legatio supervenit, quae omissa pupilli persona civitates iure belli factas populi Romani in integrum restitui iubebat. Abnuenti bellum denuntiatum, quod ille facile susceptum infeliciter gessit.

5 Eodem tempore et Nabis tyrannus multas Graeciae 6 civitates occupaverat. Igitur senatus, ne uno tempore duplici bello Romanae vires detinerentur, scripsit Flaminino, si ei videatur, sicuti Macedoniam a Philippo, ita et 7 Graeciam a Nabide liberet. Ob quam causam imperium ei prorogatum. Terribile quippe Antiochi bellum Hannibalis

---

[1] See 30.2.6ff. For the contents of this book, see Polyb. 18.49ff., 20, and 21; Diod. Sic. 28 and 29; Livy 33.38 through Book 37; Plut. *Vit. Flam.* For Flamininus see *MRR* 1.341, 344.

[2] A messy confusion between Rome's dealings with Antiochus III (the Great) in the later 190s, over his activities in the Aegean

BOOK XXXI

1. When Ptolemy Philopator, king of Egypt, died and the young son who was left expecting to succeed to the throne was overlooked because of his age and even became prey for his servants, Antiochus, king of Syria, decided to seize Egypt.[1] So after he had invaded Phoenicia and the other states that were in Syria but under Egyptian rule, the senate sent delegates to him to warn him to keep out of the kingdom of its ward who in his father's final prayers had been left in its care. When he ignored them, another legation arrived later which without mention of the ward demanded that those states that had by right of war become the property of the Roman people must be entirely restored to them. When he refused war was declared, one he lightly accepted but unsuccessfully fought.[2]

At this same time the tyrant Nabis had also seized many Greek states.[3] So not to have the Romans' strength simultaneously focused on two wars, the senate wrote to Flamininus that, if he saw fit, he should just as he had liberated Macedonia from Philip also liberate Greece from Nabis. To that end his command was prorogued. For war with Antiochus was becoming an alarming prospect

lands and Greece, and his son Antiochus IV's invasion of Egypt in 169/8.   [3] See 30.4.5.

nomen faciebat, quem aemuli eius occultis mandatis cum
Antiocho inisse societatem apud Romanos criminabantur,
8 negantes eum aequo animo sub legibus vivere adsuetum
imperio et inmoderata licentia militari; semperque taedio
9 quietis urbanae novas belli causas circumspicere. Quae
etsi falsa nuntiata fuissent, apud timentes tamen pro veris
habebantur.

2. Denique senatus metu perculsus ad speculandos
actus Hannibalis legatum in Africam Cn. Servilium mittit
eique tacitis mandatis praecipit, ut, si posset, eum per
aemulos eius interficeret metuque invisi nominis tandem
2 populum Romanum liberaret. Sed res Hannibalem non
diu latuit, virum ad prospicienda cavendaque pericula
paratum nec minus in secundis adversa quam in adversis
3 secunda cogitantem. Igitur cum tota die in oculis principum legatique Romani in foro Karthaginiensium obversa-
tus in supremum fuisset, adpropinquante vespere equum
conscendit et rus urbanum, quod propter litus maris habebat, ignaris servis iussisque ad portam revertentem oppe-
4 riri, contendit. Habebat ibi naves cum remigibus occulto
sinu litoris absconditas; erat et grandis in eo agro pecunia
praeparata, ut, cum res exegisset, nec facultas fugam
5 nec inopia moraretur. Lecta igitur servorum iuventute,
quorum copiam Italicorum captivorum numerus augebat,
navem conscendit cursumque ad Antiochum dirigit.
6 Postera die civitas principem suum ac tum temporis con-

---

[4] In 195; *MRR* 1.341. Servilius was one of three envoys; they
were hostile to Hannibal but had no plans for his murder.

[5] This estate was on the east coast near modern Mahdia, over
two hundred kilometers south of Carthage (Livy 33.48.1–2).

124

by the name of Hannibal, who his rivals were alleging in covert reports to the Romans had entered an alliance with Antiochus; they said he could not comfortably live under the rule of law since he had grown used to power and the unlimited license of military life; and from boredom with peaceful city life he was always casting around for fresh reasons for war. Although the reports had been false, among a nervous people they were still thought to be true.

2. Finally the senate, stricken with fear, sent Gnaeus Servilius as a delegate to Africa to check Hannibal's movements, and in secret instructions ordered him, if he could, to have him assassinated by his rivals and finally free the Roman people from fear of his hated name.[4] But the matter did not long escape Hannibal, a man ready to foresee and guard against danger and to consider reverses in success no less than success in adversity. So after he had spent all day under the eyes of leading citizens and the Roman delegate in the Carthaginian forum under strict observation, he mounted his horse as evening was approaching and rode to a suburban estate that he had close to the sea, his slaves unaware and ordered to await his return at the city gate. He there had ships with oarsmen hidden in a concealed bay on the shoreline;[5] and there was also a large sum of money on that land kept in readiness so that, when the situation demanded, no lack of opportunity or money should delay his flight. So choosing some young slaves, whose number he augmented with a group of Italian captives, he boarded a ship and set a course for Antiochus. The following day the city was waiting in the forum for its

7 sulem in foro expectabat. Quem ut profectum nuntiatum
est, non aliter quam si urbs capta esset, omnes trepidavere
8 exitiosamque sibi fugam eius ominati sunt. Legatus vero
Romanus, quasi iam bellum inlatum Italiae ab Hannibale
esset, tacitus Romam regreditur trepidumque nuntium
refert.

3. Interim in Graecia Flamininus iuncta cum quibusdam civitatibus societate Nabidem tyrannum duobus continuis proeliis subigit et gravibus pacis legibus fractum
2 velut exsanguem in regno reliquit. Sed libertate Graeciae
restituta deductisque ab urbibus praesidiis, cum Romanus
exercitus in Italiam reportatus esset, velut vacua rursus
possessione sollicitatus multas civitates repentino bello
3 invasit. Quibus rebus exterriti Achaei, ne vicinum malum
etiam ad se serperet bellum adversus Nabidem decernunt
ducemque praetorem suum Philopoemenem, insignis in-
4 dustriae virum, constituunt, cuius in eo bello tanta virtus
enituit, ut opinione omnium Flaminino, Romano impera-
tori, conpararetur.

5 Eodem tempore Hannibal, cum ad Antiochum perve-
6 nisset, velut deorum munus excipitur, tantusque eius adventu ardor animis regis accessit ut non tam de bello quam
7 de praemiis victoriae cogitaret. Sed Hannibal, cui nota
Romana virtus erat, negabat opprimi Romanos nisi in Ita-
8 lia posse. Ad hoc sibi centum naves et decem milia peditum mille equitum poscebat, promittens hac manu non
9 minus bellum quam gesserit Italiae restauraturum et in

---

6 Cf. Plut. *Vit. Phil.* 14ff.

7 The comparison continued to the extent that Plutarch
paired the biographies of the two men.

leading citizen, who was then also a consul. When a report 7
came that he had left, everyone panicked just as if their
city had been captured and had an ominous feeling that
his flight meant their destruction. The Roman delegate, as 8
though war had already been launched on Italy by Hannibal, then discreetly returned to Rome and brought the
disturbing news.

3. Meanwhile, in Greece Flamininus, after forging alliances with a number of cities, defeated the tyrant Nabis
in two successive battles and left him, broken by the severe peace terms, virtually exhausted in his kingdom. But 2
with the freedom of Greece restored and the garrisons
withdrawn from the cities, and since the Roman army had
been brought home to Italy, Nabis, tempted by territory
he thought again open, overran many states with a sudden
attack.[6] Alarmed by such events and to avoid a neighbor's 3
problem also reaching them, the Achaeans declared war
on Nabis and as their leader appointed their praetor Philopoemen, a man of remarkable energy, whose courage in 4
that war was so conspicuous that in everyone's view he was
to be compared with Flamininus, the Roman general.[7]

At this same time Hannibal had reached Antiochus and 5
was welcomed like a gift from the gods, and such was the 6
king's excitement at his coming that he was thinking less
about the war than the prizes of victory. But Hannibal, to 7
whom Roman valor was well known, kept insisting that the
Romans could be conquered only in Italy. For that he 8
demanded a hundred ships, ten thousand infantry and a
thousand cavalry, giving an assurance that with such a
force he would revive the war no less effectively than he
had fought it in Italy and would bring back to the king, 9
while he sat in Asia, either victory over the Romans or

127

Asia regi sedenti aut victoriam de Romanis aut aequas
10 pacis condiciones relaturum; quippe et Hispanis bello fla-
grantibus ducem tantum deesse, et Italiam notiorem sibi
nunc quam pridem fuisse; sed nec Karthaginem quietu-
ram sociamque se ei sine mora praebituram.

4. Cum regi consilia placuisset, mittitur Karthaginem
unus ex comitibus Hannibalis, qui in bellum cupidos hor-
tetur Hannibalemque cum copiis adfuturum nuntiet; nihil
dicat partibus nisi animos Karthaginiensium deesse:
2 Asiam et vires belli et sumptum praebituram. Haec cum
relata Karthaginem essent, nuntius ipse ab inimicis Hannibalis conprehenditur perductusque in senatum cum
interrogaretur, ad quem missus esset, Punico ingenio respondit se ad universum senatum missum; nec enim opus
3 hoc singulorum, sed universorum esse. Dum multis diebus deliberant, an eum Romam ad purgandam publicam
conscientiam mittant, tacitus conscensa nave ad Hannibalem revertitur. Quo cognito Karthaginienses ultro rem
4 Romam per legatum deferunt. Romani quoque legatos ad
Antiochum misere, qui sub specie legationis et regis apparatum specularentur et Hannibalem aut Romanis miti-
garent aut adsiduo conloquio suspectum invisumque
5 redderent regi. Itaque legati cum Ephesi convenissent
6 Antiochum, mandata ei senatus tradunt. Dum responsum
expectant, omnibus diebus adsidui circa Hannibalem
fuere, dicentes eum timide a patria recessisse, cum pacem
Romani non tam cum re publica eius quam cum eo factam

---

[8] He was Ariston of Tyre; but Justin cannot resist giving him
the proverbial "Carthaginian ingenuity."
[9] In 193; *MRR* 1.348f.

favorable peace terms; for with the Spaniards also burning 10 for war all they needed was a leader, and Italy was also better known to him now than it was earlier; but neither would Carthage remain at peace and would without hesitation offer herself as his ally.

4. Since the advice pleased the king, one of Hannibal's men[8] was sent to Carthage to encourage those eager for war and report that Hannibal would soon arrive with troops; he was to say that their side lacked nothing except Carthaginian support; Asia would supply both troops for the war and finances. When this news had been taken to 2 Carthage, the messenger was himself caught by Hannibal's personal enemies and brought into the senate; and when asked to whom he had been sent he replied with Carthaginian ingenuity that he had been sent to the whole senate; for this, he said, was a matter that touched not just individuals but everybody. While they were spending 3 many days considering whether to send him to Rome to clear their state of complicity, he quietly boarded a ship and returned to Hannibal. On learning of this the Carthaginians readily reported the matter to Rome through a delegate. The Romans also sent delegates to Antiochus,[9] 4 men who, purportedly on an embassy, were to both investigate the king's preparedness and also either soften Hannibal's hostility toward the Romans or by frequent conversations with him render him suspect and disliked by the king. So when the legates met Antiochus at Ephe- 5 sus, they delivered to him the dispatches from the senate. While they awaited his reply, they were every day con- 6 stantly around Hannibal, telling him he had been too fearful in leaving his country, since the Romans would with total integrity honor a peace made not so much with his

129

7   summa fide custodiant; nec bella eum Romanorum magis
odio quam patriae amore gessisse, cui ab optimo quoque
etiam spiritus ipse debeatur. Has enim publicas inter populos, non privatas inter duces bellandi causas esse. Inde
8   res gestas eius laudare. Quarum sermone laetus saepius
cupidiusque cum legatis conloquebatur, ignarus quod
familiaritate Romana odium sibi apud regem crearet.
9   Quippe Antiochus tam adsiduo conloquio reconciliatam
eius cum Romanis gratiam existimans nihil ad eum, sicuti
solebat, referre, expertemque totius consilii et veluti hostem proditoremque suum odisse coepit. Quae res tantum
10   apparatum belli cessante imperatoria arte corrupit. Senatus mandata fuerant, contentus terminis Asiae esset, ne
ipsis Asiam ingrediendi necessitatem inponeret. Quibus
spretis non accipiendum bellum statuit, sed inferendum.

    5. Dicitur, cum frequenter de bello consilium remoto
Hannibale habuisset, tandem eum vocari iussisse, non ut
ex sententia eius aliquid ageret, sed ne per omnia spre-
visse videretur, omnibusque perrogatis postremum inter-
2   rogasse. Quo ille animadverso intellegere se professus est,
non quia egeat consilio, sed ad supplendum numerum
sententiarum se vocatum; tamen et odio Romanorum
et amore regis, apud quem solum tutum exilium sibi re-
3   lictum sit, se viam gerendi belli edisserturum. Veniam
deinde libertati praefatus nihil se aut consiliorum aut
coeptorum praesentium probare ait, neque sedem belli

---

10 These conversations were later embroidered to make
Scipio Africanus one of the envoys, so as to have him and Hannibal engage in a conversation of mutual admiration (Livy 35.14.5–
12; Plut. *Vit. Flam.* 21.3–4).

state as with him; and that he had fought his wars not so   7
much from hatred of the Romans as love of his country, to
which every honorable man owed even life itself. For
these causes of wars were public and decided among na-
tions, not private and decided among generals. They then
praised his achievements. Enjoying such conversation   8
Hannibal would quite often and quite eagerly talk with the
delegates, unaware that by familiarity with the Romans he
was arousing the king's hatred.[10] For Antiochus, supposing   9
that by such frequent conversations he was reconciling
with the Romans, then refrained from disclosing anything
to him as he used to earlier, and he began to exclude him
from all his deliberations and to loathe him as an enemy
and traitor. This decision, with the loss of the expert leadership, wrecked their great preparations for the war. The   10
senate's orders had been that he remain content with the
boundaries of Asia so as not make it necessary for them to
enter Asia. Ignoring them he decided not to face a war,
but to launch one.

5. It is said that when he had held numerous councils
of war in the absence of Hannibal, he eventually had him
summoned, not to act on his advice on anything, but not
to appear to have altogether disregarded him, and that he
finally approached him when everyone else had been con-
sulted. Aware of this Hannibal said he understood it was   2
not for advice that he was being summoned, but only to
complete the number of opinions; nevertheless both from
his hatred of the Romans and his affection for the king,
the only person with whom he been left a safe exile, he
would explain the way to fight them Then after first beg-   3
ging pardon for his frankness he said he said he approved
of none the plans or schemes being proposed, and that he

131

Graeciam sibi placere, cum Italia uberior materia sit;
4 quippe Romanos vinci non nisi armis suis posse nec Italiam aliter quam Italicis viribus subigi; siquidem diversum
ceteris mortalibus esse illud et hominum et belli genus.
5 Aliis bellis plurimum momenti habere priorem aliquam
cepisse occasionem loci temporisque, agros rapuisse, urbes aliquas expugnasse; cum Romano, seu occupaveris
prior aliqua seu viceris, tamen etiam cum victo et iacente
6 luctandum esse. Quam ob rem siquis eos in Italia lacessat,
suis eos opibus, suis viribus, suis armis posse vincere, sicut
7 ipse fecerit. Sin vero quis illis Italia velut fonte virium
cesserit, proinde falli ac si quis amnes non ab ipsis fontium
primordiis derivare, sed concretis iam aquarum molibus
8 avertere vel exsiccare velit. Haec et secreto se censuisse
ultroque ministerium consilii sui obtulisse, et nunc praesentibus amicis ideo repetisse, ut scirent omnes rationem
gerendi cum Romanis belli, eosque foris invictos, domi
9 fragiles esse. Nam prius illos urbe quam imperio, prius
Italia quam provinciis exui posse; quippe et a Gallis captos
et a se prope deletos esse; neque umquam se victum prius
quam terris eorum cesserit; reverso Karthaginem statim
cum loco fortunam belli mutatam.

6. Huic sententiae obtrectatores amici regis erant, non
utilitatem rei cogitantes, sed verentes. ne probato consilio eius primum apud regem locum gratiae occuparet.

---

[11] It was at this council that Hannibal reportedly told the famous story of his oath, taken when nine years old at his father's
prompting, "never to bear goodwill to the Romans" (Polyb.
3.11.5–9; Livy 35.19.3–6; Nep. *Hann.* 2.4; et al.). Antiochus believed him.

was not pleased with Greece as a theater of war when Italy was a more fertile field; for the Romans could not be defeated other than by their own weapons and Italy only by Italian forces; they differed from all other humans both as men and in their manner of fighting. In other wars what was most important was being first to gain advantage in territory and timing, in plundering farmlands and storming a number of cities; with the Roman, whether you have preempted him or defeated him, he even when beaten and brought to the ground still has to be fought. So anyone who attacks them in Italy could use *their* resources, *their* strength and *their* arms to defeat them, just as he himself had done. But anyone leaving them Italy as a source of strength is just as misguided as someone who wishes to divert a river not by starting at its headwaters but by trying to turn its course and dry it up when the waters have already turned into a flood. Such had been his private thoughts, he said, and he had freely offered his advice, and now he had repeated it before the king's friends for all to know how war must be fought with Romans, and that they were invincible abroad but vulnerable at home. For they could be divested of their city before they could of their empire, and of Italy before their provinces; in fact they had been captured by the Gauls and also almost destroyed by himself; and he was never defeated by them before he left their country; on his return to Carthage the war's fortunes immediately changed with the location.[11]

6. This view faced criticism from the king's courtiers, who were not considering its efficacy but fearing that, if the plan were approved, he would earn first place in the

2 Et Antiocho non tantum consilium quam auctor displice-
3 bat, ne gloria victoriae Hannibalis, non sua esset. Omnia igitur variis adsentationum adulationibus corrumpebantur, nihil consilio vel ratione agebatur. Rex ipse per hiemem in luxuriam lapsus novis cotidie nuptiis deditus erat.
4 Contra Acilius, Romanus consul, qui ad hoc bellum missus erat, copias, arma ceteraque bello necessaria summa industria parabat, civitates socias confirmabat, dubias inliciebat; nec alius exitus belli quam adparatus utriusque
5 partis fuit. Itaque prima belli congressione cum cedentes suos rex cerneret, non laborantibus auxilium tulit, sed fugientibus se ducem praebuit castraque ditia victoribus
6 relinquit. Deinde cum in Asiam praeda Romanis occupatis fugiendo pervenisset, paenitere neglecti consilii coepit revocatoque in amicitiam Hannibale omnia ex sententia eius
7 agere. Interim nuntiatur ei Livium, Romanum ducem, cum LXXX rostratis navibus in bellum navale a senatu missum adventare; quae res spem illi restituendae fortunae dedit.
8 Itaque priusquam sociae civitates ad hostes deficerent, decernere navali proelio statuit, sperans cladem in Grae-
9 cia acceptam nova posse victoriae gloria aboleri. Tradita igitur Hannibali classe proelium committitur. Sed neque Asiani milites Romanis neque naves eorum pares rostratis navibus fuere; minor tamen clades ducis sollertia fuit.

---

12 Antiochus, with a small army and the royal court, had crossed to Demetrias on the coast of Thessaly in winter 192, where the king fell in love with and married a girl from nearby Chalcis in Euboea (he renamed her Euboea). In 191 he was defeated when trying to hold the pass of Thermopylae against the Romans, and returned to Asia Minor.

king's favor. Antiochus was not in favor, either, less of the ⟨2⟩
plan than its author, fearing that the glory from a victory
would go to Hannibal not him. So with the various flatter- ⟨3⟩
ing opinions everything fell apart and nothing was based
on strategy or reason. The king himself lapsed into self-
indulgence over the winter and every day was distracted
by a new marriage.[12] By contrast, Acilius,[13] the Roman ⟨4⟩
consul, who had been sent out for this war, was preparing
troops, weapons and everything else needed for a war, and
was strengthening ties with allied states and making over-
tures to the undecided; nor was the war's outcome at vari-
ance with the preparations on each side. So when in the ⟨5⟩
first clash of battle the king saw his men give way, he did
not bring aid to those in trouble but became the leader of
the men in flight and left a rich camp to the victors. Then ⟨6⟩
when he reached Asia in his flight while the Romans were
preoccupied with their plunder, he began to regret having
ignored the advice he was given, and resuming friendly
relations with Hannibal he followed all his advice. Mean- ⟨7⟩
while it was reported to him that Livius. the Roman general, was approaching,[14] sent by the senate with eighty
warships for a war at sea; and this gave him hope of reviving his fortunes. So before the allied states could defect to ⟨8⟩
his enemies, he decided to settle the issue with a sea battle, hoping that his defeat in Greece might be erased by
the fresh glory of a victory. So Hannibal was given a fleet, ⟨9⟩
and battle commenced. But neither were Asian soldiers
any match for Roman soldiers nor their ships for beaked
ships; but the defeat was narrowed by their admiral's skill.

[13] M'. Acilius Glabrio, consul 191; *MRR* 1.352; cf. Sherk
no. 12.   [14] C. Livius Salinator, praetor 191; *MRR* 1.353.

10 Romam nondum opinio victoriae venerat et idcirco in consulibus creandis suspensa civitas erat.

7. Sed adversus Hannibalem ducem quis melius quam
Africani frater crearetur, cum vincere Poenos opus Scipio-
2 num esset? Creatur igitur consul Lucius Scipio, eique
datur legatus frater Africanus, ut intellegeret Antiochus
non maiorem fiduciam se in Hannibale victo quam Roma-
3 nos in victore Scipione habere. Traicientibus in Asiam
Scipionibus exercitum iam utrubique profligatum bellum
nuntiatum est, victumque Antiochum terrestri, Hanniba-
4 lem navali bello invenerunt. Primo igitur adventu eorum
legatos pacem petentes Antiochus ad eos mittit peculiare
donum Africano ferentes filium ipsius, quem rex parvo
5 navigio traicientem ceperat. Sed Africanus privata beneficia a rebus publicis secreta dixit, aliaque esse patris officia,
alia patriae iura, quae non liberis tantum, verum etiam
6 vitae ipsi praeponantur. Proinde gratum se munus accipere privatoque inpendio munificentiae regis responsu-
rum. Quod ad bellum pacemque pertineat, nihil neque
gratiae dari neque de iure patriae decidi posse respondit.
7 Nam neque de redimendo filio umquam tractavit nec senatum de eo agere permisit, sed, ut dignum maiestate eius
8 erat, armis se recepturum dixerat. Post haec leges pacis
dicuntur: ut Asia Romanis cederet, contentus Syriae regno

---

15 Hannibal was not the admiral of Antiochus' main fleet but
of a subsidiary fleet in the waters near Rhodes. In July 190 he was
defeated by a Rhodian fleet off Side in southern Asia Minor. He
had no role in the land campaign against the Scipios.
16 In the latter stages of the war with Hannibal, P. Cornelius

Word of the victory had not yet reached Rome, and so   10
consular appointments in the city were still undecided.[15]

7. But to face their leader Hannibal what better ap-
pointment could there be than Africanus' brother, when
defeating Carthaginians was the work of Scipios?[16] So Lu-   2
cius Scipio was appointed consul, and as his legate was
given his brother Africanus, so Antiochus would understand that the confidence he had in the defeated Hannibal
was no greater than the Romans had in the victorious
Scipio. While the Scipios were transporting their army to   3
Asia it was announced that the war had now ended in both
places, and they learned that Antiochus had been defeated
in battle on land and Hannibal at sea. So immediately on   4
their arrival Antiochus sent legates to them seeking peace
and bringing to Africanus as a personal gift his son, whom
the king had taken prisoner as he was crossing the sea in
a small boat. But Africanus said private benefactions lay   5
outside his official purview, and that a father's duties were
one thing, and the fatherland's another, and these must be
set not only above children but even above life itself. So   6
he said he gratefully accepted the king's gift and would
repay the kindness from his personal resources. In the
matter of the war and peace, he replied that there could
be no favoritism and no curtailment of his country's authority. For he never discussed ransoming his son nor did   7
he allow the senate to debate it, but, as befitted his office,
he had said that he would reclaim him by force of arms.
After this peace terms were dictated: Asia would be ceded   8
to the Romans; Antiochus was to be satisfied with the

Scipio (Africanus) had led the Romans to victory. Now his brother
became consul for 190; *MRR* 1.356, 358; cf. Sherk no. 14.

esset, naves universas, captivos et transfugas traderet
9 sumptumque omnem belli Romanis restitueret. Quae
cum nuntiata Antiocho essent, nondum ita victum se esse
respondit, ut spoliari se regno pateretur, bellique ea inrita-
menta, non pacis blandimenta esse.

8. Igitur cum ab utrisque bellum pararetur ingressique
Asiam Romani Ilium venissent, mutua gratulatio Ilien-
sium ac Romanorum fuit, Iliensibus Aenean ceterosque
cum eo duces a se profectos, Romanis se ab his procreatos
2 referentibus; tantaque laetitia omnium fuit, quanta esse
3 post longum tempus inter parentes et liberos solet. Iuva-
bat Ilienses nepotes suos Occidente et Africa domita
Asiam ut avitum regnum vindicare, optabilem Troiae rui-
4 nam fuisse dicentes, ut tam feliciter renasceretur. Contra
Romanos avitos lares et incunabula maiorum templaque
ac deorum simulacra inexplebile desiderium videndi tene-
5 bat. Profectis ab Ilio Romanis Eumenes rex cum auxiliis
occurrit, nec multo post proelium cum Antiocho commis-
6 sum. Cum in dexteriore cornu pulsa legio Romana maiore
dedecore quam periculo ad castra fugeret, M. Aemilius,
tribunus militum, ad tutelam castrorum relictus armare se
milites suos et extra vallum progredi iubet strictisque gla-
diis fugientibus minari, morituros dicens, ni in proelium
revertantur, infestioraque sua quam hostium castra inven-
7 turos. Adtonita tam ambiguo periculo legio comitantibus

---

[17] Eumenes II Soter (197–160); see Sherk nos. 7 and 13. Antiochus was defeated at Magnesia in 190, and the peace settlement was finalized in 188.

kingdom of Syria and surrender all ships, captives and deserters and repay the Romans all their war expenses. When this was reported to Antiochus, he replied that he 9 was not yet so utterly defeated as to allow himself to be stripped of his kingdom, and that these were incitements to war, not inducements to peace.

8. So when war was being prepared by both sides and after entering Asia the Romans had reached Ilium, there was mutual rejoicing by the people of Ilium and the Romans, those of Ilium recalling Aeneas and the other leaders that had set off with him from their land, and the Romans recalling their descent from these heroes; and the 2 joy among them was as there might be between parents and children reunited after a long absence. The Trojans 3 were pleased that after subduing the West and Africa their descendants were now claiming Asia as their hereditary empire, saying that the fall of Troy had been welcome for heralding such an auspicious rebirth. For their part the 4 Romans were taken with an insatiable desire to see the home of their ancestors, the cradle of their forefathers, and the temples and statues of their gods. After the Romans had set off from Ilium, King Eumenes joined them 5 with some auxiliary forces, and not much later a battle was fought with Antiochus.[17] When a Roman legion was re- 6 pulsed on the right wing and was fleeing back to camp more in disgrace than danger, Marcus Aemilius, a military tribune who had been left to protect the camp, ordered his men to arm themselves, proceed beyond the rampart and with swords drawn threaten men who were fleeing, saying they would die if they refused to return to battle and would find their own camp more dangerous than their enemy's. Shaken by such a twofold danger the legion, ac- 7

commilitonibus, qui fugere eos prohibuerant, in proelium
revertitur, magnaque caede edita initium victoriae fuit.
8 Caesa hostium L milia, capta XI. Antiocho pacem petenti
nihil ad superiores condiciones additum, Africano praedi-
cante, Romanos neque, si vincantur, animis minui neque,
9 si vincant, secundis rebus insolescere. Captas civitates
inter socios divisere, muneri Romano aptiorem Asiam
quam possessioni voluptariae iudicantes; quippe victoriae
gloriam Romano nomini vindicandam, opum luxuriam
sociis relinquendam.

companied by the comrades who had held them from flight, returned to the battle, and with great carnage paved the way to victory. Fifty thousand of the enemy were killed and eleven thousand captured. When Antiochus sued for 8 peace nothing was added to the earlier conditions, Africanus declaring that Romans were neither demoralized if defeated nor overbearing if victorious. Captured towns 9 they distributed among the allies, judging it more appropriate that Asia be granted as a gift from Rome than kept for their pleasure; for the glory of victory must claimed for the Roman name, they said, extravagant riches left to allies. ·

·

LIBER XXXII

1. Aetoli, qui Antiochum in bella Romana inpulerant, victo eodem soli adversus Romanos et viribus inpares et omni
2 auxilio destituti remanserunt; nec multo post victi libertatem, quam inlibatam adversus dominationem Atheniensium Spartanorumque inter tot Graeciae civitates soli re-
3 tinuerant, amiserunt. Quae condicio tanto amarior illis, quanto serior fuit, reputantibus tempora illa, quibus tantis Persarum opibus domesticis viribus restiterint, quibus Gallorum violentiam Asiae Italiaeque terribilem Delphico bello fregerint; quae gloriosa recordatio maius desiderium libertatis augebat.
4 Dum haec aguntur, medio tempore inter Messenios et Achaeos de principatu primo dissensio, mox bellum ortum
5 est. In eo nobilis Achaeorum imperator Philopoemen capitur, non quia pugnando vitae pepercerit, sed, dum suos in proelium revocat, in transitu fossae equo praecipitatus
6 a multitudine hostium oppressus est. Quem Messenii iacentem seu metu virtutis seu verecundia dignitatis inter-
7 ficere ausi non fuerunt. Itaque laeti velut in illo omne

---

[1] This continues events from 189. Other sources are Polyb. 21.25ff., 40ff., and 22–25; Diod. Sic. 29.11ff.; Livy 38–40; Plut. *Vit. Phil.* 18ff. Philopoemen died in 183.

BOOK XXXII

1. The Aetolians, who had pushed Antiochus into his Roman wars, were on his defeat left isolated against the Romans, being both unequal in strength and also left with no support;[1] and when they were defeated not much later, 2 they lost the liberty that only they, among so many Greek city-states, had maintained against the hegemony of the Athenians and Spartans. Their predicament was all the 3 more distressing for coming so late, since they thought back on those days when they had resisted such mighty Persian power with their own forces, and when they had in the Delphic War broken the ferocity of the Gauls that was terrifying Asia and Italy; and that glorious memory was increasing their longing for freedom.

While this was going on, meanwhile between the Messenians and Achaeans first dissension arose over leadership, and soon a war. In it the famous Achaean general 5 Philopoemen was captured, not because he tried to save himself when fighting but because while rallying his men to battle, he was thrown from his horse when crossing a ditch and overpowered by a crowd of the enemy. As he lay 6 prostrate the Messenians either from fear of his courage or respect for his distinction did not dare kill him. And so 7 as if they had with him ended the entire war, they paraded

EPITOME OF POMPEIUS TROGUS

bellum confecissent, captivum per universam civitatem in
modum triumphi circumduxerunt effuso obviam populo,
8 ac si suus, non hostium imperator adventaret, nec victorem Achaei avidius vidissent, quam victum hostes vide-
runt. Igitur eundem in theatrum duci iusserunt, ut omnes
contuerentur, quem potuisse capi incredibile singulis vi-
9 debatur. Inde in carcerem ducto verecundia magnitudinis
eius venenum dederunt, quod ille laetus, ac si vicisset,
accepit, quaesito prius, an Lycortas, praefectus Achaeorum, quem secundum a se esse scientia militari sciebat,
incolumis effugisset. Quem ut accepit evasisse, non in
10 totum dicens male consultum Achaeis expiravit. Nec
multo post reparato bello Messenii vincuntur poenasque
interfecti Philopoemenis pependerunt.

2. Interea in Syria rex Antiochus, cum gravi tributo
pacis a Romanis victus oneratus esset, seu inopia pecuniae
conpulsus seu avaritia sollicitatus, qui sperabat se sub specie tributariae necessitatis excusatius sacrilegia commissu-
rum, adhibito exercitu nocte templum Elymaei Iovis ad-
2 greditur. Qua re prodita concursu incolarum cum omni
militia interficitur.

3 Romae, cum multae Graeciae civitates questum de
iniuriis Philippi, regis Macedonum, venissent et disceptatio in senatu inter Demetrium, Philippi filium, quem pater
ad satisfaciendum senatui miserat, et legatos civitatium
esset, turba querelarum confusus adulescens repente ob-
4 ticuit. Tunc senatus verecundia eius motus, quae probata

---

2 See 31.8.5ff. Antiochus' death came in 187.
3 The year is 185. The death of Demetrius occurred in 181,
that of Philip in 179.

their captive throughout the city as in a triumph, with people streaming out to meet him as if it were their own general coming and not their enemy's, nor would the Achaeans have been more excited at seeing him victorious than their enemies were on seeing him defeated. So they ordered him brought into the theater for all to see the man whose capture everyone thought impossible. Then when he was taken to prison, from respect for his greatness they gave him poison, which he happily took as if he were the victor, first asking whether Lycortas, the Achaean commander whom he knew to be second only to him in military science, had got away unharmed. When told that he had escaped he died, saying that not everything had gone badly for the Achaeans. Not much later when the war restarted the Messenians were defeated and paid the price for killing Philopoemen.

2. Meanwhile, in Syria, King Antiochus had been burdened with a heavy war tax as a condition of peace following his defeat by the Romans,[2] and either pressed by lack of money or tempted by greed he was hoping that with the excuse of having to pay the tribute he could the more easily be forgiven for sacrilege, and so he raised an army and made a night attack on the temple of Elymaian Jupiter. When word of that got out he was killed in an attack by the local people together with all his troops.

In Rome many Greek states had come to complain of wrongs suffered at the hands of Philip, king of Macedon, and there was then a dispute in the senate between Demetrius, Philip's son, whom his father had sent to exonerate him before the senate, and legates from the city-states;[3] and bewildered by the mass of complaints the young man suddenly fell silent. Then the senate, touched by his

etiam antea, cum obses Romae esset, omnibus fuerat, causam illi donavit. Atque ita modestia sua Demetrius veniam patri, non iure defensionis, sed patrocinio pudoris ob-

5 tinuit, quod ipsum decreto senatus significatum est, ut appareret non tam absolutum regem quam donatum filio

6 patrem. Quae res Demetrio non gratiam legationis, sed

7 odium obtrectationis conparavit. Nam et apud fratrem Perseum aemulatio illi invidiam contraxit, et apud patrem nota absolutionis causa offensae fuit, indignante Philippo plus momenti apud senatum personam filii quam auctori-

8 tatem patris ac dignitatem regiae maiestatis habuisse. Igitur Perseus perspecta patris aegritudine cotidie absentem Demetrium apud eum criminari et primo invisum, post etiam suspectum reddere; nunc amicitiam Romanorum,

9 nunc proditionem patris ei obiectare. Ad postremum insidias sibi ab eo paratas confingit, ad cuius rei probationem inmittit indices, testes subornat et facinus, quod obicit,

10 admittit. Quibus rebus conpulso ad parricidium patre funestam omnem regiam facit.

3. Occiso Demetrio sublatoque aemulo non neglegentior tantum Perseus in patrem, verum etiam contumacior

2 erat, nec heredem regni, sed regem gerebat. His rebus offensus Philippus inpatientius in dies mortem Demetrii dolebat, tunc et insidiis circumventum suspicari, testes

3 indicesque torquere. Atque ita cognita fraude non minus scelere Persei quam innoxia Demetrii morte cruciabatur,

modesty, which had also earlier won its approval when he was a hostage at Rome, decided the case in his favor. And so by his own modesty Demetrius secured pardon for his father not by a formal defense but the evidence of his own decency, which was itself demonstrated by a decree of the senate that made it clear that it was not a king being absolved but a father being made a gift of his son. The matter earned Demetrius no gratitude for his commission but malice. For with his brother Perseus competition brought him jealousy, and by his father, when he learned why he was pardoned, he was also resented, since Philip was angry that his son's character had had more influence with the senate than his father's authority and regal majesty. So observing his father's chagrin, Perseus would daily slander Demetrius before him in his absence and first made him unpopular, and later even under suspicion; he would accuse him now of friendship with the Romans, now of betraying his father. Finally he claimed a plot had been hatched against him by his brother, and to corroborate it he brought in informers, suborned witnesses, and committed the very crime that he was denouncing. Driving his father to parricide in this way he gave the whole palace a funereal atmosphere.

3. With Demetrius killed and his rival removed Perseus became not only more neglectful toward his father but even quite offensive, and he started behaving not as the heir to the kingdom but as the king. Offended by this, Philip began to regret the death of Demetrius more bitterly every day and then to suspect that he had been the victim of a plot, and so he had witnesses and informers tortured. And so when he learned of the foul play, he was tormented no less by the criminal act of Perseus than by

peregissetque ultionem, nisi morte praeventus fuisset.
4 Nam brevi post tempore morbo ex aegritudine contracto
decessit, relicto magno belli apparatu adversus Romanos,
5 quo postea Perseus usus est. Nam et Gallos Scordiscos ad
belli societatem perpulerat, fecissetque Romanis grave
bellum, nisi decessisset.

6   Namque Galli bello adversus Delphos infeliciter gesto,
in quo maiorem vim numinis quam hostium senserant,
amisso Brenno duce pars in Asiam, pars in Thraciam ex-
7 torres fugerant. Inde per eadem vestigia, qua venerant,
8 antiquam patriam repetivere. Ex his manus quaedam in
confluente Danuvii et Savi consedit Scordiscosque se ap-
9 pellari voluit. Tectosagi autem, cum in antiquam patriam
Tolosam venissent conprehensique pestifera lue essent,
non prius sanitatem recuperavere quam aruspicum re-
sponsis moniti aurum argentumque bellis sacrilegiisque
10 quaesitum in Tolosensem lacum mergerent, quod omne
magno post tempore Caepio, Romanus consul, abstulit.
Fuere autem argenti pondo centum decem milia, auri
11 pondo quinquies decies centum milia. Quod sacrilegium
causa excidii Caepioni exercituique eius postea fuit. Romanos quoque Cimbrici belli tumultus velut ultor sacrae
12 pecuniae insecutus est. Ex gente Tectosagorum non me-
diocris populus praedae dulcedine Illyricum repetivit spo-
liatisque Histris in Pannonia consedit.

---

4 See 24.6ff.; 25.2.   5 Q. Servilius Caepio, consul 106,
proconsul 105, when he suffered the defeat; *MRR* 1.553, 557.
Tolosa today is Toulouse. *Quinquies decies centum milia* is liter-
ally "five times ten times one hundred thousand"; but other esti-
mates exist—Orosius (5.15.25) has one hundred thousand pounds
of gold, as well as the one hundred and ten thousand of silver;
Strabo (2.188C) cites Posidonius, a contemporary of the event,

the undeserved death of Demetrius, and he would have exacted vengeance had he not been prevented by his own death. For a little later he died from a malady brought on 4 by remorse, leaving behind great preparations for war against the Romans that Perseus later put to use. For he 5 had also induced the Scordiscan Gauls to join him in a war and would have brought a serious war on the Romans had he not died.

For after their unsuccessful war on Delphi, in which 6 they had felt more violence from the god than from their enemy, the Gauls, having lost their leader Brennus, had fled into exile, some into Asia and some into Thrace.[4] Then 7 following the paths by which they had come, they returned to their old homeland. One of their tribes settled at the 8 confluence of the Danube and Save and chose to be called the Scordisci. The Tectosagi, however, when they reached 9 their old homeland of Tolosa and were struck by a deadly plague, did not regain their health until on their soothsayers' advice they sank the silver and gold they had acquired by war and sacrilege in the lake of Tolosa, all of which was 10 much later removed by the Roman consul Caepio. There were a hundred and ten thousand pounds of silver, and five million pounds of gold. That sacrilege was later the cause 11 of the destruction of Caepio and his army.[5] The Romans were also overtaken by a violent war with the Cimbri as if it were revenge for the sacred money. Of the tribe of the 12 Tectosagi no small number returned to Illyricum from their love of plunder and after pillaging the Istrians settled in Pannonia.

for an estimate of fifteen thousand talents in all, a much smaller (though still huge) amount. Modern editors too have varied in their suggested emendations to the Latin text.

13   Histrorum gentem fama est originem a Colchis ducere,
missis ab Aeeta rege ad Argonautas, raptores filiae, per-
14 sequendos; qui ut a Ponto intraverunt Histrum, alveo Savi
fluminis penitus invecti vestigia Argonautarum insequentes naves suas umeris per iuga montium usque ad
litus Adriatici maris transtulerunt, cognito quod Argonautae idem propter magnitudinem navis priores fecissent;
15 quo ut avectos Colchi non reppererunt, sive metu regis
sive taedio longae navigationis iuxta Aquileiam con sedere
Histrique ex vocabulo amnis, quo a mari concesserant,
appellati.
16   Daci quoque suboles Getarum sunt, qui cum Orole
rege adversus Bastarnas male pugnassent, ad ultionem
segnitiae capturi somnum capita loco pedum ponere iussu
regis cogebantur ministeriaque uxoribus, quae ipsis ante
fieri solebant, facere. Neque haec ante mutata sunt quam
ignominiam bello acceptam virtute delerent.

    4. Igitur Perseus, cum imperio Philippi patris succes-
sisset, omnes has gentes adversum Romanos in societatem
belli sollicitabat.
2   Interim inter Prusiam regem, ad quem Hannibal post
pacem Antiocho a Romanis datam profugerat, et Eumenen bellum ortum est, quod Prusias Hannibalis fiducia
3   rupto foedere prior intulit. Namque Hannibal, cum ab
Antiocho Romani inter ceteras condiciones pacis deditio-

----

6 The Black Sea.   7 Perseus ruled from 179 until the
defeat of 168. Prusias is Prusias II of Bithynia (ca. 182–149). For
Hannibal see Livy 39.51, for the Roman embassy *MRR* 1.380 (the
year 183). In reality, it was Rome that decided to launch the war,
while Perseus strove to avoid it.

The Istrian people are said to be descended from the   13
Colchians sent by King Aëtes in pursuit of the Argonauts,
the abductors of his daughter; after entering the Ister   14
from the Pontus,[6] they sailed far inland up the River Save
following the tracks of the Argonauts, and carried their
ships on their shoulders over mountain ranges right to the
coast of the Adriatic Sea, aware that the Argonauts had
earlier done the same because of the size of their ship; and   15
when the Colchians could not find them after they had
sailed off, they were either so frightened of their king or
so tired of their long sea journey that they settled near
Aquileia and were called Istrians, after the name of the
river by which they had left the sea.

The Dacians are also descendants of the Getae, who   16
had fought poorly with King Oroles against the Bastarnae.
As punishment for their cowardice, they were forced by
order of the king to sleep with their heads placed where
they normally put their feet and to provide for their wives
services earlier provided for them by the wives. And this
did not change until they erased by their valor the ignominy they incurred in the war.

4. So Perseus, after he acceded to the empire of his
father Philip, began enticing all these peoples into a war
alliance against the Romans.[7]

Meanwhile war had arisen between King Prusias, to   2
whom Hannibal had fled after Antiochus was granted a
peace treaty by the Romans, and Eumenes, one that Prusias started by breaking the peace treaty through his confidence in Hannibal. For since the Romans were among   3
their peace conditions demanding his surrender, Hanni-

nem eius poscerent, admonitus a regc in fugam versus
4 Cretam defertur. Ibi cum diu quietam vitam egisset in-
vidiosumque se propter nimias opes videret, amphoras
plumbo repletas in templo Dianae, quasi fortunae suae
5 praesidia, deponit atque ideo nihil de illo sollicita civitate,
quoniam velut pignus opes eius tenebat, ad Prusiam contendit, auro suo statuis, quas secum portabat, infuso, ne
6 conspectae opes vitae nocerent. Dein, cum Prusias terrestri bello ab Eumene victus esset et proelium in mare
transtulisset, Hannibal novo commento auctor victoriae
fuit; quippe omne serpentium genus in fictiles lagoenas
7 coici iussit medioque proelio in naves hostium mittit. Id
primum Ponticis ridiculum visum, fictilibus dimicare, qui
ferro nequeant. Sed ubi serpentibus coepere naves re-
pleri, ancipiti periculo circumventi hosti victoriam cesse-
8 runt. Quae ubi Romam nuntiata sunt, missi a senatu legati
sunt, qui utrumque regem in pacem cogerent Hannibalemque deposcerent. Sed Hannibal re cognita sumpto
veneno legationem morte praevenit.

9   Insignis hic annus trium toto orbe maximorum impe-
ratorum mortibus fuit, Hannibalis et Philopoemenis et
10 Scipionis Africani. Ex quibus constat Hannibalem nec
tum, cum Romano tonantem bello Italia contremuit, nec
cum reversus Karthaginem summum imperium tenuit,
11 aut cubantem cenasse aut plus quam sextario vini indul-
sisse pudicitiamque eum tantam inter tot captivas ha-

---

8 That is, from the snakes as well as their enemy.

9 The coincidence was irresistible; see also Polyb. 23.12ff.;
Diod. Sic. 29.18ff.; Livy 39.50.10f.

bal, warned by the king, fled to Crete for refuge. There he   4
saw that despite leading a peaceful life he was envied for
his excessive wealth, so he filled some wine jars with lead
and deposited them in the temple of Diana as protection
for his fortune; and when the people were no longer con-   5
cerned about him since they were holding his wealth as a
guarantee, he hurried away to Prusias, first filling with
gold some statues that he was taking with him, so that if
detected his riches would not be a threat to his life. Then,   6
when Prusias was defeated in a land battle by Eumenes
and had switched to war at sea, Hannibal won a victory
with an extraordinary stratagem; for he had all sorts of
snakes thrown into earthenware jars and in the middle of
the battle hurled them onto the enemy ships. That seemed   7
at first ridiculous to the Pontic soldiers—men fighting
with earthenware pots who could not with the sword! But
when the ships started filling with snakes and they were
surrounded by a twofold threat,[8] they conceded victory to
their enemy. When this was reported in Rome, legates   8
were sent by the senate to force both kings into a peace
treaty and demand Hannibal's surrender. But Hannibal on
learning of it took poison and by his death preempted the
embassy.

This year was remarkable for the deaths of the three   9
greatest generals in the whole world, Hannibal, Philopoemen and Scipio Africanus.[9] Of these it is believed that in   10
the case of Hannibal not even when Italy trembled before
him as he thundered in his Roman war, and not even when
he held supreme command on his return to Carthage—
not even then would he dine reclining or indulge in more
than a pint of wine; and such was his abstinence when   11
surrounded by so many female captives that one would say

153

12 buisse, ut in Africa natum quivis negaret. Moderationis certe eius fuit, ut, cum diversarum gentium exercitus rexerit, neque insidiis suorum militum sit petitus umquam neque fraude proditus, cum utrumque hostes saepe temptassent.

he was not a man born in Africa. Such for sure was his   12
evenhandedness that, although he commanded armies of
different races, he faced neither conspiracy among his
men nor treacherous betrayal, although his enemies had
often tried both against him.

LIBER XXXIII

1. Minore quidem rerum motu Romani Macedonicum quam Punicum bellum gesserunt, sed tanto clarius, quanto nobilitate Macedones Poenos antecesserunt; quippe cum gloria Orientis domiti, tum et auxilio omnium regum iuva-
2 bantur. Itaque Romani et legiones plures numero conscripserunt et auxilia a Masinissa, rege Numidarum, et ceteris omnibus sociis acciverunt; et Eumeni, regi Bithy-
3 niae, denuntiatum, ut bellum summis viribus iuvaret. Perseo praeter Macedonicum invictae opinionis exercitum decennis belli sumptus a patre paratus in thesauris et horreis erat. Quibus rebus inflatus oblitus fortunae paternae veterem . Alexandri gloriam considerare suos iubebat.
4 Prima equitum congressio fuit, qua victor Perseus suspen-
5 sam omnium exspectationem in favorem sui traxit; misit tamen legatos ad consulem, qui pacem peterent, quam patri suo Romani etiam victo dedissent, inpensas belli lege victi suscepturus. Sed consul P. Licinius non minus graves

---

1 The friction between Rome and Macedon began in 174, but war broke out in 171, ending with Perseus' defeat at Pydna in 168. Other sources are Polyb. 27–30; Diod. Sic. 29.33f., 30–31.14; Livy 41.22ff. through to the end of Book 45; Plut. *Vit. Aem*. That Perseus had the support of "all the kings" is not the only overstatement here—the Macedonian army could hardly claim invincibil-

BOOK XXXIII

1. The Macedonian War that the Romans fought was less momentous than the Punic War, but it was more famous since the Macedonians had greater renown than the Carthaginians; for they were helped both by the glory of their Eastern conquest and also by being aided by all the kings.[1] So the Romans both enrolled a greater number of legions 2 and also sent for assistance from Masinissa, king of Numidia, and all their other allies; and Eumenes, king of Bithynia, was ordered to assist the campaign with his finest troops. Apart from his reputedly invincible Macedonian 3 army, Perseus also had reserves sufficient for a ten-year war laid up by his father in his treasury and granaries. Made overconfident by this and forgetting his father's misfortune, he told his men to think of Alexander's glory of old. First came a cavalry battle, in which a victorious Per- 4 seus won over any who had been wavering and awaiting the outcome; but he still sent delegates to the consul to 5 request peace terms that the Romans had granted his father even in defeat, undertaking to indemnify the war expenses as if himself defeated. But the consul Publius Licinius dictated terms no less severe than for a defeated

ity. Justin makes Eumenes II, like his father (27.3.2), king not of Pergamum but wrongly of Bithynia.

6 quam victo leges dixit. Dum haec aguntur, metu tam peri-
culosi belli Romani Aemilium Paulum consulem creant
eique extra ordinem Macedonicum bellum decernunt; qui
cum ad exercitum venisset, non magnam moram pugnae
7 fecit. Pridie quam proelium consereretur, luna nocte defecit, id portentum Perseo omnibus praesagantibus finem-
que Macedonici regni portendi vaticinantibus.

2. In ea pugna M. Cato, oratoris filius, dum inter confertissimos hostes insigniter dimicat, equo delapsus pe-
2 destre proelium adgreditur. Nam cadentem manipulus
hostium cum horrido clamore veluti iacentem obtrunca-
turus circumsteterat; at ille citius corpore collecto magnas
3 strages edidit. Cum ad unum opprimendum undique hostes convolarent, dum procerum quendam petit, gladius
ei e manu elapsus in mediam cohortem hostium decidit;
4 ad quem recuperandum umbone se protegens inspectante
utroque exercitu inter hostium mucrones sese inmersit
recollectoque gladio multis vulneribus exceptis ad suos
cum clamore hostium revertitur. Huius audaciam ceteri
5 imitati victoriam peperere. Perseus rex fuga cum decem
milibus talentum Samothraciam defertur, quem Cn. Octavius ad persequendum missus a consule cum duobus filiis,
Alexandro et Philippo, cepit captumque ad consulem
duxit.

6 Macedonia a Carano, qui primus in ea regnavit, usque

---

2 P. Licinius Crassus, consul in 171; *MRR* 1.416.

3 L. Aemilius Paullus, consul in 168; *MRR* 1.427.

4 The eclipse occurred on the night of June 22, 168; Livy's date
(September 3: 44.37.8) is due to the complex Roman calendar
being out by some ten weeks in this period.

enemy.[2] While this was happening, the Romans, from fear 6
of such a dangerous war, elected Aemilius Paullus consul
and decreed to him the Macedonian war as an extraordinary command;[3] and when he reached his army he did not
long delay the fight. On the day before battle was joined 7
there was a lunar eclipse, which everyone took as an omen
for Perseus and predicting the end of the Macedonian
Kingdom.[4]

2. In that conflict Marcus Cato, the orator's son,[5] was
putting up a remarkable fight in the thick of the enemy
when he fell from his horse and started to fight on foot.
For as he fell an enemy maniple had surrounded him with 2
a bloodcurdling yell, intending to kill him where he lay;
but he, swiftly pulled himself together and inflicted serious damage on them. When his enemies flocked around 3
to bring down the one man and he lunged at some tall
fellow, his sword slipped from his hand and fell amid an
enemy cohort; and to recover it he, protecting himself 4
with his shield, plunged among the sword tips of his enemies before the eyes of both armies, and after retrieving
the sword and receiving many wounds he returned to his
comrades amid an uproar from the enemy. Copying his
brave example, the others secured the victory. King Per- 5
seus left in flight for Samothrace together with ten thousand talents, but, sent in pursuit by the consul, Gnaeus
Octavius[6] captured him with his two sons, Alexander and
Philip, and after capturing him brought him to the consul.

From Caranus,[7] who first ruled there, to the time of 6

[5] *MRR* 1.431.   [6] Praetor in 168 and commander of the
Roman fleet in the Aegean; *MRR* 1.428.
[7] See 7.1.7.

Perseum XXX reges habuit. Quorum sub regno fuit quidem annis DCCCCXXIV, sed rerum non nisi CL duobus
7 annis potita. Ita cum in dicionem Romanorum cessisset,
magistratibus per singulas civitates constitutis libera facta
8 est legesque, quibus adhuc utitur, a Paulo accepit. Aetolorum universarum urbium senatus cum coniugibus et liberis, qui dubia fide fuerant, Romam missus, ibique, ne in
patria aliquid novaret, diu detentus, aegreque per multos
annos legationibus civitatium senatu fatigato in patriam
quisque suam remissus est.

Perseus, Macedonia had thirty kings. It was under their rule for nine hundred and twenty-four years, but their power lasted no more than a hundred and fifty-two years.[8] So when it fell under Roman authority it became free, with magistracies established in each of its cities, and the legal system still in use today it received from Paullus. The senates of all the Aetolian cities whose loyalty had been dubious were sent to Rome together with their wives and children, and they were kept there a long time for them not to foment unrest in their country; and only reluctantly, after the senate had for many years been entreated by deputations from their states, were they all returned to their various homes.[9]

[8] A curious figure, leaving one to wonder what Trogus felt to be the limiting dates of Macedonian control. Some editors think that Trogus had written *CLXXXX duobus annis* (i.e., "192"), counting from the accession of Philip II in 360/59, and that Justin or a later copyist miswrote the numeral; this is plausible. Livy (45.9.7) gives a rounded 150 years from the death of Alexander to the end of the kingdom, and this may have influenced Justin's figure.

[9] Not the Aetolian leaders (Aetolia was by now a cipher) but a thousand Achaean notables, among them the future historian Polybius. The surviving three hundred were allowed home in 150; Polyb. 35.6.

LIBER XXXIV

1. Poenis ac Macedonibus subactis Aetolorumque viribus principum captivitate debilitatis soli adhuc ex Graecia universa Achaei nimis potentes tunc temporis Romanis videbantur, non propter singularum civitatium nimias
2 opes, sed propter conspirationem universarum. Namque Achaei, licet per civitates veluti per membra divisi sint, unum tamen corpus et unum imperium habent singularumque urbium pericula mutuis viribus propulsant.
3 Quaerentibus igitur Romanis causam belli tempestive Fortuna querelam Spartanorum obtulit, quorum agros
4 Achaei propter mutuum odium populabantur. Spartanis a senatu responsum est, legatos se ad inspiciendas res socio-
5 rum et ad iniuriam demendam in Graeciam missuros; sed legatis occulta mandata data sunt, ut corpus Achaeorum dissolverent singulasque urbes proprii iuris facerent, quo facilius et ad obsequium cogerentur et, si quae urbes
6 contumaces essent, traicerentur. Igitur legati omnium civitatium principibus Corinthum evocatis decretum sena-

---

1 Justin offers some inaccuracies here. Carthage was overcome only in 146, though the Macedonian pretender Andriscus had been dealt with in 148. See Polyb. 36, 38–39. Rome's conflict with the Achaean League occurred in 147/6. On the "Aetolians," see previous note.

BOOK XXXIV

1. With the Carthaginians and Macedonians subdued and the Aetolians' strength blunted by the capture of their leaders,[1] in all Greece only the Achaeans at that time still seemed too powerful to the Romans, not because of the excessive strength of individual states but because they all acted together. For although divided into states—into 2 separate limbs, as it were—the Achaeans are nevertheless one body and one power, and they repel threats to all of their cities by pooling their strength. So when the Romans 3 sought some pretext for war Fortune opportunely offered a complaint from the Spartans, whose territory the Achaeans were plundering through hatred each of the other. The 4 reply the Spartans received from the senate was that they would send delegates to Greece to examine the situation of their allies and remove any injustice;[2] but the delegates 5 were given secret orders to dissolve the Achaean league and make the cities autonomous so they could be more easily forced into submission and any recalcitrant cities moved elsewhere. So summoning the leading citizens of 6 all the states to Corinth, the delegates read out the senato-

[2] In 147; *MRR* 1.464.

7 tus recitant, quid consilii habeant aperiunt; expedire omnibus dicunt, ut singulae civitates sua iura et suas leges
8 habeant. Quod ubi omnibus innotuit, veluti in furorem
9 versi universum peregrinum populum trucidant; legatos
quoque ipsos Romanorum violassent, ni audito tumultu
trepidi fugissent.

2. Haec ubi Romam nuntiata sunt, statim senatus
Mummio consuli bellum Achaicum decernit, qui extem-
plo exercitu deportato et omnibus strenue provisis pug-
2 nandi copiam hostibus fecit. Sed Achaei veluti nihil negotii Romano bello suscepissent, ita apud eos neglecta et
3 soluta omnia fuere. Itaque praedam, non proelium cogitantes et vehicula ad spolia hostium reportanda adduxe-
runt et coniuges liberosque suos ad spectaculum certami-
4 nis in montibus posuerunt. Sed proelio commisso ante
oculos suorum caesi lugubre his spectaculum et gravem
5 luctus memoriam reliquerunt. Coniuges quoque liberique
eorum de spectatoribus captivi facti praeda hostium fuere.
6 Urbs ipsa Corinthus diruitur, populus omnis sub corona
venditur, ut hoc exemplo ceteris civitatibus metus nova-
rum rerum inponeretur.

7 Dum haec aguntur, rex Syriae Antiochus Ptolomeo,
maiori sororis suae filio, regi Aegypti, bellum infert, segni
admodum et cotidiana luxuria ita marcenti, ut non solum

---

3 L. Mummius, consul in 146; *MRR* 1.465f. But before he
arrived, the propraetor Q. Caecilius Metellus from Macedonia
defeated the main Achaean army in central Greece. Mummius
finished the war and on the senate's instructions sacked and razed
Corinth, which was not refounded until 46 BC.

4 Affairs begin in 170 with Polyb. 27.19. Justin strangely

rial decree and explained its plan; it was in everyone's in- 7
terests for the various states to have their own rights and
their own laws. When this became generally known, they, 8
as if in a fit of lunacy, killed the entire foreign population;
and they would also have manhandled the Roman dele- 9
gates had they not fled in panic on hearing the uproar.

2. When news of this reached Rome, the senate immediately assigned the Achaean War to the consul Mummius,[3] who promptly shipped over an army and after
swiftly preparing everything gave the enemy opportunity
for battle. But just as the Achaeans had taken war with 2
Rome as being a minor affair, so everything on their side
was in neglect and disorder. So focusing on plunder, not 3
battle, they brought wagons to haul off spoils from their
enemies, and also placed their wives and children on hills
to view the fight. But cut down before the eyes of their 4
families at the start of battle they left them a sad spectacle
and a grim and doleful memory. Their wives and their 5
children, too, now made captives instead of spectators,
became the plunder of their enemy. The city of Corinth 6
itself was destroyed and its whole population sold into
slavery, so that by this example the other states would fear
insurrection.

While this was going on, King Antiochus of Syria 7
launched a war on his sister's eldest son Ptolemy, king of
Egypt,[4] a rather listless man and so languid with his daily

makes these eastern events contemporary with those thirty years
later in Greece. The monarchs are Antiochus IV Epiphanes (175–
164) and Ptolemy VI Philometor (180–145). The latter exercised
joint rule with Ptolemy VIII and Cleopatra II from 170 and was
temporarily expelled in 164 (Polyb. 31.10, 17ff.).

regiae maiestatis officia intermitteret, verum etiam sensu
8 hominis nimia sagina careret. Pulsus igitur regno ad fratrem minorem Ptolomeum Alexandream confugit partici-
patoque cum eo regno legatos Romam ad senatum mittunt, auxilium petunt, fidem societatis inplorant. Movere
senatum preces fratrum.

3. Mittitur itaque legatus Popilius ad Antiochum, qui
abstinere illum Aegypto aut, si iam incessisset, excedere
2 iuberet. Cum in Aegypto eum invenisset osculumque ei
rex obtulisset (nam coluerat inter ceteros Popilium Antiochus, cum obses Romae esset), tunc Popilius facessere
interim privatam amicitiam iubet, cum mandata patriae
3 intercedant; prolatoque senatus decreto et tradito, cum
cunctari eum videret consultationemque ad amicos referre, ibi Popilius virga, quam in manu gerebat, amplo
circulo inclusum, ut amicos caperet, consulere eos iubet
nec prius inde exire, quam responsum senatui daret, aut
4 pacem aut bellum cum Romanis habiturum. Adeoque
haec austeritas animum regis fregit, ut pariturum se senatui responderet.

5 Reversus in regnum Antiochus decedit relicto parvulo
6 admodum filio, cui cum tutores dati a populo essent, pa-
truus eius Demetrius, qui obses Romae erat, cognita

---

5 In 168; *MRR* 1.430. C. Popillius Laenas had been consul in
172. He met Antiochus on the shore at Eleusis, just outside Alexandria; crucially, this was after the Roman victory at Pydna, news
of which had reached both men.   6 This was the famous
Day of Eleusis, which struck all the eastern states like a thunder-
clap. Antiochus IV, still the most powerful ruler in the eastern
Mediterranean, did not dare refuse a direct order from Rome.

excesses that he not only neglected his regal duties but
from his obesity lacked even normal human feelings. So   8
when driven from his kingdom he fled to his younger
brother Ptolemy in Alexandria and sharing his kingdom
with him sent delegates to the senate in Rome, sought its
aid, and appealed to the honor of their alliance. The senate
was swayed by the brothers' entreaties.

3. So Popillius was sent as a delegate to Antiochus to
order him to stay out of Egypt or, if he had already invaded, to withdraw from it.[5] When he met Antiochus in   2
Egypt and the king went to kiss him (for Popillius was one
of the people whose friendship Antiochus had cultivated
when a hostage in Rome), Popillius then said their personal friendship must cease for a time since his country's
demands stood in its way; and when, after bringing out and   3
handing him the senate's decree, he saw him hesitate and
refer the matter to his friends for discussion, Popillius,
with the staff that he had in his hand, traced a circle
around the king large enough to include his friends, and
ordered them to discuss the matter and not leave it until
he gave the senate his answer on whether he would have
peace or war with the Romans. Such firmness so broke the   4
king's will that he replied that he would obey the senate.[6]

On returning to his kingdom Antiochus died, leaving a   5
son who was just a child, and when guardians were as-   6
signed to him by the people[7] his uncle, Demetrius, who
was a hostage in Rome, approached the senate after learn-

[7] Antiochus V Eupator (163–162); Demetrius I Soter (162–
150). See Polyb. 31.2, 9, 11ff.; App. *Syr.* 46f.

morte fratris Antiochi senatum adiit: obsidem se vivo
fratre venisse, quo mortuo cuius obses sit, se ignorare.
7 Dimitti igitur se ad regnum petendum aequum esse,
quod, sicut iure gentium maiori fratri cesserit, ita nunc
8 sibi, qui pupillum aetate antecedat, deberi. Cum se non
dimitti animadverteret a senatu, tacito iudicio tutius apud
pupillum quam apud eum regnum futurum arbitrante,
specie venandi ab urbe profectus Ostiis tacitus cum fugae
9 comitibus navem conscendit. Delatus in Syriam secundo
favore omnium excipitur, regnumque ei occiso pupillo ac
tutoribus traditur.

4. Eodem fere tempore Prusias, rex Bithyniae, consilium cepit interficiendi Nicomedis filii, quem a se ablega-
tum, studens minoribus filiis, quos ex noverca eius susce-
2 perat, Romae habebat. Sed res adulescenti ab iis, qui
facinus susceperant, proditur hortatique sunt, ut crudelitate patris provocatus occupet insidias et in auctorem re-
3 torqueat scelus. Nec difficilis persuasio fuit. Igitur cum
accitus in regnum patris venisset, statim rex appellatur.
4 Prusias regno spoliatus a filio privatusque redditus etiam
5 a servis deseritur. Cum in latebris ageret, non minore scelere, quam filium occidi iusserat, a filio interficitur.

---

8 Demetrius was helped in his flight by none other than Polybius, who tells the story (31.11–15). He was unable to stop the
decline and shrinkage of the once-huge Seleucid Empire.

9 For Prusias II, see 32.4.2. His successor is Nicomedes II
Epiphanes (149–ca. 127). See Diod. Sic. 32.20f.; Zonaras 9.28.
The coup is the source for Corneille's tragedy *Nicomède* (1651),
which, however, takes great liberties with the facts.

ing of the death of his brother Antiochus; he had come as
a hostage while his brother was alive, he said, but with his
death he did not know for whom he stood hostage. He   7
therefore thought it fair that he be released to claim the
throne, he said, because since he had followed international law in ceding it to his elder brother that throne
should now be his as he was older than the orphan. When   8
he saw that he was not gaining his release from the senate,
which secretly judged the kingdom would be safer with
the orphan than with him, he left the city ostensibly to go
hunting and with a number accompanying him in his flight
furtively boarded a ship at Ostia.[8] Sailing to Syria he re-   9
ceived a warm welcome from everyone and after killing
the orphan and his guardians was given the throne.

4. At about the same time Prusias, king of Bithynia,
decided on killing his son Nicomedes, whom he had kept
banished in Rome, since he favored the younger sons that
he had fathered by the boy's stepmother.[9] But the affair   2
was leaked to the young man by those who had undertaken
to commit the crime, and these urged him, since he had
become a target of his father's cruelty, to forestall the trap
and have crime recoil on its author. Persuasion was not
difficult. So when he was summoned and arrived in his   3
father's kingdom, he was immediately proclaimed king.
Prusias, deprived of his throne by his son and becoming a   4
private citizen again, was deserted even by his slaves.
When he was living in hiding, he was—by a crime no   5
worse than ordering his son's murder—killed by his son.

LIBER XXXV

1. Demetrius occupato Syriae regno novitati suae otium periculosum ratus ampliare fines regni et opes augere fini-
2 timorum bellis statuit. Itaque Ariarathi, regi Cappadociae, propter fastiditas sororis nuptias infestus fratrem eius Orophernen per iniuriam regno pulsum supplicem rece- pit, datumque sibi honestum belli titulum gratulatus resti-
3 tuere eum in regnum statuit. Sed Orophernes ingrato animo inita cum Antiochensibus pactione, offensis tunc Demetrio, pellere ipsum regno, a quo restituebatur, con-
4 silium cepit. Quo cognito Demetrius vitae quidem eius, ne Ariarathes metu fraterni belli liberaretur, pepercit, ipsum autem conprehensum vinctum Seleuciae custodiri
5 iubet. Nec Antiochenses indicio territi a defectione desti-
6 terunt. Itaque adiuvantibus et Ptolomeo, rege Aegypti, et Attalo, rege Asiae, et Ariarathe Cappadociae, bello a De- metrio lacessiti subornant Balam quendam, sortis extre- mae iuvenem, qui Syriae regnum velut paternum armis

---

[1] See 34.3.5ff. Other sources are Polyb. 31.33ff.; Diod. Sic. 31.32–32.10. Besides Demetrius and Ptolemy VI, the monarchs involved are Ariarathes V Eusebes Philopator of Cappadocia (ca. 163–ca. 130); Attalus II of Pergamum (160–139; he was not "king of Asia," though Justin commonly uses this term for the Per-

BOOK XXXV

1. When Demetrius came to the kingdom of Syria and
thought that as a novice inactivity could prove dangerous
for him, he decided to increase the extent of his kingdom
and his power by wars with his neighbors.[1] So since he was   2
angry with Ariarathes, king of Cappadocia, for rejecting
marriage to his sister he accepted an appeal from his
brother Orophernes, who had been unjustly dethroned by
him, and pleased with being given an honorable pretext
for war, he decided to restore him to his kingdom. But   3
Orophernes with no gratitude made a pact with the people
of Antioch, who were then hostile to Demetrius, and
planned to drive from the throne the very man by whom
he was being restored. When he heard of this Demetrius   4
still spared his life so Ariarathes should not be free of fear
of war with his brother, but he ordered him arrested and
kept prisoner at Seleucia. But the people of Antioch were   5
not deterred from revolt by the betrayal of the plot. So   6
with help of both Ptolemy, king of Egypt, Attalus, king of
Asia, and Ariarathes of Cappadocia, they, following an attack by Demetrius, recruited a certain Bala, a young man
of the lowest station, to reclaim by war the kingdom of

gamene rulers); Alexander Balas (150–145); Demetrius II Nicator (145–140, and see 36.1).

7 repeteret, et ne quid contumeliae deesset, nomen ei Alex-
8 andri inditur genitusque ab Antiocho rege dicitur. Tantum
odium Demetrii apud omnes erat, ut aemulo eius non
vires tantum regiae, verum etiam generis nobilitas con-
9 sensu omnium tribueretur. Igitur Alexander admirabili
rerum varietate, pristinarum sordium oblitus, totius ferme
Orientis viribus succinctus bellum Demetrio infert vic-
10 tumque vita pariter ac regno spoliat. Quamquam nec
Demetrio animus in propulsando bello defuit. Nam et
primo proelio hostem fugavit et regibus bellum restituen-
11 tibus multa milia in acie cecidit. Ad postremum tamen
invicto animo inter confertissimos fortissime dimicans
cecidit.

2. Initio belli Demetrius duos filios apud Gnidium hos-
pitem suum cum magno pondere auri commendaverat, ut
belli periculis eximerentur et, si ita fors tulisset, paternae
2 ultioni servarentur. Ex his maior, Demetrius, annos pubertatis egressus audita Alexandri luxuria, quem insperatae
opes et alienae felicitatis ornamenta velut captum inter
scortorum greges desidem in regia tenebant, auxiliantibus
Cretensibus securum ac nihil hostile metuentem adgredi-
3 tur. Antiochenses quoque veterem patris offensam novis
meritis correcturi se ei tradunt; sed et milites paterni favore iuvenis accensi prioris sacramenti religionem novi
regis superbiae praeferentes signa ad Demetrium trans-

Syria as his paternal property; and as a final touch to the   7
insult, Bala was given the name Alexander and said to
be born of King Antiochus. Such was everyone's hatred   8
for Demetrius that his rival was ascribed not only royal
power but also noble birth with everyone's approval. Thus   9
through an amazing turn of events, Alexander, forgetting
his former humble rank and equipped with the strength
of almost all the East, made war on Demetrius and after
defeating him took his life as well his throne. But neither   10
did Demetrius lack spirit in repelling the war. For in the
first battle he routed his enemy and when the kings renewed the war he also killed many thousands in battle.
Finally, however, with a still unbroken spirit he fell fight-   11
ing valiantly in the thick of the fray.

2. At the start of the war Demetrius had entrusted his
two sons to a friend on Cnidus together with a large sum
of gold so they would be spared the dangers of the war
and, if fate so decided, be preserved to avenge the death
of their father. The elder of them, Demetrius, who was   2
past the years of puberty, heard of the dissipation of Alexander, whom unexpected wealth and the trappings of another's success was keeping virtually captive, idling amid
scores of whores in the palace; and with the help of some
Cretans, he attacked him when felt secure and was fearing
no attack. The people of Antioch also, in order to correct   3
by fresh kindnesses the earlier wrong they had done his
father, put themselves in his service; but in addition his
father's soldiers, fired with enthusiasm for the young man
and preferring the sanctity of their former oath of alle-
giance to the new king's arrogance, also shifted their sup-

4   ferunt. Atque ita Alexander, non minore impetu fortunae destructus quam elatus, primo proelio victus interficitur; deditque poenas et Demetrio, quem occiderat, et Antiocho, cuius mentitus originem fuerat.

port to Demetrius. And so it was that Alexander, brought 4
down by no less a stroke of fortune than the one by which
he had been elevated, was defeated and killed in the first
battle; and he paid a penalty both to Demetrius, whom he
had killed, and to Antiochus, from whom he had falsely
claimed descent.

LIBER XXXVI

1. Recuperato paterno regno Demetrius, et ipse rerum successu corruptus, vitiis adulescentiae in segnitiam labitur tantumque contemptum apud omnes inertiae, quan-
2 tum odium ex superbia pater habuerat, contraxit. Itaque cum ab imperio eius passim civitates deficerent, ad abolendam segnitiae maculam bellum Parthis inferre sta-
3 tuit; cuius adventum non inviti Orientis populi videre et propter Arsacidae, regis Parthorum, crudelitatem et quod veteri Macedonum imperio adsueti novi populi superbiam
4 indigne ferebant. Itaque cum et Persarum et Elymaeorum Bactrianorumque auxiliis iuvaretur, multis proeliis Par-
5 thos fudit. Ad postremum tamen pacis simulatione deceptus capitur traductusque per ora civitatium populis, qui
6 desciverant, in ludibrium favoris ostenditur. Missus deinde in Hyrcaniam benigne et iuxta cultum pristinae fortunae habetur.

---

1 Posidonius took up where Polybius finished and may have been an ultimate source for Trogus, even if mixed with others and mediated by another writer (Timagenes?). We have, in general, Diod. Sic. 33–34/35; App. *Syr.* 67ff. Demetrius II Nicator was a Parthian prisoner from 139 to 129. Antiochus VI Epiphanes was killed in 142, and Antiochus VII Sidetes ruled from 138 to 129.

2 The Parthian king was Mithridates I, whose dynasty, founded by Arsaces I in the mid-third century, was called the Arsacids (see

BOOK XXXVI

1. On recovering his father's throne, Demetrius himself also becoming corrupted by success,[1] lapsed into idleness with adolescent vices and among everyone aroused as much contempt for his inertia as his father had aroused hatred for his arrogance. So since cities were everywhere 2 defecting from his authority he decided to remove the stigma of indolence by making war on the Parthians; and 3 his coming was not unwelcome to the peoples of the East because of the ruthlessness of Arsacides, king of the Parthians, and also because being accustomed to the old Macedonian Empire they resented the new people's arrogance.[2] So when he received help with reinforcements 4 from the Persians and also from the Elymaeans and Bactrians, he routed the Parthians in many battles. Finally, 5 however, duped by a bogus offer of peace, he was captured, paraded before peoples in cities that had deserted, and put on display before rebellious peoples to mock their support for him. Then sent into Hyrcania he was treated 6 kindly and in a manner suited to his former status.

Book 41). Under these kings the Parni people of the central Asian steppe had taken over more and more of the Seleucid Empire, and by Demetrius II's time were rulers of Iran and even Mesopotamia. Hyrcania, mentioned below, was a region in northeastern Persia by the Caspian Sea.

7   Dum haec aguntur, interim in Syria Trypho, qui se
tutorem Antiocho, Demetrii privigno, substitui a populo
8 laboraverat, occiso pupillo regnum Syriae invadit. Quo diu
potitus tandem exsolescente favore recentis imperii ab
Antiocho, puero admodum, Demetrii fratre, qui in Asia
educabatur, bello vincitur, rursusque regnum Syriae ad
9 subolem Demetrii revertitur. Igitur Antiochus, memor
quod et pater propter superbiam invisus et frater propter
segnitiam contemptus fuisset, ne in eadem vitia incideret,
recepta in matrimonium Cleopatra, uxore fratris, civitates,
quae initio fraterni imperii defecerant, summa industria
10 persequitur, domitasque rursus regni terminis adicit; Iudaeos quoque, qui in Macedonico imperio sub Demetrio
patre armis se in libertatem vindicaverant, subegit. Quorum vires tantae fuere, ut post haec nullum Macedonum
regem tulerint domesticisque imperiis usi Syriam magnis
bellis infestaverint.

   2. Namque Iudaeis origo Damascena, Syriae nobilis-
sima civitas, unde et Assyriis regibus genus ex regina Sa-
2 mirami fuit. Nomen urbi a Damasco rege inditum, in cuius
honorem Syri sepulcrum Atarathes, uxoris eius, pro templo coluere, deamque exinde sanctissimae religionis ha-
3 bent. Post Damascum Azelus, mox Adores et Abrahames
4 et Israhel reges fuere. Sed Israhelem felix decem filiorum
5 proventus maioribus suis clariorem fecit. Itaque populum

---

   3 Trypho, also named Diodotus, was not a Seleucid kinsman
but made himself king circa 140, only to be overthrown a few
years later (the chronology is obscure).
   4 That is, Demetrius I.   5 Diod. Sic. 34/35.1 (the year
134); Joseph. *AJ* 13.8.2ff.   6 See 1.2.

While this was happening, meanwhile in Syria Trypho, 7
who had been endeavoring to have himself installed by the
people as guardian for Antiochus, stepson of Demetrius,
killed his ward and seized the kingdom of Syria.[3] After 8
holding it for some time he was, as favor for the new regime began to wane, finally defeated in battle by Antiochus, Demetrius' brother, who was just a boy being
brought up in Asia, and the kingdom of Syria then re-
verted to the line of Demetrius.[4] So remembering that his 9
father had been hated for his arrogance and his brother
despised for his idleness, and not to lapse into the same
vices himself, Antiochus married Cleopatra, his brother's
widow, and took vigorous action against cities that had
defected at the start of his brother's reign, and subduing
them he annexed them again to his kingdom's territory. He 10
also conquered the Jews, who had been part of the Macedonian Empire under Antiochus' father Demetrius, but
had regained independence by force of arms.[5] Such was
their strength that after this they accepted to no Macedonian king and with their own power harassed Syria with
major wars.

2. Now the Jews came originally from Damascus, Syria's most renowned city, from which also came the Assyr-
ian kings, through the line of Queen Semiramis.[6] The 2
name of the city derives from King Damascus, in whose
honor the Syrians venerate as a temple the tomb of Ata-
rathe, his wife, and since her time they hold her as a goddess of the holiest sanctity. After Damascus Azelus was 3
king, and after him Adores, Abraham and Israhel. Israhel, 4
however, fortunate in having ten sons born to him, gained
greater fame than his forebears. So dividing his people 5

179

in decem regna divisum filiis tradidit, omnesque ex nomine Iudae, qui post divisionem decesserat, Iudaeos appellavit colique memoriam eius ab omnibus iussit, cuius
6 portio omnibus accesserat. Minimus aetate inter fratres
Ioseph fuit, cuius excellens ingenium fratres veriti clam
7 interceptum peregrinis mercatoribus vendiderunt. A quibus deportatus in Aegyptum, cum magicas ibi artes sollerti
8 ingenio percepisset, brevi ipsi regi percarus fuit. Nam et
prodigiorum sagacissimus erat et somniorum primus in-
tellegentiam condidit, nihilque divini iuris humanique ei
9 incognitum videbatur, adeo ut etiam sterilitatem agrorum
ante multos annos providerit; perissetque omnis Aegyptus
fame, nisi monitu eius rex edicto servari per multos annos
10 fruges iussisset; tantaque experimenta eius fuerunt, ut
non ab homine, sed a deo responsa dari viderentur.
11   Filius eius Moyses fuit, quem praeter paternae sci-
entiae hereditatem etiam formae pulchritudo commenda-
12 bat. Sed Aegyptii, cum scabiem et vitiliginem paterentur,
responso moniti eum cum aegris, ne pestis ad plures ser-
13 peret, terminis Aegypti pellunt. Dux igitur exulum factus
sacra Aegyptiorum furto abstulit, quae repetentes armis
14 Aegyptii domum redire tempestatibus conpulsi sunt. Itaque Moyses Damascena, antiqua patria, repetita montem
Sinam occupat, in quo septem dierum ieiunio per deserta
Arabiae cum populo suo fatigatus cum tandem venisset,
septimum diem more gentis Sabbata appellatum in omne

into ten kingdoms, he passed them on to his sons and
called them all Jews (Judaei) after Juda, who had died
after the division, and he ordered his memory to be cher-
ished by all to whom a portion had been given. The young-   6
est among the brothers was Joseph, whose brothers from
fear of his outstanding intellect waylaid him and sold him
to foreign merchants. Taken away into Egypt by these   7
people he there mastered the art of magic by his quick
intelligence and soon became very close to the king himself. For he was both very expert in prodigies and also the   8
first to understand dreams, and no aspect of any divine or
human order seemed beyond his knowledge, so much so   9
that he even foresaw barrenness in the fields many years
before it occurred; and all Egypt would have perished in
a famine had the king not issued an edict on his advice and
ordered crops to be stockpiled over many years; and so   10
accurate was he when put to the test that his predictions
seemed be given not by a man but a god.

His son was Moses, who apart from inheriting his fa-   11
ther's knowledge also had good looks favoring him. But   12
when the Egyptians were afflicted with mange and lep-
rosy, they on an oracle's advice drove him from the borders
of Egypt along with the sick in order to prevent further
spread of the plague. Then when he became the exiles'   13
leader he stole objects of worship of the Egyptians, and
while trying to retrieve them by armed force the Egyptians were forced to return home by storms. So Moses,   14
returning to the area of Damascus, his ancient homeland,
halted on Mount Sinai, on which, exhausted after finally
reaching it with his people after seven days without food
in the Arabian desert, he established for all time the seventh day, traditionally called the Sabbath by that people,

15 aevum ieiunio sacravit, quoniam illa dies famem illis er-
roremque finierat. Et quoniam metu contagionis pulsos se
ab Aegypto meminerant, ne eadem causa invisi apud incolas forent, caverunt, ne cum peregrinis converent; quod
ex causa factum paulatim in disciplinam religionemque
16 convertit. Post Moysen etiam filius eius Arruas sacerdos
sacris Aegyptiis, mox rex creatur; semperque exinde hic
mos apud Iudaeos fuit, ut eosdem reges et sacerdotes
haberent, quorum iustitia religione permixta incredibile
quantum coaluere.

3. Opes genti ex vectigalibus opobalsami crevere, quod
2 in his tantum regionibus gignitur. Est namque vallis, quae
continuis montibus velut muro quodam ad instar castrorum clauditur (spatium loci ducenta iugera; nomine Ari-
3 cus dicitur); in ea silva est et ubertate et amoenitate in-
4 signis, siquidem palmeto et opobalsameto distinguitur. Et
arbores opobalsami similem formam piceis arboribus habent, nisi quod sunt humiles magis et in vinearum morem
excoluntur. Hae certo anni tempore balsamum sudant.
5 Sed non minor loci eius apricitatis quam ubertatis admiratio est; quippe cum toto orbe regionis eius ardentissimus
sol sit, ibi tepidi aeris ‹flatu› naturalis quaedam ac perpe-
6 tua opacitas inest. In ea regione latus lacus est, qui propter
magnitudinem aquae et inmobilitatem Mortuum Mare
7 dicitur. Nam neque ventis movetur resistente turbinibus
bitumine, quo aqua omnis stagnatur, neque navigationis
patiens est, quoniam omnia vita carentia in profundum
merguntur; nec materiam ullam sustinet, nisi quae bitumine incrustatur.

---

7 Jericho; see Strabo 16.763C, who calls it Hiericus.
8 Text uncertain, but Ruehl's *bitumine* gives better sense than
the transmitted *(a)lumine*, "unguent."

as a holy day of fasting, since that day had brought an end
to their hunger and wandering. And since they remem-   15
bered that it was from fear of contagion that they were
driven from Egypt, they, in order not to be shunned by the
inhabitants for the same reason, avoided all social contact
with strangers; and though done for a specific purpose this
gradually turned into a religious practice. After Moses his   16
son Arruas was also made priest of the Egyptian religious
ceremonies, and soon became king; and ever since the
practice among Jews has been to have their kings also as
their priests, and the integration of judicial and religious
systems has made them amazingly unified.

3. The wealth of the people grew from taxes on balsam,
which is found only in those regions. For there is a valley   2
which is enclosed by an unbroken mountain range resem-
bling a wall and forming the shape of a camp (it has an
area of two hundred acres—its name is Aricus);[7] and   3
within it is a forest noted for both its fertility and its charm,
being studded with palm and balsam trees. Balsam trees   4
also have a similar shape to pine trees, except that they are
shorter and cultivated like vines. At a certain time of year,
they secrete balsam. But the area is no less remarkable for   5
its sunniness than its fruitfulness; in fact, although the sun
in the region is hotter than anywhere on earth, there is
there a kind of natural and sustained relief produced by a
mild breeze. In that region is a broad lake, which because   6
of the extent and stillness of its waters is called the Dead
Sea. For it is neither moved by wind since its pitch makes   7
it resistant to storms and makes its waters viscous even in
a whirlwind, nor is it navigable because all lifeless objects
sink to the bottom; and it will keep no wood afloat unless
it is coated with pitch.[8]

8   Primum Xerxes, rex Persarum, Iudaeos domuit; postea
cum ipsis Persis in dicionem Alexandri Magni venere
diuque in potestate Macedonici imperii subiecti Syriae
9   regno fuere. A Demetrio cum descivissent, amicitia Romanorum petita primi omnium ex Orientalibus libertatem
acceperunt, facile tunc Romanis de alieno largientibus.

4. Per eadem tempora, quibus in Syria regni mutatio
inter novos reges alternabatur, in Asia rex Attalus florent-
issimum ab Eumene patruo acceptum regnum caedibus
amicorum et cognatorum suppliciis foedabat, nunc matrem anum, nunc Beronicen sponsam maleficiis eorum
2   necatam confingens. Post hanc scelestam violentiae rabiem squalidam vestem sumit, barbam capillumque in
modum reorum submittit, non in publicum prodire, non
populo se ostendere, non domi laetiora convivia inire aut
aliquod signum sani hominis habere, prorsus ut poenas
3   pendere manibus interfectorum videretur. Omissa deinde
regni administratione hortos fodiebat, gramina serebat et
noxia innoxiis permiscebat, eaque omnia veneni suco in-
4   fecta velut peculiare munus amicis mittebat. Ab hoc studio
aerariae artis fabricae se tradit, cerisque fingendis et aere
5   fundendo procudendoque oblectatur. Matri deinde sepulcrum facere instituit, cui operi intentus morbum ex solis
fervore contraxit et septima die decessit. Huius testamento heres populus Romanus tunc instituitur.
6   Sed erat ex Eumene Aristonicus, non iusto matrimonio, sed ex paelice Ephesia, citharistae cuiusdam filia,

---

9 In 161; 1 Maccabees 8; Joseph. *AJ* 12.417ff.; *MRR* 1.444 n. 1.
10 Attalus III of Pergamum (138–133); Diod. Sic. 34/35.3f.

It was Xerxes, king of Persia, who first conquered the 8
Jews; subsequently these together with the Persians themselves fell under the rule of Alexander the Great and long
remained under the Macedonian Empire subject to Syrian rule. After they defected from Demetrius, they sought 9
friendship with the Romans and were the first of all Eastern peoples to gain their freedom, the Romans at that time
readily distributing the property of others.[9]

4. In this same period, in which regime changes in
Syria had the kingdom alternating between new kings, in
Asia King Attalus[10] was defiling the flourishing kingdom
that he had inherited from his uncle Eumenes by murdering friends and persecuting kinsmen, lying now that his
aged mother and now his wife Berenice had been murdered by their criminal acts. After this wicked and insane 2
outburst of violence he put on shabby clothing, let his
beard and hair grow long like men on trial, and would not
appear in public before the people, hold cheerful dinners
at home or give any indication of being a sane man, clearly
seeming to be paying a penalty to the shades of the people
he had murdered. Then ignoring the administration of the 3
kingdom he would be cultivating his gardens, planting
herbs, mixing the poisonous with the harmless, and send
them all impregnated with the sap of poisonous ones as
special presents to his friends. From this hobby he moved 4
on to working with bronze, and he took delight in wax
modeling and pouring and forging bronze. He then started 5
work on a tomb for his mother, but while busy with it he
fell ill from sunstroke and died six days later. In his will the
Roman people were then named his heirs.

But from Eumenes Aristonicus was born, not in legiti- 6
mate marriage but from his mistress Ephesia, a certain

185

genitus, qui post mortem Attali velut paternum regnum
7 Asiam invasit. Cum multa secunda proelia adversus civitates, quae metu Romanorum tradere se eidem nolebant,
fecisset iustusque iam rex videretur, Asia Licinio Crasso
8 consuli decernitur, qui intentior Attalicae praedae quam
bello, cum extremo anni tempore inordinata acie proelium
conseruisset, victus poenas inconsultae avaritiae sanguine
9 dedit. In huius locum missus Perpenna consul prima
congressione Aristonicum superatum in potestatem suam
redegit Attalicasque gazas, hereditarias populi Romani,
10 navibus inpositas Romam deportavit. Quod aegre ferens
successor eius M'. Aquilius consul ad eripiendum Aristonicum Perpennae, veluti sui potius triumphi munus esse
11 deberet, festinata velocitate contendit. Sed contentionem
12 consulum mors Perpennae diremit. Sic Asia Romanorum
facta cum opibus suis vitia quoque Romam transmisit.

lyre player's daughter, and he after the death of Attalus seized Asia as being his father's kingdom.[11] After he had 7 fought numerous successful battles against cities that from fear of the Romans refused to yield to him and he already seemed established as king, Asia was assigned to the consul Licinius Crassus,[12] who being more focused on Attalus' 8 treasure than the war, at the end of the year joined battle with his army in disorder, and in defeat paid for his reckless greed with his blood. Sent out as his replacement, the 9 consul Perpenna[13] defeated Aristonicus in the first encounter and took him prisoner, and the treasure of Attalus, the inheritance of the Roman people, he loaded on ships and brought back to Rome. Displeased with this, his successor, the consul M'. Aquilius,[14] hastened with all speed 10 to seize Aristonicus from Perpenna, thinking he should instead be gracing his own triumph. The consular rivalry, 11 however, was cut short by the death of Perpenna. Thus 12 Asia, now made the property of the Romans, passed its vices as well as its riches on to Rome.

[11] As Eumenes III (133–129).

[12] P. Licinius Crassus Dives Mucianus, consul 131; *MRR* 1.500, 503.

[13] M. Perperna, consul 130; *MRR* 1.501f., 504.

[14] Consul 129; *MRR* 1.504.; Perpenna was now proconsul.

LIBER XXXVII

1. Capto Aristonico Massilienses pro Phocaeensibus, conditoribus suis, quorum urbem senatus et omne nomen, quod et tunc et antea Antiochi bello infesta contra populum Romanum arma tulerant, deleri iusserat, legatos Romam deprecatum misere veniamque his a senatu obti-
2 nuere. Post haec regibus, qui adversus Aristonicum auxilia tulerant, praemia persoluta: Mithridati Pontico Syria maior, filiis Ariarathis, regis Cappadociae, qui eodem bello
3 occiderat, Lycaonia et Cilicia datae. Fidiorque populus Romanus in socii filios quam mater in liberos fuit; quippe
4 hinc parvulis auctum regnum, inde vita adempta. Namque Laodice ex numero sex filiorum, quos virilis sexus ex Ariarathe rege susceperat, timens, ne non diutina administratione regni adultis quibusdam potiretur, quinque parri-
5 cidali veneno necavit; unum parvulum sceleri matris cognatorum custodia eripuit, qui post necem Laodices (nam propter crudelitatem eam populus extinxerat) solus regno potitus est.

---

[1] See 36.4.6ff. The triumphal records show Aquilius was still in Asia in 126, and the settlement was perhaps not made until 123; *MRR* 1.509, 513. Mithridates V Euergetes was king of Pontus circa 150 to 121/0 and was succeeded by Mithridates VI Eupator, who ruled until 63.

BOOK XXXVII

1. After Aristonicus was captured the senate had ordered the city and entire people of the Phocaeans to be destroyed for having taken up arms against the Roman people both at that time and earlier in the war with Antiochus; and since these were their founders, the Massiliots sent delegates to Rome to appeal and obtained pardon for them from the senate.[1] After this, kings who had brought 2 the Romans aid against Aristonicus had rewards paid out to them: Mithridates of Pontus was given Greater Syria, and the sons of Ariarathes (the king of Cappadocia, who had fallen in the same war) were given Lycaonia and Cilicia. The Roman people were more loyal to the sons of their 3 ally than their mother was toward her children, since by the one the young boys had their kingdoms extended, and by the other their lives taken away. For Laodice had had 4 six children of male sex by King Ariarathes and, fearing that she would not long maintain charge of the kingdom if any grew up, she killed five with a murderous poison; one youngster was rescued from his mother's villainy by 5 some protective relatives, and after the murder of Laodice (for because of her ruthlessness the people had killed her) he alone came to reign.[2]

[2] Ariarathes VI Epiphanes Philopator (ca. 120–ca. 111).

6   Mithridates quoque repentina morte interceptus fi-
7 lium, qui et ipse Mithridates dictus est, reliquit; cuius ea
postea magnitudo fuit, ut non sui tantum temporis, verum
etiam superioris aetatis omnes reges maiestate superaverit
bellaque cum Romanis per XLVI annos varia victoria ges-
8 serit, cum eum summi imperatores, Sylla, Lucullus ceterique, in summa Cn. Pompeius ita vicerit, ut maior cla-
riorque in restaurando bello resurgeret damnisque suis
9 terribilior redderetur. Denique ad postremum non vi hostili victus, sed voluntaria morte in avito regno senex herede filio decessit.

2. Huius futuram magnitudinem etiam caelestia os-
2 tenta praedixerant. Nam et eo quo genitus est anno et eo
quo regnare primum coepit stella cometes per utrumque
tempus LXX diebus ita luxit, ut caelum omne conflagrare
3 videretur. Nam et magnitudine sui quartam partem caeli
occupaverat et fulgore sui solis nitorem vicerat; et cum
oreretur occumberetque, IV horarum spatium consume-
4 bat. Puer tutorum insidias passus est, qui eum fero equo
5 inpositum equitare iacularique cogebant; qui conatus cum
eos fefellissent supra aetatem regente equum Mithridate,
6 veneno eum appetivere. Quod metuens antidota saepius
bibit et ita se adversus insidias, exquisitis tutioribus reme-
diis, stagnavit, ut ne volens quidem senex veneno mori

3 For Sulla (whose name is spelled "Sylla" in Seel's text), see
MRR under the years 88–84; for Lucullus, under 74–67; for Pompey, under 66–63.
4 Mithridates VI (r. 120–63 BC) died not in his ancestral kingdom of Pontus but in a dependent city in the Crimea, committing
suicide to avoid capture and death from his rebel son Pharnaces.

Mithridates who was also taken by a sudden death left 6
a son, who was also called Mithridates; his subsequent 7
greatness was such that he surpassed all other kings in
majesty, not only those of his own day but even those of
earlier times, and he fought wars with the Romans over
forty-six years with intermittent success and although the 8
greatest generals—Sulla, Lucullus and the others, especially Gnaeus Pompeius[3]—did defeat him, the result was
that he reemerged even greater and more glorious in renewing war and after his losses returned even more terrifying. Finally not defeated by any enemy force but 9
committing suicide, he died an old man in his ancestral
kingdom, leaving a son as his heir.[4]

2. This man's forthcoming greatness had been foretold
even by celestial phenomena. For both in the year he was 2
born and the one in which he began his reign a comet
burned so brightly on both occasions for seventy days that
the whole sky appeared to be aflame. For in its magnitude 3
it had filled a quarter of the heavens and with its brilliance
also outshone the sun; and its rising and setting took a
period of four hours. As a boy he faced plots from his 4
guardians, who put him on an unbroken horse and made
him ride and throw javelins; but when the scheme failed 5
since Mithridates rode the horse with skill beyond his
years, they tried to poison him. From fear of that he often 6
drank antidotes and thus immunized himself against their
plots, taking exotic preventive agents in ever stronger
amounts, so that as an old man he could not die by poison

191

7 potuerit. Timens deinde, ne inimici, quod veneno non potuerant, ferro peragerent, venandi studium finxit, quo per septem annos neque urbis neque ruris tecto usus est,
8 sed per silvas vagatus diversis montium regionibus pernoctabat ignaris omnibus, quibus esset locis, adsuetus feras cursu aut fugere aut persequi, cum quibusdam etiam
9 viribus congredi. Quibus rebus et insidias vitavit et corpus ad omnem virtutis patientiam duravit.

3. Ad regni deinde administrationem cum accessisset, statim non de regendo, sed de augendo regno cogitavit.
2 Itaque Scythas invictos antea, qui Zopyriona, Alexandri Magni ducem, cum XXX milibus armatorum deleverant, qui Cyrum, Persarum regem, cum CC milibus trucidaverant, qui Philippum, Macedonum regem, fugientem
3 fecerant, ingenti felicitate perdomuit. Auctus igitur viribus Pontum quoque ac deinceps Cappadociam occupavit.
4 Cum de Asia tractaret, tacitus cum quibusdam amicis regno profectus universam nemine sentiente pervagatus
5 est omniumque urbium situm ac regiones cognovit. Inde in Bithyniam transcendit et quasi dominus Asiae opportuna quaeque victoriae suae metatus est. Post haec in regnum, cum iam perisse crederetur, reversus est invento parvulo filio, quem per absentiam eius soror uxorque Laodice enixa fuerat. Sed inter gratulationem post longam
7 peregrinationem adventus sui et filii geniti veneno pericli-

---

5 See 1.8; 2.3.1ff.; 9.1.9ff.; 12.2.16ff.   6 Pontus was his own kingdom; Justin probably means Galatia, while Asia in the next sentence means, as often, Pergamum. These events occurred decades after the birth of his first son.   7 Around the year 112. Laodice was executed by her brother in 105.

even when he wanted to. Fearing then that his enemies 7
might accomplish with the sword what they had been unable to with poison, he feigned interest in hunting, by
which he for seven years avoided being under a roof either
in town or country, but roaming through forests he would 8
pass the nights in various parts of the mountains with everyone unaware of where he was, becoming accustomed
to avoiding or chasing wild beasts and even pitting his
strength against some. In this way he both avoided traps 9
and hardened his body to face any test of courage.

3. When he then came to administering the kingdom,
his immediate thought was not for ruling it but extending
it. So he turned to the as yet undefeated Scythians, who 2
had destroyed Alexander the Great's general Zopyrion together with thirty thousand soldiers, massacred the Persian king Cyrus and twenty thousand men, and put Philip
king of Macedon to flight,[5] and with great good fortune he
conquered them. So with his strength thus augmented he 3
also seized Pontus and then Cappadocia.[6] When he was 4
considering Asia, he secretly set off from his kingdom with
some friends and with no one aware roamed all over that
country and took note of the site of all its cities and regions. He then crossed into Bithynia and as if lord of Asia 5
traversed areas likely to favor his victory. After this he 6
returned to his kingdom, when it was already believed that
he was dead, finding there a baby boy to whom Laodice,
his sister and wife, had given birth during his absence.[7]
But while being congratulated on his return from the long 7
expedition and the birth of his son, he faced danger of

tatus est, siquidem Laodice soror, cum perisse eum crederet, in concubitus amicorum proiecta, quasi admissum
facinus maiori scelere tegere posset, venenum advenienti
8 paravit. Quod cum ex ancillis Mithridates cognovisset,
facinus in auctores vindicavit.

4. Hieme deinde adpetente non in convivio, sed in
campo, nec in avocationibus, sed in exercitationibus, nec
inter sodales, sed inter coaequales aut equo aut cursu aut
2 viribus contendebat. Exercitum quoque suum ad parem
laboris patientiam cotidiana exercitatione durabat, atque
3 ita invictus ipse inexpugnabilem exercitum fecerat. Inita
deinde cum Nicomede societate Paphlagoniam invadit
4 victamque cum socio dividit. Quam cum teneri a regibus
senatui nuntiatum esset, legatos ad utrumque misit, qui
5 gentem restitui in pristinum statum iuberent. Mithridates,
cum se iam parem magnitudini Romanorum crederet,
superbo responso hereditarium patri suo regnum obve-
nisse respondit; mirari se, quod cum ei relata controversia
6 non fuerit, sibi referatur. Nec territus minis Galatiam quo-
7 que occupat. Nicomedes, quoniam se tueri iure non pot-
8 erat, iusto regi redditurum respondit. Atque ita filium
suum mutato nomine Pylaemenen, Paphlagonum regum
nomine, appellat et quasi stirpi regiae reddidisset regnum,
9 falso nomine tenet. Sic ludibrio habiti legati Romam revertuntur.

---

8 Nicomedes III Euergetes of Bithynia (ca. 127–ca. 94); the
year is 104.

9 That is, his father.

poisoning, for his sister Laodice, as she believed him dead, had started sleeping with his friends, and as if she could conceal her offense by a greater crime, prepared poison for him on his return. When Mithridates heard of it from 8 maidservants he inflicted punishment for the crime on its authors.

4. As winter then approached, he was not spending his time in dining but on the plain, not on relaxation but on training, not among cronies but among brothers-in-arms, and was competing in horse or foot racing or tournaments of strength. He was also strengthening his army with daily 2 exercise to endure hardship to his level, and so, indomitable himself, he had also created an unbeatable army. Then forming an alliance with Nicomedes[8] he overran 3 Paphlagonia, and on conquering it divided it with his ally. When the Senate was notified that it was being occupied 4 by the two kings, it sent delegates to both of them to order the people restored to its former status. Mithridates, since 5 he now thought himself equal to the might of the Romans, arrogantly replied that his kingdom had come to his father by inheritance: he was surprised that since *he*[9] had faced no problem he was himself doing so. And undaunted by 6 threats he also seized Galatia. Nicomedes, since he could 7 offer no justification, replied that he would restore the country to its legitimate king. And so, he changed his son's 8 name and called him Pylaemenes, a Paphlagonian royal name, and as if he had restored the throne to the royal line he held it under a false name. After facing ridicule like this 9 the delegates returned to Rome.

LIBER XXXVIII

1. Mithridates parricidia nece uxoris auspicatus sororis alterius Laodices filios, cuius virum Ariarathen, regem Cappadociae, per Gordium insidiis occiderat, tollendos statuit, nihil actum morte patris existimans, si adulescentes paternum regnum, cuius ille cupiditate flagrabat,
2 occupassent. Igitur dum in his cogitationibus versatur, interim Nicomedes, rex Bithyniae, vacuam morte regis
3 Cappadociam invadit. Quod cum nuntiatum Mithridati fuisset, per simulationem pietatis auxilia sorori ad ex-
4 pellendum Cappadocia Nicomeden mittit. Sed iam Laodice per pactionem se Nicomedi in matrimonium tradide-
5 rat. Quod aegre ferens Mithridates praesidia Nicomedis Cappadocia expellit regnumque sororis filio restituit,
6 egregium prorsus factum, ni subsecuta fraus esset; siquidem interiectis mensibus simulat se Gordium, quo ministro usus in Ariarathe interficiendo fuerat, restituere in patriam velle, sperans, si obsisteret adulescens, causas belli futuras, aut, si permitteret, per eundem filium tolli

---

[1] For general consideration of Mithridates and the early first century, see Memnon *FGrH* 434 F 22 (Sherk no. 56); also App. *Mith.* 10ff. For Nicomedes see 37.4.3. In Cappadocia Ariarathes VII Philometor was monarch from circa 111 to circa 100; then Mithridates installed his son as Ariarathes Eusebes Philopator.

BOOK XXXVIII

1. After initiating his parricides with the murder of his wife, Mithridates then decided that the sons of his other sister, Laodice, whose husband, Ariarathes, king of Cappadocia, he had killed in a trap set by Gordius, should also be removed, thinking the father's death had served no purpose if the young men gained the father's throne, which he was passionately coveting.[1] Now while he was 2 occupied with such thoughts, Nicomedes, the king of Bithynia, overran Cappadocia, now left with no ruler after the death of its king. When this was reported to Mithri- 3 dates, he, feigning sympathy, sent help to his sister to drive Nicomedes out of Cappadocia. But Laodice had already 4 made a treaty with Nicomedes and married him. Angry 5 over that Mithridates drove Nicomedes' garrisons from Cappadocia and restored the kingdom to his sister's son, a truly commendable action but for the treachery that followed it; for some months later he pretended that he 6 wished to restore Gordius to his native land, the man whose services he had used for murdering Ariarathes, hoping that, if the young man objected, he would have a pretext for war, and if he agreed the son could also be

7 posse, per quem interfecerat patrem. Quod ubi Ariarathes
iunior moliri cognovit, graviter ferens interfectorem patris
per avunculum potissimum ab exilio revocari, ingentem
8 exercitum contrahit. Igitur cum in aciem eduxisset Mithridates peditum LXXX milia, equitum X, currus falcatos
sexcentos, nec Ariarathi auxiliantibus finitimis regibus
minores copiae essent, incertum belli timens consilia ad
insidias transfert sollicitatoque iuvene ad conloquium,
9 cum ferrum occultatum inter fascias gereret, scrutatore ab
Ariarathe regio more misso, curiosius imum ventrem per-
tractanti ait: caveret, ne aliud telum inveniret quam quae-
10 reret. Atque ita risu protectis insidiis sevocatum ab amicis
velut ad secretum sermonem inspectante utroque exercitu
interficit; regnum Cappadociae octo annorum filio in-
posito Ariarathis nomine additoque ei rectore Gordio tradidit.

2. Sed Cappadoces crudelitate ac libidine praefecto-
rum vexati a Mithridate deficiunt fratremque regis, et ipsum Ariarathen nomine, ab Asia, ubi educabatur, revo-
2 cant, cum quo Mithridates proelium renovat victumque
regno Cappadociae expellit. Nec multo post adulescens ex
3 aegritudine collecta infirmitate decedit. Post huius mortem Nicomedes timens, ne Mithridates accessione Cappadociae etiam Bithyniam finitimam invaderet, subornat
puerum eximiae pulchritudinis, quasi Ariarathes tres, non
duos filios genuisset, qui a senatu Romano paternum reg-

---

[2] "One who searches (a place, also a person) for something
hidden" (*OLD*). This was around 100 BC.

[3] Ariarathes VIII (ca. 96).

removed by the same agent by whom he had killed the
father. When the young Ariarathes understood what was 7
happening, he was angry that his father's assassin was being brought out of exile by his uncle of all people, and he
assembled a huge army. So when Mithridates led eighty 8
thousand infantry, ten thousand cavalry and six hundred
scythed chariots into battle, and Ariarathes' troops as-
sisted by neighboring kings were no less numerous, he saw
the outcome of the war being in doubt, changed his tactics
to subterfuge, and lured the young man to a meeting
where he was carrying a dagger hidden in his undergar- 9
ment; then when a *scrutator*[2] was sent over by Ariarathes
to search him, the usual practice of royalty, and he started
feeling the lower part of his abdomen quite attentively,
Mithridates said he should be careful not to find a weapon
other than the one he was looking for. And so with his plot 10
concealed with a joke he took him aside from his courtiers
as if for a private talk and killed him before the eyes of
both armies; the kingdom of Cappadocia he then passed
on to his eight-year-old son, giving him the name Ariarathes and adding Gordius as his regent.

2. But vexed by the cruelty and lust of their rulers the
Cappadocians defected from Mithridates and recalled
their late king's brother, also named Ariarathes, from Asia,
where he was being brought up.[3] Mithridates renewed his 2
conflict with him, defeated him, and drove him from the
kingdom of Cappadocia. And not much later the young
man died from an illness brought on by grief. After his 3
death Nicomedes feared that having acquired Cappadocia
Mithridates might also overrun its neighbor Bithynia, and
he bribed a very good-looking boy to claim his "father's
kingdom" from the Roman senate, alleging that Ariarathes

199

4 num peteret. Vxorem quoque Laodicen Romam mittit ad
testimonium trium ex Ariarathe susceptorum filiorum.

5 Quod ubi Mithridates cognovit, et ipse pari inpudentia
Gordium Romam mittit, qui senatui adseveret puerum,
cui Cappadociae regnum tradiderat, ex eo Ariarathe geni-
tum, qui bello Aristonici auxilia Romanis ferens cecidisset.

6 Sed senatus studio regum intellecto, aliena regna falsis
nominibus furantium, Mithridati Cappadociam et Nico-

7 medi ad solacia eius Paphlagoniam ademit. Ac ne contumelia regum foret ademptum illis, quod daretur aliis, uter-

8 que populus libertate donatus est. Sed Cappadoces munus
libertatis abnuentes negant vivere gentem sine rege posse.
Itaque rex illis a senatu Ariobarzanes statuitur.

3. Erat eo tempore Tigranes rex Armeniae, obses Parthis ante multum temporis datus, nec olim ab eisdem in
regnum paternum remissus. Hunc Mithridates mire ad
societatem Romani belli, quod olim meditabatur, perli-

2 cere cupiebat. Nihil igitur de offensa Romanorum sen-
tientem per Gordium inpellit, ut Ariobarzani, segni admodum, bellum inferat, et ne quis dolus subesse videatur,

3 filiam suam ei Cleopatram in matrimonium tradit. Primo
igitur adventu Tigranis Ariobarzanes sublatis rebus suis
Romam contendit, atque ita per Tigranen rursus Cappa-

4 docia iuris esse Mithridatis coepit. Eodem tempore mortuo Nicomede etiam filius eius, et ipse Nicomedes, regno
a Mithridate pellitur, qui cum supplex Romam venisset,

---

4 Ariobarzanes I Philoromaios (ca. 95–ca. 62).

5 Tigranes II ("the Great"; ca. 95–55).

had had three children, not two. He also sent his wife   4
Laodice to Rome to confirm a story of three sons being
born to Ariarathes. When Mithridates discovered this, he   5
himself with similar effrontery also sent Gordius to Rome
to affirm before the senate that the boy to whom he had
delivered the throne of Cappadocia was born of the Ariarathes who had died bringing aid to the Romans in the war
with Aristonicus. But the senate, discerning the intent of   6
the kings, who were stealing others' thrones with false
claims, took Cappadocia from Mithridates and to assuage
him took Paphlagonia from Nicomedes. And not to offend   7
the kings by taking something from them to give to others,
each people was granted freedom. But the Cappadocians,   8
refusing the gift of freedom, said their people could not
live without a king. So Ariobarzanes was appointed their
king by the senate.[4]

3. At that time the king of Armenia was Tigranes,[5] who
had much earlier been given as hostage to the Parthians
and only recently been returned by them to his father's
kingdom. Mithridates was very eager to entice him into
joining him in a war with Rome that he had long been
contemplating. So not realizing that he might offend the   2
Romans he, through Gordius, induced him to make war
on Ariobarzanes, a quite indolent man, and to avoid suspicion of any duplicity he gave him his daughter Cleopatra
in marriage. Then at Tigranes' first approach Ariobarzanes   3
took his possessions and hastened to Rome, and so through
Tigranes Cappadocia again began to come under the jurisdiction of Mithridates. At this same time, on the death   4
of Nicomedes, his son, also himself named Nicomedes,
was driven from his kingdom by Mithridates, and when he
came to Rome as a suppliant it was decided in the senate

decernitur in senatu, ut uterque in regnum restituantur; in quod tum missi M'. Aquilius et Mallius ‹Malthinus› legati.

5   His cognitis Mithridates societatem cum Tigrane bellum adversus Romanos gesturus iungit, pactique inter se sunt, ut urbes agrique Mithridati, homines vero et quae-

6 cumque auferri possent, Tigrani cederent. Post haec Mithridates intellecto quantum bellum suscitaret, legatos ad Cimbros, alios ad Gallograecos et Sarmatas Bastarnasque

7 auxilium petitum mittit. Nam omnes has gentes Romanum meditabundus bellum variis beneficiorum muneribus iam ante inlexerat. Ab Scythia quoque exercitum venire iubet omnemque Orientem adversus Romanos armat.

8 Non magno igitur labore Aquilium et ‹Malthinum› Asiano exercitu instructos vincit, quibus simul cum Nicomede

9 pulsis ingenti favore civitatium excipitur. Multum ibi auri argentique studio veterum regum magnumque belli apparatum invenit, quibus instructus debita civitatibus publica privataque remittit et vacationem quinquennii concedit.

10 Tunc ad contionem milites vocat eosque variis exhortatio-

11 nibus ad Romana bella sive Asiana incitat. Quam orationem dignam duxi, cuius exemplum brevitati huius operis insererem; quam obliquam Pompeius Trogus exposuit, quoniam in Livio et in Sallustio reprehendit, quod contiones directas pro sua oratione operi suo inserendo historiae modum excesserint.

---

6 The new king is Nicomedes IV Philopator (ca. 94–74). See *MRR* 2.35f., 43 (the years 89 and 88).

7 Justin seems to be saying that he is actually copying what he found in Trogus, but scholarly opinion remains divided; see especially Mineo ad loc. Perhaps, "instead of using their own words"?

that they each be restored to their kingdoms; and for that Manius Aquilius and Mallius Malthinus were sent out as legates.[6]

On learning of this Mithridates made an alliance with Tigranes to prosecute the war against the Romans, and they agreed between them that cities and land should go to Mithridates, captives and all movable goods to Tigranes. After that Mithridates, aware of the great war he was fomenting, sent legates to the Cimbri to seek support, and others to the Gallograeci, Sarmatae and Bastarnae. For all these peoples he had already courted with various gifts and favors when considering war with Rome. He also summoned troops from Scythia, and armed all of the East against the Romans. So with no great effort he defeated Aquilius and Malthinus who had an army of Asian soldiers, and when they were routed together with Nicomedes he was welcomed with great favor by the city-states. There he found large amounts of gold and silver carefully amassed by kings of old, and much military equipment; and with it he remitted all debts public and private to the cities and granted five years of tax exemption. He then called his soldiers to a meeting and with various kinds of exhortation roused them to the Roman or rather "Asian" wars. His speech I have thought worthy of inclusion in this abridgment; Pompeius Trogus presented it as indirect discourse, since he criticized Livy and Sallust for overstepping the proper bounds of history by inserting in their work speeches in direct discourse but composed in their own style.[7]

5

6

7

8

9

10

11

4. Optandum sibi fuisse ait, ut de eo liceret consulere,
2 bellumne sit cum Romanis an pax habenda; quin vero sit
resistendum inpugnantibus, ne eos quidem dubitare, qui
spe victoriae careant; quippe adversus latronem, si nequeant pro salute, pro ultione tamen sua omnes ferrum
3 stringere. Ceterum quia non id agitur, an liceat quiescere
non tantum animo hostiliter, sed etiam proelio congressis,
consulendum, qua ratione ac spe coepta bella sustineant.
4 Esse autem sibi victoriae fiduciam, si sit illis animus; Ro-
manosque vinci posse cognitum non sibi magis quam ipsis
militibus, qui et in Bithynia Aquilium et ‹Malthinum› in
5 Cappadocia fuderint. Ac si quem aliena magis exempla
quam sua experimenta moveant, audire se a Pyrro, rege
Epiri, non amplius quinque milibus Macedonum instructo
6 fusos tribus proeliis Romanos. Audire Hannibalem sedecim annis Italiae victorem inmoratum, et quin ipsam caperet urbem, non Romanorum illi vires restitisse sed domes-
7 ticae aemulationis atque invidiae studium. Audire populos
transalpinae Galliae Italiam ingressos maximis eam pluri-
busque urbibus possidere et latius aliquanto solum finium,
quam in Asia, quae dicatur inbellis, idem Galli occupa-
8 vissent. Nec victam solum dici sibi Romam a Gallis, sed
etiam captam, ita ut unius illis montis tantum cacumen
9 relinqueretur; nec bello hostem, sed pretio remotum. Gallorum autem nomen, quod semper Romanos terruit, in
partem virium suarum ipse numeret. Nam hos, qui Asiam

---

[8] Here and elsewhere in the speech is demonstrated the rhetorical advantage of referring to the past with less than accuracy;
cf. the Aetolians at 28.2.

4. He would have preferred, he said, to be allowed to consider whether to have war or peace with the Romans; but when aggressors must be faced, not even those with 2 no hope of victory can hesitate; for against a robber everyone, even if they cannot for their safety, still draws a sword for vengeance. But since it was no longer a matter of 3 whether they could have peace, having now gone beyond hostile feelings to the point of clashing in battle, they must consider with what strategy and prospects they could sustain a war they had already begun. He was himself confi- 4 dent of victory if they took courage; and that the Romans could be defeated his soldiers themselves also knew since they put both Aquilius to flight in Bithynia and Malthinus in Cappadocia. And should anyone be more impressed by 5 foreign examples than by their own, he heard that the Romans had been routed in three battles by Pyrrhus, king of Epirus, who had had no more than five thousand Macedonians with him.[8] He was told that Hannibal had re- 6 mained victorious in Italy for sixteen years, and that what had prevented him taking the city was not the strength of the Romans but the bitter rivalry and jealousy among his own people. He was told that the peoples of Transalpine 7 Gaul had on entering Italy occupied it, settled in most of its largest cities, and seized much more territory there than those same Gauls had taken in Asia, which is called unwarlike. Nor had Rome only been defeated by the 8 Gauls, he was told, but was also captured by them, so completely that they were left only the top of one hill; and that it was not by war but payment that their enemy was removed. Now the Gallic name, which always terrified the 9 Romans, he could himself count on as part of his strength. For the Gauls who live in Asia are different from those

205

incolunt, Gallos ab illis, qui Italiam occupaverant, sedibus
10 tantum distare, originem quidem ac virtutem genusque
pugnae idem habere; tantoque his acriora esse quam illis
ingenia, quod longiore ac difficiliore spatio per Illyricum
Thraciamque prodierint, paene operosius transitis eorum
finibus quam ubi consedere possessis.

11 Iam ipsam Italiam audire se numquam, ut Roma condita sit, satis illi pacatam, sed adsidue per omnes annos pro
libertate alios, quosdam etiam pro vice imperii bellis
12 continuis perseverasse; et a multis civitatibus Italiae deletos Romanorum exercitus ferri, a quibusdam novo contu-
13 meliae more sub iugum missos. Ac ne veteribus inmo-
remur exemplis, hoc ipso tempore universam Italiam bello
Marsico consurrexisse, non iam libertatem, sed consor-
14 tium imperii civitatisque poscentem; nec gravius vicino
Italiae bello quam domesticis principum factionibus urbem premi, multoque periculosius esse Italico civile bel-
15 lum. Simul et a Germania Cimbros, inmensa milia fero-
rum atque inmitium populorum, more procellae inundasse
16 Italiam; quorum etsi singula bella sustinere Romani possent, universis tamen obruantur, ut ne vacaturos quidem
bello suo putet.

5. Utendum igitur occasione et rapienda incrementa
virium, ne, si illis occupatis quieverint, mox adversus va-
2 cuos et quietos maius negotium habeat. Non enim quaeri,

---

9 See Livy 9.1ff. The humiliation of being paraded under the
enemy yoke was inflicted on the Roman army defeated by the
Samnites at the Caudine Forks in 321 BC, and on one defeated
by the Helvetii (in Switzerland) in 107.

10 The Marsi, having shown their loyalty in the Hannibalic

that settled in Italy only in their location, since they have 10
the same descent, valor, and way of fighting; and they are
much fiercer than them because they went through Illyricum and Thrace on a longer and more difficult journey,
facing almost more hardship in traversing those areas than
in conquering those where they settled.

He was now hearing that Italy itself had never been 11
fully subdued since Rome was founded, but that throughout all the years it had always been at war, some fighting
for freedom, others even challenging her leadership; and 12
that Roman armies had been wiped out by many states and
by some sent under the yoke as a new form of humiliation.[9]
And not to linger over old examples, at this very time all 13
Italy had revolted in the Marsian War,[10] no longer demanding freedom but a share in government and citizenship;[11] nor was the city suffering more seriously from a 14
local war in Italy than from infighting among the leaders
and a civil war far more dangerous than their Italian war.
At the same time the Cimbri—countless thousands of 15
savage, pitiless peoples—had also flooded into Italy from
Germany;[12] and even if the Romans could sustain separate 16
wars they would be overwhelmed by them as a whole, so
he thought they would not even be free for war with him.

5. So they must seize the opportunity and swiftly build
up their strength, since if they remained inactive while the
enemy was preoccupied, they could later have greater difficulty with them when they were disengaged and at peace.

War, demanded Roman citizenship in the so-called "Social War"
(Vell. Pat. 2.21).

[11] The Social War of 91 to 89.

[12] And had been defeated by Marius in 101.

an capienda sint arma, sed utrum sua potius occasionem
3 an illorum. Nam bellum quidem iam tunc secum ab illis
geri coeptum, cum sibi pupillo maiorem Phrygiam ade-
merint, quam patri suo praemium dati adversus Aristonicum auxilii concesserant, gentem quam et proavo suo
4 Mithridati Seleucus Callinicus in dotem dedisset. Quid,
cum Paphlagonia se decedere iusserint, non alterum illud
genus belli fuisse? Quae non vi, non armis, sed adoptione
testamenti et regum domesticorum interitu hereditaria
5 patri suo obvenisset. Cum inter hanc decretorum amari-
tudinem parendo non tamen eos mitigaret, quin acerbius
6 in dies gerant, non obtinuisse. Quod enim a se non prae-
bitum illis obsequium? Non Phrygiam Paphlagoniamque
dimissas? Non Cappadocia filium eductum, quam iure
7 gentium victor occupaverat? Raptum tamen sibi esse victoriae ius ab illis, quorum nihil est nisi bello quaesitum.
8 Non regem Bithyniae Chreston, in quem senatus arma
decreverat, a se in gratiam illorum occisum? Tamen nihilo
minus inputari sibi, si qua Gordius aut Tigranes faciat.
9 Libertatem etiam in contumeliam sui a senatu ultro dela-
tam Cappadociae, quam reliquis gentibus abstulerunt;
dein populo Cappadocum pro libertate oblata Gordium
regem orante ideo tantum, quoniam amicus suus esset,
10 non obtinuisse. Nicomeden praecepto illorum bellum sibi
intulisse; quia ultum ierit se, ab ipsis ventum obviam in
eo; et nunc eam secum bellandi illis causam fore, quod

---

13 Seleucus II Callinicus (246–225).

14 See 38.3.4.

15 Socrates Chrestus, brother of Nicomedes III, was installed,
then removed, by Mithridates in 91/0.

For it was not a question of whether they should take up 2
arms, but whether to do so at a time favoring them or the
enemy. For their war with him had already started when 3
they took Greater Phrygia from him while he was a boy;
they had given it to his father in reward for help against
Aristonicus, and it was a country that Seleucus Callinicus
had even given as dowry to his great-grandfather Mithridates.[13] Well, when they ordered him to leave Paphlago- 4
nia, had that not been another form of war? It had come
to his father not through force or war, but as an inheritance
through adoption after the country's royal line died out.
Even by obeying these harsh decrees[14] he had not molli- 5
fied them or prevented them from becoming more op-
pressive every day. For how had he not complied with 6
them? Were Phrygia and Paphlagonia not relinquished?
Had he not removed his son from Cappadocia, which he
had by international convention taken as victor? Yet his 7
right to the victory had been wrested from him by men
whose acquisitions had come only from war. Had not the 8
Bithynian king Chrestus, on whom the senate had declared war, been killed by him to please them?[15] Yet he
was still made personally accountable for anything Gordius or Tigranes might do. To insult him even Cappadocia 9
had been granted its freedom by the senate, something
they usually took away from other races; then when, instead of the freedom they were offered, the Cappadocian
people begged for Gordius as their king, the only reason
for their not gaining it was that Gordius was his friend.
Nicomedes had made war on him at their bidding; be- 10
cause he started defending himself, they came to obstruct
him; and now their reason for war with him would be that

non inpune se Nicomedi lacerandum, saltatricis filio, praebuerit.

6. Quippe non delicta regum illos, sed vires ac maiestatem insequi, neque in uno se, sed in aliis quoque omni-
2 bus hac saepe arte grassatos. Sic et avum suum Pharnacen per cognitionum arbitria succidaneum regi Pergameno
3 Eumeni datum; sic rursus Eumenen, cuius classibus primo in Asiam fuere transiecti, cuius exercitu magis quam suo et Magnum Antiochum et Gallos in Asia et mox
4 in Macedonia regem Perseum domuerant, et ipsum pro hoste habitum eique interdictum Italia, et quod cum ipso deforme sibi putaverant, cum filio eius Aristonico bellum gessisse. Nullius apud eos maiora quam Masinissae, regis
5 Numidarum, haberi merita; huic inputari victum Hannibalem, huic captum Syphacem, huic Karthaginem deletam, hunc inter duos illos Africanos tertium servatorem
6 urbis referri: tamen cum huius nepote bellum modo in Africa gestum adeo inexpiabile, ut ne victum quidem patris memoriae donarent, quin carcerem ac triumphi spectaculum experiretur.
7 Hanc illos omnibus regibus legem odiorum dixisse, scilicet quia ipsi tales reges habuerint, quorum etiam nominibus erubescant, aut pastores Aboriginum, aut aruspices Sabinorum, aut exules Corinthiorum, aut servos

---

16 Pharnaces I (ca. 185–ca. 170). This claim seems invented.

17 See 31.8; 33.

18 See 36.4.6ff. "He himself" means Perseus, not Mithridates.

19 Masinissa contributed to the Roman victory in 202, but died in 149, before the destruction of Carthage, even though he had played a part in the resumption of hostilities. The "two fa-

he did not offer himself abjectly to be mangled by Nicomedes, the son of a dancing girl.

6. In fact it was not the misdeeds of kings that they
punished, but their strength and majesty, he said, and not
only against him had they had often run wild but everyone
else as well. So too their treatment of his grandfather 2
Pharnaces,[16] made successor to Eumenes, king of Pergamum, with a formal inquiry; so again Eumenes, whose 3
fleets the Romans had used when first crossing to Asia and
on whose army they had relied more than their own to
overcome Antiochus the Great and the Gauls in Asia, and
later King Perseus in Macedonia,[17] and he himself had 4
been deemed an enemy and forbidden access to Italy, and
since they had felt it unbecoming to fight a war with him
directly, they had done so with his son Aristonicus.[18] None
among them was thought to have been of greater service
than Masinissa, king of the Numidians: he was the one 5
credited with Hannibal's defeat, he with Syphax's capture
and he with Carthage's destruction; and he together with
the two famous Africani was hailed as the third savior of
the city;[19] and yet they had recently in Africa fought such 6
a deadly war with his grandson that even after defeating
him they made no concession to his grandfather's memory
to spare him imprisonment and being paraded in a triumph.[20]

This principle of hatred for all kings they had of course 7
adopted because such were the kings that they had themselves that even their names made them blush—they were
either Aboriginal shepherds, Sabine soothsayers, Corin-

mous Africani" are the conqueror of Hannibal and Scipio Aemi-
lianus.   [20] A reference to the defeat of Jugurtha in 105.

vernasque Tuscorum, aut, quod honoratissimum nomen
8 fuit inter haec, Superbos; atque ut ipsi ferunt conditores
suos lupae uberibus altos, sic omnem illum populum lupo-
rum animos inexplebiles sanguinis, atque imperii divitia-
rumque avidos ac ieiunos habere.

7. Se autem, seu nobilitate illis conparetur, clariorem
illa conluvie convenarum esse, qui paternos maiores suos
a Cyro Darioque, conditoribus Persici regni, maternos a
magno Alexandro ac Nicatore Seleuco, conditoribus imperii Macedonici, referat, seu populus illorum conferatur
suo, earum se gentium esse, quae non modo Romano
imperio sint pares, sed Macedonico quoque obstiterint.
2 Nullam subiectarum sibi gentium expertam peregrina imperia; nullis umquam nisi domesticis regibus paruisse,
Cappadociam velint an Paphlagoniam recensere, rursus
Pontum an Bithyniam, itemque Armeniam maiorem mi-
noremque; quarum gentium nullam neque Alexander ille,
qui totam pacavit Asiam, nec quisquam successorum eius
3 aut posterorum attigisset. Scythiam duos umquam ante se
reges non pacare, sed tantum intrare ausos, Darium et
Philippum, aegre inde fugam sibi expedisse, unde ipse
4 magnam adversus Romanos partem virium haberet. Multoque se timidius ac diffidentius bella Pontica ingressum,
cum ipse rudis ac tiro esset, Scythiae praeter arma virtu-

---

21 "The Proud," a sobriquet applied usually only to the last
Tarquin king, expelled at the end of the sixth century. The founders are, of course, Romulus and Remus. "Aborigines" was the
name of Italy's legendary earliest dwellers; the Sabine soothsayer
was Rome's second king Numa; the "Etruscan" slave was Servius
Tullius, sixth king (not an Etruscan but a Latin).

thian exiles, or Etruscan slaves, captured or homebred, or, what was the most honored name among them, the Superbi;[21] and as even they admit themselves their founders 8 were suckled at a she-wolf's teats, so that all those people have wolf-like temperaments with an insatiable thirst for blood and ravenous hunger for power and riches.

7. He, however, if compared with them in breeding, was superior to that motley crowd of refugees and able to trace his line back to Cyrus and Darius, founders of the Persian Empire, on his father's side, and to Alexander the Great and Seleucus Nicator, founders of the Macedonian Empire, on his mother's; nor were their people to be compared with his, coming as he did from races[22] that had not only equaled Roman power but also resisted Macedonia's. No people subject to him had faced foreign domination, 2 he said; never had they been under kings not of their race, whether they looked at Cappadocia or Paphlagonia, or Pontus or Bithynia, and likewise Greater and Lesser Armenia—none of these peoples had been touched either by that famous Alexander who subdued all Asia nor by any of his successors or predecessors. Only two kings before him, 3 Darius and Philip, had ever dared enter Scythia, much less subdue it, and these had had difficulty escaping from where he would be drawing most of his strength to face the Romans. He had felt far more anxious and diffident 4 entering his Pontic wars, when he was only a raw novice himself, but Scythia, even apart from its weapons and

[22] Or, possibly, "he was the king of races" if, as Ruehl conjectured, *regem* has been lost between *se* and *gentium*.

temque animi locorum quoque solitudinibus vel frigori-
bus instructae, per quae denuntiaretur ingens militiae
5 periculum ac labor. Inter quas difficultates ne spes quidem praemii foret ex hoste vago nec tantum pecuniae, sed
etiam sedis inope.

6 Nunc se diversam belli condicionem ingredi. Nam neque caelo Asiae esse temperatius aliud, nec solo fertilius
nec urbium multitudine amoenius; magnamque temporis
partem non ut militiam, sed ut festum diem acturos bello
7 dubium facili magis an ubere, si modo aut proximas regni
Attalici opes aut veteres Lydiae Ioniaeque audierint, quas
8 non expugnatum eant, sed possessum; tantumque se avida
expectat Asia, ut etiam vocibus vocet: adeo illis odium
Romanorum incussit rapacitas proconsulum, sectio publi-
canorum, calumniae litium.

9 Sequantur se modo fortiter et colligant, quid se duce
possit efficere tantus exercitus, quem sine cuiusquam
militum auxilio suamet unius opera viderint Cappadociam
caeso rege cepisse, qui solus mortalium Pontum omnem
Scythiamque pacaverit, quam nemo ante transire tuto at-
10 que adire potuit. Nam iustitiae atque liberalitatis suae ne
ipsos milites quin experiantur testes refugere et illa indicia
habere, quod solus regum non paterna solum, verum
etiam externa regna hereditatibus propter munificentiam
adquisita possideat, Colchos, Paphlagoniam, Bosphorum.

8. Sic excitatis militibus post annos tres et XX sumpti

---

23 In 97, the proconsul in Asia, Q. Mucius Scaevola, and his
legate, P. Rutilius Rufus, had taken steps to curtail abuses, but
suffered at the hands of the offended interest group; *MRR* 2.7f.
24 The actual figure should be thirty-three years.

courage, also had desert wastes and a freezing climate, all
of which presaged a campaign of great risk and hardship. Amid such obstacles there could be no hope even of 5
plunder from a nomadic enemy that lacked not only
money but even a fixed habitation.

Now he was starting out on a different kind of war, he 6
said. For there was no climate milder than Asia's, no soil
more fertile, no place more pleasant with its numerous
cities; and much of their time they would spend not fighting but feasting, in a war one hesitated between describing
as easy or profitable, if they only heard of the wealth of 7
Attalus' neighboring kingdom or of the long-established
riches of Lydia and Ionia, which they would not storm but
appropriate; and so impatiently was Asia awaiting him that 8
she was even calling him to come—such hatred for the
Romans had been instilled in its peoples by the avarice of
their proconsuls, the public auctioning of property by the
publicani, and their fraudulent litigation.[23]

They need only to follow him bravely and be aware 9
what such a great army could achieve under his leadership, a man they had seen capture Cappadocia after killing
its king and without any of his men's help, and the only
mortal to have subdued all Pontus and Scythia, which no
one before could traverse or safely enter. Now as to his 10
fairness and generosity he did not object to having the
soldiers themselves called witnesses, and he had this as
further evidence, that he alone of kings possessed not only
the kingdoms of his forefathers but also foreign kingdoms
inherited through his generosity—Colchis, Paphlagonia
and the Bosphorus.

8. After thus stimulating the men Mithridates, twenty-
three years after taking power,[24] embarked on his Roman

2   regni in Romana bella descendit. Atque in Aegypto mortuo rege Ptolomeo ei, qui Cyrenis regnabat, Ptolomeo per
legatos regnum et uxor Cleopatra regina, soror ipsius,
3   defertur. Laetus igitur hoc solo Ptolomeus, quod sine certamine fraternum regnum recepisset, in quod subornari
et a matre Cleopatra et favore principum fratris filium
cognoverat, ceterum infestus omnibus, statim ubi Alexan-
4   driam ingressus est, fautores pueri trucidari iussit. Ipsum
quoque die nuptiarum, quibus matrem eius in matrimonium recipiebat, inter apparatus epularum et sollemnia
religionum in conplexu matris interficit atque ita torum
5   sororis caede filii eius cruentus ascendit. Post quod non
mitior in populares, qui eum in regnum vocaverant, fuit,
siquidem peregrinis militibus licentia caedis data omnia
sanguine cotidie manabant; ipsam quoque sororem filia
eius virgine per vim stuprata et in matrimonium adscita
6   repudiat. Quibus rebus territus populus in diversa labitur
7   patriamque metu mortis exul relinquit. Solus igitur in
tanta urbe cum suis relictus Ptolomeus, cum regem se non
hominum, sed vacuarum aedium videret edicto peregrinos sollicitat.
8   Quibus confluentibus obvius legatis Romanorum,
Scipioni Africano et Spurio Mummio et L. Metello, qui
9   ad inspicienda sociorum regna veniebant, procedit. Sed
quam cruentus civibus, tam ridiculus Romanis fuit. Erat
enim et vultu deformis et statura brevis et sagina ventris

---

25 We go back to the accession of Ptolemy VIII Euergetes
Physcon (145–116).   26 Diod. Sic. 33.28.1ff. This embassy
seems to belong about 140; *MRR* 1.480f. Scipio Africanus Aemi-
lianus was the general who had destroyed Carthage in 146.

wars. And in Egypt, on the death of King Ptolemy, dele-   2
gates were sent to that Ptolemy who reigned in Cyrene to
offer him both the kingdom and the queen Cleopatra, his
sister, as his wife.[25] So with this alone Ptolemy felt pleased,   3
because with no dispute he had recovered his brother's
kingdom, for which he knew his brother's son was being
groomed both by his mother Cleopatra and by the leading
citizens who supported him, but as he hated everybody he,
on entering Alexandria, immediately had the boy's sup-
porters brutally murdered. The boy himself, on the day of   4
the wedding at which he was marrying his mother, he
killed in his mother's arms amid the banquet preparations
and religious rites and thus climbed into his sister's bed
bloody from murdering her son. After that he was no more   5
lenient with the commoners who had called him to the
kingdom, for with his foreign troops given license to murder, blood was daily flowing everywhere; and he also divorced his sister, raping her virgin daughter and taking her
in marriage. Terrified by such behavior the people slipped   6
off in all directions and fearing for their lives left their
country as exiles. So left isolated with his entourage in   7
such a large city, Ptolemy, seeing himself as a king not of
a people but of empty buildings, started encouraging foreign immigrants by edict.

While these were flocking in he went out to meet the   8
Roman legates, Scipio Africanus, Spurius Mummius and
Lucius Metellus, who were coming to inspect kingdoms of
Roman allies.[26] But while cruel to his citizens, to the Ro-   9
mans he looked just ridiculous. For he had an ugly face,
short stature, and a pot belly, looking less like a man than

10 non homini, sed beluae similis. Quam foeditatem nimia
    subtilitas perlucidae vestis augebat, prorsus quasi astu in-
    spicienda praeberentur, quae omni studio occultanda
11 pudibundo viro erant. Post discessum deinde legatorum
    (quorum Africanus, dum inspicit urbem, spectaculo Alex-
    andrinis fuit) iam etiam peregrino populo invisus cum fi-
    lio, quem ex sorore susceperat, et cum uxore, matris pae-
    lice, metu insidiarum tacitus in exilium proficiscitur
    contractoque mercenario exercitu bellum sorori pariter
12 ac patriae infert. Arcessitum deinde maximum a Cyrenis
    filium, ne eum Alexandrini contra se regem crearent,
    interficit. Tunc populus statuas eius et imagines detrahit.
13 Quod factum studio sororis existimans filium, quem ex
    ea susceperat, interficit, corpusque in membra divisum et in
    cista conpositum matri die natalis eius inter epulas offerri
14 curat. Quae res non reginae tantum, verum etiam univer-
    sae civitati acerba et luctuosa fuit tantumque maerorem
    festivissimo convivio intulit, ut regia omnis repentino
15 luctu incenderetur. Verso igitur studio principum ab epu-
    lis in exsequias membra lacera populo ostendunt et quid
    sperare de rege suo debeant, filii caede demonstrant.

    9. Finito luctu orbitatis Cleopatra, cum urgeri se fra-
    terno bello videret, auxilium a Demetrio, rege Syriae, per
    legatos petit, cuius et ipsius varii et memorabiles casus
2   fuere. Namque Demetrius, sicut supra dictum est, cum
    bellum Parthis intulisset et multis congressionibus victor
    fuisset, repente insidiis circumventus amisso exercitu ca-

---

27 Possibly late 131; Diod. Sic. 34/35.14.
28 At 36.1. Demetrius returned in 129 and ruled until 125.
Phraates II was king of Parthia from 139 to 129.

an animal. His ugliness was heightened by clothing too   10
finespun and almost transparent, just as if he was putting
on display what any decent man would have done everything to hide. Then after the departure of the delegates   11
(among whom, Africanus provided a sight for the Alexandrians while he was inspecting the city) he, being now
hated even by his immigrant population and fearing a plot
on his life, slipped off into exile with a son he had had by
his sister and accompanied also by his wife, her mother's
rival, and raising a mercenary force launched an attack on
both his sister and his country. Then summoning his eldest   12
son from Cyrene, he killed him so the Alexandrians could
not make him a king to oppose him.[27] After that the people
tore down his statues and busts. Believing this was done   13
from affection for his sister, he killed the son he had by
her, dismembered his body, put it in a basket and had it
offered to the mother at her birthday feast. The affair was   14
bitterly distressing not only for the queen but the whole
city and it cast such gloom over a most joyous feast that
the whole palace was aflame with sudden grief. So with   15
the leading citizens' attention turned from feasting to a
funeral they displayed the mangled limbs to the people,
and by the son's murder showed them what they must
expect from their king.

9. When the grieving for her loss ended, Cleopatra,
since she saw she faced war with her brother, sought help
through delegates from King Demetrius of Syria, whose
own fortunes were also both varied and remarkable. For   2
Demetrius, as noted above,[28] after he had attacked the
Parthians and been victorious in many engagements, was
suddenly caught in an ambush and captured, with the loss

3   pitur. Cui Arsacides, Parthorum rex, magno et regio animo
misso in Hyrcaniam non cultum tantum regium praestitit,
sed et filiam in matrimonium dedit regnumque Syriae,
quod per absentiam eius Trypho occupaverat, restitutu-
rum promittit.

4   Post huius mortem desperato reditu non ferens captivitatem Demetrius, privatam etsi opulentam vitam per-
5   taesus, tacitus in regnum fugam meditatur. Hortator illi et
comes Callimander amicus erat, qui post captivitatem eius
a Syria per Arabiae deserta ducibus pecunia conparatis
6   Parthico habitu Babyloniam pervenerat. Sed fugientem
Phrahates, qui Arsacidae successerat, equitum celeritate
7   per conpendiosos tramites occupatum retrahit. Ut est
deductus ad regem, Callimandro quidem non tantum
venia, verum etiam praemium fidei datum, Demetrium
autem et graviter castigatum ad coniugem in Hyrcaniam
8   remittit artioribusque custodiis observari iubet. Interiecto
deinde tempore, cum fidem illi etiam suscepti liberi facerent, eodem amico comite repetita fuga est, sed pari infe-
licitate prope fines regni sui deprehenditur ac denuo per-
9   ductus ad regem ut invisus a conspectu submovetur. Tunc
quoque uxori et liberis donatus in Hyrcaniam, poenalem
sibi civitatem, remittitur talisque aureis in exprobratio-
10   nem puerilis levitatis donatur. Sed hanc Parthorum tam
mitem in Demetrium clementiam non misericordia gentis
faciebat nec respectus cognationis, sed quod Syriae reg-

---

[29] Mithridates I, of the Arsacid dynasty; see above, 36.1.3.

of his army. Arsacides, the Parthian king,[29] having a great 3
and regal spirit sent him into Hyrcania and not only provided him with a regal lifestyle but also gave him his
daughter in marriage and promised to restore to him his
kingdom of Syria, which Trypho had seized in his absence.

After this man's death Demetrius despaired of ever 4
returning, and unable to bear his captivity and weary of
private life, luxurious though it was, he secretly began to
consider fleeing to his kingdom. The man who encouraged 5
and accompanied him was his friend Callimander, who
after his capture had hired guides and come through the
Arabian deserts from Syria to Babylon in Parthian clothes.
But as he fled, Phraates, who had succeeded Arsacides, 6
took shorter roads and by bed his horsemen's speed,
caught him and brought him back. When he was brought 7
to the king, Callimander was not only pardoned but even
rewarded for his loyalty, but Demetrius, after severely
reprimanding him, he sent back to his wife in Hyrcania
and ordered him kept under stricter guard. Sometime 8
later, when having had children also earned him some
confidence, he once more ran off with the same friend, but
with similar misfortune he was apprehended almost at the
frontier of his kingdom, brought back to the king again,
and in disgust taken away from his sight. Then also re- 9
stored to his wife and children, he was sent back to Hyrcania, the community of his punishment, and presented
with golden dice to show disapproval of his puerile flight-
iness. But this humane, lenient treatment of Demetrius by 10
the Parthians came not from any innate compassion of the
race nor regard for family ties, but rather because they
were aiming at mastery of Syria and intended to use De-

num adfectabant usuri Demetrio adversus Antiochum fratrem, prout res vel tempus vel fortuna belli exegisset.

10. His auditis Antiochus occupandum bellum ratus exercitum, quem multis finitimorum bellis induraverat,
2 adversus Parthos ducit. Sed per luxuriam non minor apparatus quam militiae fuit, quippe octoginta milia armatorum secuta sunt trecenta lixarum, ex quibus cocorum pis-
3 torum maior numerus fuit. Argenti certe aurique tantum, ut etiam gregarii milites auro caligas figerent proculcarentque materiam, cuius amore populi ferro dimicant.
4 Culinarum quoque argentea instrumenta fuere, prorsus
5 quasi ad epulas, non ad bellum pergerent. Advenienti Antiocho multi orientales reges occurrere tradentes se regnaque sua cum exsecratione superbiae Parthicae. Nec
6 mora congressioni fuit. Antiochus tribus proeliis victor cum Babyloniam occupasset, Magnus haberi coepit. Itaque ad eum omnibus populis deficientibus nihil Parthis
7 reliqui praeter patrios fines fuit. Tunc Phrahates Demetrium in Syriam ad occupandum regnum cum Parthico praesidio mittit, ut eo pacto Antiochus ad sua tuenda a Parthia revocaretur. Interim, quoniam viribus non poterat, insidiis Antiochum ubique temptabat.
8 Propter multitudinem hominum exercitum suum Antiochus per civitates in hiberna diviserat, quae res exitii causa fuit. Nam cum gravari se copiarum praebitione et iniuriis militum civitates viderent, ad Parthos deficiunt et

---

30 Antiochus VII Sidetes.

31 See Diod. Sic. 34/35.15ff.

32 In the manuscripts the word "scaenicorum" ([and] entertainers) appears, deleted by Seel.

metrius against his brother Antiochus[30] as circumstances, time, or the fortunes of war required.

10. On hearing about this Antiochus, thought he should strike the first blow and led out against the Parthians an army that he had reinforced for his many wars with his neighbors.[31] But there was no less provision for luxury 2 than for war since eighty thousand soldiers were attended by three hundred thousand camp followers, most of them being cooks and bakers.[32] For sure there was so much 3 silver and gold that even the common soldiers fastened their boots with gold and were treading underfoot something from love of which people fight with iron. Cooking 4 vessels were also made of silver, as if it were for dinner, not war that they were heading. As Antiochus approached, 5 many eastern princes came to meet him, surrendering themselves and their kingdoms with curses on Parthian arrogance. There was no delaying the encounter. Victori- 6 ous in three battles, Antiochus after seizing Babylon began to be seen as "the Great." And so, with all peoples defecting to him the Parthians were left with nothing beyond their ancestral lands. Phraates then sent Demetrius into 7 Syria with a Parthian escort to seize the kingdom, so that Antiochus would thus be brought back from Parthia to defend his own territory. Meanwhile, since he could not take him by force, he was everywhere trying to catch Antiochus with a trap.

Because of his large numbers of men Antiochus had 8 distributed his army in winter quarters throughout the cities, and that brought about his downfall. For when cities saw themselves burdened with supplying provisions and being mistreated by soldiers, they defected to the Parthians and on a prearranged day all made surprise at-

die statuta omnes apud se divisum exercitum per insidias,
9 ne invicem ferre auxilia possent, adgrediuntur. Quae cum
nuntiata Antiocho essent, auxilium proximis laturus cum
ea manu, quae secum hiemabat, progreditur. In itinere
obvium regem Parthorum habuit, adversus quem fortius
10 quam exercitus eius dimicavit. Ad postremum tamen, cum
virtute hostes vincerent, metu suorum desertus occiditur,
cui Phrahates exequias regio more fecit filiamque Demetrii, quam secum Antiochus advexerat, captus amore vir-
11 ginis uxorem duxit. Paenitere deinde dimissi Demetrii
coepit; ad quem retrahendum cum turmas equitum festi-
nato misisset, Demetrium hoc ipsum metuentem iam in
regno missi invenerunt frustraque omnia conati ad regem
suum reversi sunt.

tacks on the section of the army quartered with them, so that the various divisions could not reinforce each other. When this was reported to Antiochus, he went forward to 9 assist those closest at hand with the contingent that was wintering with him. On the way he was met by the Parthian king, against whom he fought more courageously than his army did. Finally, however, when his enemies 10 were prevailing by their valor, he was deserted by his demoralized troops and killed; and Phraates gave him a royal funeral and took as his wife the daughter of Demetrius (for he had fallen in love with the girl), whom Antiochus had brought with him. He then started to regret letting 11 Demetrius go free; but when he then swiftly sent cavalry squadrons to bring him back, they found Demetrius, who feared that very thing, already in his kingdom, and after trying everything in vain they returned to their king.

LIBER XXXIX

1. Antiocho in Parthia cum exercitu deleto frater eius
Demetrius obsidione Parthorum liberatus ac restitutus in
regnum, cum omnis Syria in luctu propter amissum exer-
2 citum esset, quasi Parthica ipsius ac fratris bella, quibus
alter captus, alter occisus erat, prospere cessissent, ita
Aegypto bellum inferre statuit, regnum Aegypti Cleopatra
socru pretium auxilii adversus fratrem suum pollicente.
3 Sed dum aliena adfectat, ut adsolet fieri, propria per defectionem Syriae amisit, siquidem Antiochenses primi
duce Tryphone, execrantes superbiam regis, quae conversatione Parthicae crudelitatis intolerabilis facta erat, mox
Apameni ceteraeque civitates exemplum secutae per ab-
4 sentiam regis a Demetrio defecere. Ptolomeus quoque,
rex Aegypti, bello ab eodem petitus, cum cognovisset
Cleopatram, sororem suam, opibus Aegypti navibus inpo-
· sitis ad filiam et Demetrium generum in Syriam profu-
gisse, inmittit iuvenem quendam Aegyptium, Protarchi

---

1 See 38.9ff. This book, along with Book 40, is the only reason-
ably coherent narrative to survive for the events it covers. It has
been concluded that the ultimate source was quite good, though
again the mediation of Timagenes is suggested. See also Diod.
Sic. 34/35.24, 28f., 34, 39a; App. *Syr.* 68ff. The Syrian succession
is Demetrius II Nicator (restored 129–125); Seleucus V (125);

BOOK XXXIX

1. When Antiochus and his army were wiped out in Parthia and his brother Demetrius was released from confinement among the Parthians and restored to his kingdom, all Syria was in mourning over the loss of the army;[1] and as if his own and his brother's Parthian wars had been successful, in which one was taken prisoner and the other killed, he decided to make war on Egypt since his mother-in-law Cleopatra promised him the kingdom of Egypt as reward for help against her brother. But while trying to seize other people's possessions he, as often happens, lost his own when Syria defected; for the people of Antioch, led by Trypho, rebelled first from hatred of the king's tyrannical behavior, which had become unbearable from his contact with Parthian brutality, and soon the Apamenians and the rest of the cities followed their lead and defected from Demetrius in the king's absence. When Ptolemy, king of Egypt,[2] also under attack from the same man, learned that his sister Cleopatra had put Egyptian treasures aboard ships and fled to Syria to her daughter and son-in-law Demetrius, he sent some young Egyptian, son of the mer-

Antiochus VIII Grypos (125–96), with Cleopatra Thea (125–121); Antiochus IX Cyzicenus (115–95).

2 Ptolemy VIII Euergetes Physcon (145–116).

negotiatoris filium, qui regnum Syriae armis peteret.
5 Conposita fabula, quasi per adoptionem Antiochi regis
receptus in familiam regiam esset, nec Syris quemlibet
regem aspernantibus, ne Demetrii superbiam paterentur,
nomen iuveni Alexandri inponitur auxiliaque ab Aegypto
ingentia mittuntur.
6   Interea corpus Antiochi interfecti a rege Parthorum in
loculo argenteo ad sepulturam in Syriam remissum pervenit, quod cum ingenti studio civitatum et regis Alexandri
ad confirmandam fabulae fidem excipitur. Quae res illi
magnum favorem popularium conciliavit omnibus non
7 fictas in eo, sed veras lacrimas existimantibus. Demetrius
autem victus ab Alexandro, cum undique circumstantibus
malis premeretur, ad postremum etiam ab uxore filiisque
8 deseritur. Relictus igitur cum paucis servulis cum Tyrum
religione se templi defensurus petisset, navi egrediens
9 praefecti iussu interficitur. Alter ex filiis, Seleucus, quoniam sine matris auctoritate diadema sumpsisset, ab eadem interficitur; alter, cui propter nasi magnitudinem
cognomen Grypos fuit, rex a matre hactenus constituitur,
ut nomen regis penes filium, vis autem omnis imperii
penes matrem esset.
    2. Sed Alexander occupato Syriae regno, tumens suc-
cessu rerum, spernere iam etiam ipsum Ptolomeum, a quo
subornatus in regnum fuerat, superba insolentia coepit.
2 Itaque Ptolomeus reconciliata sororis gratia destruere
Alexandri regnum, quod odio Demetrii viribus suis adqui-
3 sierat, summis opibus instituit. Mittit igitur ingentia Grypo

---

³ The word is the Greek for "hook-nosed." He was Antiochus
VIII, king from 115 to 95.   ⁴ The year is 122.

chant Protarchus, to launch an armed attack on the kingdom of Syria. A story was concocted suggesting that he   5
had been adopted into the royal family by King Antiochus,
and since the Syrians would refuse no king to escape Demetrius' tyrannical behavior, the young man was given the
name Alexander and sent massive reinforcements from
Egypt.

Meanwhile the body of Antiochus, who had been killed   6
by the king of Parthia, arrived in a silver casket, sent back
to Syria for burial, and it was received with great emotion
by the cities and by King Alexander as confirming his story.
This won him great popular support, everyone thinking
his tears not to be fake but genuine. Demetrius, however,   7
defeated by Alexander and now afflicted with misfortune
everywhere, was finally abandoned even by his wife and
children. So left with a few slaves he made for Tyre to   8
protect himself with the sanctity of the temple, and while
leaving the ship he was killed on the prefect's orders. One   9
of his sons, Seleucus, then assumed the diadem without
his mother's authority and was killed by her; the other,
who was nicknamed Grypos from the size of his nose,[3]
was installed as king by the mother, but with the royal
title remaining with the son and regal authority with the
mother.

2. But seizing the kingdom of Syria and being flushed
with success, Alexander now began to look down even on
Ptolemy himself, by whom his accession to the kingdom
had been prepared.[4] So, reconciling with his sister, Ptol-   2
emy did all he could to destroy Alexander's kingdom,
which he had acquired through hatred for Demetrius. So   3
he sent Grypos massive auxiliary troops and his daughter

auxilia et filiam Tryphaenam Grypo nupturam, ut populos
in auxilium nepotis non societate tantum belli, verum et
4 adfinitate sua sollicitet. Nec res frustra fuit. Nam cum
omnes Grypum instructum Aegypti viribus viderent, pau-
5 latim ab Alexandro deficere coepere. Fit deinde inter reges proelium, quo victus Alexander Antiochiam profugit.
Ibi inops pecuniae, cum stipendia militibus deessent, in
templo Iovis solidum ex auro signum Victoriae tolli iubet,
facetis iocis sacrilegium circumscribens; nam Victoriam
6 commodatam sibi ab Iove esse dicebat. Interiectis deinde
diebus, cum ipsius Iovis aureum simulacrum infiniti pon-
deris tacite evelli iussisset deprehensusque in sacrilegio
concursu multitudinis esset in fugam versus, magna vi
tempestatis oppressus ac desertus a suis a latronibus capitur; perductus ad Grypum interficitur.
7   Grypos porro recuperato patrio regno externisque
periculis liberatus insidiis matris adpetitur. Quae cum
cupiditate dominationis prodito marito Demetrio et altero
filio interfecto huius quoque victoria inferiorem dignitatem suam factam doleret, venienti ab exercitatione po-
8 culum veneni obtulit. Sed Grypos praedictis iam ante insidiis, veluti pietate cum matre certaret, bibere ipsam iubet;
abnuenti instat; postremum prolato indice eam arguit,
solam defensionem sceleris superesse adfirmans, si bibat,
quod filio obtulit. Sic victa regina scelere in se verso ve-
9 neno, quod alii paraverat, extinguitur. Parta igitur regni
securitate Grypos octo annis quietem et ipse habuit et

Tryphaena in marriage, in order to induce peoples to support his grandson not only by a military alliance but also family ties. Nor was this unsuccessful. For when everyone 4 saw Grypos furnished with the resources of Egypt they began gradually to abandon Alexander. There was then a 5 battle between the kings, in which Alexander was defeated and then fled to Antioch. There, short of money and his troops without pay, he ordered the solid gold statue of Victory in the temple of Jupiter removed, cloaking his sacrilege with witty jokes: for he would say that Victory was on loan to him from Jupiter. Then some days later, 6 when he ordered the gold statue of Jupiter himself, a thing of enormous weight, to be quietly dragged off, and when, caught in the act of sacrilege, he turned to flee a gathered crowd and, overtaken by a violent storm and deserted by his men, he was captured by bandits; when brought to Grypos he was executed.

Grypos, having recovered his father's realm and being 7 free of external threats, then became a target of his mother's treachery. Although through her lust for power she had already betrayed her husband Demetrius and killed her other son, she resented seeing her station diminished by his victory, and as he was returning from exercise, she set a cup of poison before him. But Grypos, already fore- 8 warned of the plot, bade her, as if he were rivaling his mother in courtesy, to drink it herself; when she refused, he insisted; and finally bringing forward the informant he openly accused her, insisting her only defense against the crime was if she drank what she offered her son. Thus the queen, overcome by her crime recoiling on herself, died by the poison she had prepared for someone else. So, his 9 kingdom secured, Grypos both had eight years of peace

10   regno praestitit. Natus deinde illi est aemulus regni, frater
ipsius Cyzicenus, eadem matre genitus, sed ex Antiocho
patruo susceptus, quem cum veneno tollere voluisset, ut
maturius armis cum eo de regno contenderet, excitavit.

    3. Inter has regni Syriae parricidales discordias moritur
rex Aegypti Ptolomeus, regno Aegypti uxori et alteri ex
filiis quem illa legisset relicto; videlicet quasi quietior
Aegypti status quam Syriae regnum esset, cum mater al-

2   tero ex filiis electo alterum hostem esset habitura. Igitur
cum pronior in minorem filium esset, a populo conpellitur
maiorem eligere. Cui prius quam regnum daret, uxorem
ademit conpulsumque repudiare carissimam sibi sororem
Cleopatram minorem sororem Selenen ducere iubet, non
materno inter filias iudicio, cum alteri maritum eriperet,

3   alteri daret. Sed Cleopatra non tam a viro repudiata quam
a matre divortio viri dimissa Cyziceno in Syria nubit, eique
ne nudum uxoris nomen adferret, exercitum Cypri solli-

4   citatum velut dotalem ad maritum deducit. Par igitur iam
viribus fratris Cyzicenus proelium committit ac victus in

5   fugam vertitur. Tunc Antiochiam Grypos, in qua erat Cyziceni uxor Cleopatra, obsidere coepit, qua capta Tryphaena,
uxor Grypi, nihil antiquius quam sororem Cleopatram

---

    [5] Antiochus VII Sidetes (138–129).   [6] Cleopatra III and
Ptolemy IX Soter II (Lathyrus) ruled from 116 to 107.

    [7] Antiochus IX, so nicknamed because he was brought up in
Cyzicus in Bithynia; another son of Antiochus VII and Cleopatra
Thea (the Cleopatra murdered by her son Antiochus VIII Grypos,
39.2.7–8). His wife Cleopatra (IV), and her sister Cleopatra Tryphaena, were therefore cousins of both him and his brother Grypos. Cyzicenus' further adventures are mentioned in *Prol*. 40.

himself and granted it to his kingdom as well. Then a rival   10
for the kingdom appeared for him, his own brother Cyzicenus, born of the same mother but adopted by his uncle
Antiochus,[5] and in trying to remove him with poison, he
only provoked him all the sooner to armed struggle for the
kingdom.

3. During these murderous schisms in the kingdom of
Syria King Ptolemy of Egypt died, leaving the kingdom of
Egypt to his wife and whichever of their two sons she
might choose,[6] as if indeed the situation would be more
settled in Egypt than Syria, when the mother in choosing
one of the sons would have the other as an enemy! Now,   2
although she leaned more toward the younger son, she was
forced by the people to choose the elder. Before she gave
him the kingdom, she took away his wife, and forcing to
him divorce his sister Cleopatra whom he dearly loved
ordered him to marry his younger sister Selene, no moth-
erly decision for her daughters, since she was taking a
husband from one to give to the other. But Cleopatra, not   3
so much repudiated by her husband as dismissed with a
divorce by her mother, married Cyzicenus in Syria,[7] and
not to bring him only the bare title of wife, she also brought
an army procured from Cyprus as dowry for her husband.
So being then a match for his brother, Cyzicenus commit-   4
ted to battle and when defeated turned to flight. Then   5
Grypos began to besiege Antioch, where Cyzicenus' wife
Cleopatra could be found, and when it was taken Tryphaena,[8] the wife of Grypos, ordered nothing to take pre-

[8] More correctly (Cleopatra) Tryphaena, married to Antiochus IX Cyzicenus from 115 to 112.

requiri iussit, non ut captivae opem ferret, sed ne effugere captivitatis mala posset, quae sui aemulatione in hoc potissimum regnum invaserit hostique sororis nubendo hostem

6 se eius effecerit. Tunc peregrinos exercitus in certamina fratrum adductos, tum repudiatam a fratre contra matris

7 voluntatem extra Aegyptum nuptam accusat. Contra Grypos orare, ne tam foedum facinus facere cogatur. A nullo umquam maiorum suorum inter tot domestica, tot externa bella post victoriam in feminas saevitum, quas sexus ipse et periculis bellorum et saevitiae victorum exi-

8 mat; in hac vero praeter commune bellantium fas accedere necessitudinem sanguinis; quippe ipsius, quae tam cruente saeviat, sororem equidem germanam esse, suam vero consobrinam, liberorum deinde communium mater-

9 teram. His tot necessitudinibus sanguinis adicit superstitionem templi, quo abdita profugerit, tantoque religiosius colendos sibi deos, quo magis his propitiis ac faventibus vicisset; tum neque occisa illa virium se quicquam Cyzi-

10 ceno dempturum, nec servaturum reddita. Sed quanto Grypos abnuit, tanto soror muliebri pertinacia accenditur, rata non misericordiae haec verba, sed amoris esse. Itaque

11 vocatis ipsa militibus mittit qui sororem confoderent. Qui ut in templum intraverunt, cum evellere eam non possent, manus amplexantis deae simulacrum praeciderunt. Tunc Cleopatra execratione parricidarum mandata violatis nu-

12 minibus ultione sui decedit. Nec multo post repetita proelii congressione victor Cyzicenus uxorem Grypi Tryphae-

·

cedence over finding her sister Cleopatra, not to help the
captive but so she should not escape the miseries of captivity, since it was as her rival that she had entered this par-
ticular kingdom and in marrying her sister's enemy had
made herself *her* enemy. Then she accused her of bringing   6
foreign armies into a dispute between brothers, and then,
after being repudiated by her brother, of marrying outside
Egypt against her mother's wishes. Grypos, however,   7
begged not to be forced into such a terrible crime. By
none of his ancestors, amid so many domestic and so many
foreign wars, had cruelty ever been inflicted on women
after a victory, their sex itself sufficing to spare them the
perils of war and savagery of victors; and in *her* case, in- 8
deed, apart from the ethical code of combatants, there was
also a blood relationship; for the object of her vindictive
fury was her own sister, his cousin, and then also aunt to
the children they shared. To all these family ties he added   9
awe for the temple where she sought refuge, saying its
gods must be all the more respected by him for his victory
came through their favor and support; and then by killing
her he would not be weakening Cyzicenus' strength, nor
would he be supporting it by returning her. But the more   10
Grypos refused, the more the sister was fired with female
obstinacy, thinking these comments arose not from pity
but love. So she personally summoned the soldiers and
sent men to run her sister through. When these entered   11
the temple and were unable to drag her out, they hacked
off her hands as she clung to the goddess's statue. Then,
cursing her assassins and calling for revenge for her death,
Cleopatra died. And not much later, victorious in a second   12
battle, Cyzicenus captured Grypos' wife Tryphaena, who

nam, quae paulo ante sororem interfecerat, capit eiusque
supplicio uxoris manibus parentavit.

4. At in Aegypto Cleopatra cum gravaretur socio regni,
filio Ptolomeo, populum in eum incitat, abductaque ei
Selene uxore eo indignius, quod ex Selene iam duos filios
habebat, exulare cogit, arcessito minore filio Alexandro et
2 rege in locum fratris constituto. Nec filium regno expulisse
contenta bello Cypri exulantem persequitur. Vnde pulso
interficit ducem exercitus sui, quod vivum eum e manibus
emisisset, quamquam Ptolomeus verecundia materni
3 belli, non viribus minor ab insula recessisset. Igitur Alexander territus hac matris crudelitate et ipse eam relinquit,
periculoso regno securam ac tutam vitam anteponens.
4 Cleopatra vero timens, ne maior filius Ptolomeus a Cyziceno ad recuperandam Aegyptum auxiliis iuvaretur, ingentia Grypo auxilia et Selenen uxorem, nupturam hosti
5 prioris mariti, mittit Alexandrumque filium per legatos in
regnum revocat; cui cum occultatis insidiis exitium machi-
naretur, occupata ab eodem interficitur spiritumque non
6 fato, sed parricidio dedit; digna prorsus hac mortis infamia, quae et matrem toro expulit et duas filias viduas al-
terno fratrum matrimonio fecit et filio alteri in exilium
acto bellum intulit, alteri erepto regno exitium per insidias
machinata est.

5. Sed nec Alexandro caedes tam nefanda inulta fuit.
Nam ubi primum conpertum est scelere filii matrem inter-

---

9 Cleopatra III and Ptolemy X Alexander ruled from 107 to
101; the latter ruled with Cleopatra Berenice from 101 to 88; then
Ptolemy IX Soter II returned and ruled until 81.

10 In addition to the immediately preceding narrative, see
38.8.5, 11.

had recently murdered her sister, and executing her appeased his wife's shades.

4. Now in Egypt Cleopatra, unhappy with sharing the kingdom with her son Ptolemy, incited the people against him, and after taking his wife Selene from him—all the more cruel because he already had two children by Selene—she drove him into exile, summoning her younger son Alexander and making him king in place of his brother.[9] Not satisfied even with driving her son from his kingdom she persecuted him with war when he was in exile in Cyprus. When he was driven from there she executed the leader of her own army for allowing to him slip through his hands alive, although Ptolemy (ashamed to fight his mother and not from lack of strength) had left the island. So Alexander, frightened by such ruthlessness on his mother's part, also abandoned her, preferring a secure and stable life to a perilous throne. Cleopatra then, fearing her elder son Ptolemy might have help from Cyzicenus to recover Egypt, sent to Grypos massive reinforcements and his wife Selene, who was to marry her former husband's enemy, and through legates she had her son Alexander recalled to the kingdom; but when caught secretly plotting against his life, she was killed by him and she surrendered her life not to fate but parricide. It was an infamous death that she certainly deserved—she had driven her mother from her marriage, made two daughters widows by marrying them to their brothers in turn, made war on one son after driving him into exile, and treacherously plotted the other's death after robbing him of his throne.[10]

5. But neither did Alexander escape punishment for so foul a murder. For as soon as it became known that the queen had died by her son's murderous hand, he was

fectam, concursu populi in exilium agitur revocatoque
Ptolomeo regnum redditur, qui neque cum matre bellum
gerere voluisset, neque a fratre armis repetere, quod prior
possedisset.

2   Dum haec aguntur, frater eius ex paelice susceptus, cui
pater Cyrenarum regnum testamento reliquerat, herede
3 populo Romano instituto decedit. Iam enim fortuna Romana porrigere se ad orientalia regna, non contenta Italiae terminis, coeperat. Itaque et ea pars Libyae provincia
facta est; postea Creta Ciliciaque piratico bello perdomi-
4 tae in formam provinciae rediguntur. Quo facto et Syriae
et Aegypti regna Romana vicinitate artata, quae incrementa de finitimis bellis quaerere solebant, adempto
vagandi arbitrio vires suas in perniciem mutuam conver-
5 terunt, adeo ut adsiduis proeliis consumpti in contemptum finitimorum venerint praedaeque Arabum genti,
6 inbelli antea, fuerint; quorum rex Herotimus fiducia sep-
tingentorum filiorum, quos ex paelicibus susceperat, divisis exercitibus nunc Aegyptum, nunc Syriam infestabat
magnumque nomen Arabum viribus finitimorum exsan-
guibus fecerat.

driven into exile by a revolt of the people, Ptolemy was recalled, and the throne was restored to him, since he had been willing neither to fight a war with his mother nor recover from his brother by force what he had earlier possessed.

In the course of these events, his brother, who was born 2 of a concubine, died, and when left the kingdom of Cyrene in his father's will he had appointed as heirs the Roman people.[11] For by now Roman fortune, no longer content 3 with being confined to Italy had begun to reach out to the eastern kingdoms. So this part of Libya also became a province; then Crete and Cilicia, conquered in the war with the pirates, were reduced to provinces. After that 4 both the Syrian and Egyptian kingdoms, cramped by their Roman neighbor, often tried to extend their territories through wars with their neighbors, but as their freedom of movement became more restricted, they turned their strength to destroying each other, to the point that, ex- 5 hausted from incessant battles they became despised by their neighbors and fell prey to the previously unwarlike Arabic race. Their king Herotimus, confident in seven 6 hundred sons that he had had by his concubines, divided his armies, overran Egypt at one time, and Syria at another and had made great the Arab name by draining the strength of his neighbors.[12]

[11] In 74. Crete and Cilicia were part of Pompey's settlement of the East in 63, ratified in 59. Cyprus was not annexed until 58/7.

[12] Herotimus was probably Aretas III, king of the Nabataeans (capital Petra), who harassed both Syria and Egypt for two decades, until forced to make peace by Pompey's lieutenant Scaurus in 62.

LIBER XL

1. Mutuis fratrum odiis et mox filiis inimicitiis parentum
succedentibus cum inexpiabili bello et reges et regnum
Syriae consumptum esset, ad externa populus auxilia
concurrit peregrinosque reges sibi circumspicere coepit.
2 Itaque cum pars Mithridatem Ponticum, pars Ptolomeum
ab Aegypto arcessendum censeret, occurreretque quod et
Mithridates inplicitus bello Romano esset, Ptolomeus
3 quoque hostis semper fuisset Syriae, omnes in Tigranen,
regem Armeniae, consensere, instructum praeter domesticas vires et Parthica societate et Mithridatis adfinitate.
4 Igitur accitus in regnum Syriae per X et VIII annos tran-
quillissimo regno potitus est; neque bello alium lacessere
neque lacessitus inferre alii bellum necesse habuit.

2. Sed sicut ab hostibus tuta Syria fuit, ita terrae motu
vastata est, quo centum septuaginta milia hominum et
multae urbes perierunt. Quod prodigium mutationem re-
2 rum portendere aruspices responderunt. Igitur Tigrane a

---

1 See Book 39 n. 1. The brothers are Grypos and Cyzicenus
(39.1ff.); no fewer than six claimants followed their deaths in 96
and 95, respectively, until Tigranes (Bickerman 160). Tigranes II
was king of Armenia circa 95 to 55, and ruler of the Syrian Kingdom from 83 to 69; then Lucullus replaced him with Antiochus
XIII Asiaticus (*MRR* 2.133). He, in turn, experienced varying
fortunes until Pompey removed him in 64 (*MRR* 2.163f.). For

BOOK XL

1. With mutual hatreds growing among the brothers and then soon between sons who were inheriting their parents' enmities, and since the kings and kingdom of Syria had been consumed with implacable war, people sought assistance from abroad and began to look around for foreign kings for themselves.[1] So since some were for inviting 2 Mithridates of Pontus, some Ptolemy from Egypt, and they also knew that Mithridates was embroiled in war with Rome and also that Ptolemy had always been an enemy of Syria, everyone agreed on Tigranes, king of Armenia, who 3 apart from his own domestic power had the further advantage of a Parthian alliance and a family tie with Mithridates. So he was summoned to the throne of Syria and 4 ruled his kingdom very peacefully for eighteen years; and he was obliged neither to attack anyone nor defend himself against anyone.

2. But while Syria was secure against enemies, it was also devastated by an earthquake, in which a hundred and seventy thousand people and many cities perished. This prodigious event foretold a change in circumstances according to the soothsayers. Now after Tigranes' defeat by 2

Mithridates see, above, Book 38. The Egyptian monarch was still (until 81) Ptolemy IX Soter II. See App. *Syr.* 48f.

Lucullo victo rex Syriae Antiochus, Cyziceni filius, ab eo-
3 dem Lucullo appellatur. Sed quod Lucullus dederat,
postea ademit Pompeius, qui poscenti regnum respondit
ne volenti quidem Syriae, nedum recusanti daturum se
regem, qui X et VIII annos, quibus Tigranes Syriam tenuit,
in angulo Ciliciae latuerit, victo autem eodem Tigrane a
4 Romanis alieni operis praemia postulet. Igitur ut habenti
regnum non ademerit, ita quo cesserit Tigrani, non daturum, quod tueri nesciat, ne rursus Syriam Iudaeorum et
5 Arabum latrociniis infestam reddat. Atque ita Syriam in
provinciae formam redegit, paulatimque Oriens Romanorum discordia consanguineorum regum factus est.

Lucullus, King Antiochus of Syria, son of Cyzicenus, was deemed king by that same Lucullus. But what Lucullus 3 had granted was later taken from him by Pompey who, when he claimed the kingdom, replied that even if Syria wanted him he would not install him as king, and he certainly would not if it opposed him; in the eighteen years that Tigranes ruled Syria, he said, he had lain hidden in a corner of Cilicia, but when that same Tigranes was defeated by the Romans he came demanding the rewards of another's efforts. So since he had not deprived him of the 4 kingdom he held, he said, he would not give him a kingdom that he had ceded to Tigranes and which he could not defend, for fear of his again exposing it to the marauding of Jews and Arabs. And so he reduced Syria to a regular 5 province, and gradually the East became Roman territory through the quarreling of its blood-related kings.

LIBER XLI

1. Parthi, penes quos velut divisione orbis cum Romanis
facta nunc Orientis imperium est, Scytharum exules fuere.
2 Hoc etiam ipsorum vocabulo manifestatur, nam Scythico
3 sermone exules "parthi" dicuntur. Hi et Assyriorum et
Medorum temporibus inter Orientis populos obscurissimi
4 fuere. Postea quoque, cum imperium Orientis a Medis ad
Persas translatum est, veluti vulgus sine nomine praeda
5 victorum fuere. Postremum Macedonibus triumphato
6 Oriente servierunt, ut cuivis mirum videatur ad tantam
eos felicitatem per virtutem provectos, ut imperent gentibus, sub quarum imperio veluti servile vulgus fuere.

7   A Romanis quoque trinis bellis per maximos duces flo-
rentissimis temporibus lacessiti soli ex omnibus gentibus
8 non pares solum, verum etiam victores fuere; quamquam
plus gloriae est inter Assyria et Medica Persicaque memo-
rata olim regna et opulentissimum illud mille urbium Bac-

---

1 It is supposed that Trogus' sources for Parthian (and Indian)
history were Timagenes, Posidonius, and Apollodorus of Ar-
temita. Romans of the late Republic and Augustan era had par-
ticular reason to be interested in the Parthians, who continued to
be a concern through the following centuries. For previous mention of the Parthians, see 2.1.3, 3.6; 11.15.2; 12.4.12; 13.4.23;
36.1.2ff.; 38.9.2ff.; 39.1.1ff.

244

BOOK XLI

1. The Parthians, between whom and the Romans the world is more or less divided, and who now rule the East, were exiles from Scythia.[1] This is clear even from their name, for in the Scythian language exiles are called "Parthi." In the time of both the Assyrians and the Medes they were the most obscure all the peoples of the east. Later on too, when power in the East shifted from the Medes to the Persians, they were merely a nameless crowd and prey for their conquerors. Finally they were subject to the Macedonians after their eastern conquest, so one might be surprised that by their valor they achieved such success as to dominate peoples under whose rule they had been only a servile horde.[2]

Attacked in three wars by the Romans with their greatest leaders when these were at height of their power, only they of all the races came off not just on equal terms but even victorious; yet greater still is their renown for having been able to arise among the once-renowned kingdoms of Assyria, Media and Persia and that opulent Bactrian Em-

[2] On the Parthians and their empire, see U. Ellerbrock, *The Parthians: The Forgotten Empire* (London, 2021); V. S. Curtis and S. Stewart, *The Age of the Parthians* (London, 2007).

trianum imperium emergere potuisse quam longinqua
9 bella vicisse, praeterea cum gravibus Scythicis et vicinali-
bus bellis· adsidue vexati variis periculorum certaminibus
10 urgerentur. Hi domesticis seditionibus Scythia pulsi solitudines inter Hyrcaniam et Dahas et Areos et ‹Sparnos›
11 et Margianos furtim occupavere. Fines deinde non inter-
cedentibus primo finitimis, postea etiam prohibentibus in
tantum protulere, ut non inmensa tantum ac profunda
camporum, verum etiam praerupta collium montiumque
12 ardua occupaverint. Ex quo fit, ut Parthiae pleraque finium aut aestus aut frigoris magnitudo possideat, quippe
cum montes nix et campos aestus infestet.

2. Administratio gentis post defectionem Macedonici
2 imperii sub regibus fuit. Proximus maiestati regum pro-
bulorum ordo est; ex hoc duces in bello, ex hoc in pace
3 rectores habent. Sermo his inter Scythicum Medicumque
4 medius et utrisque mixtus. Vestis olim sui moris; postea-
quam accessere opes, ut Medis perlucida ac fluida. Armo-
5 rum patrius ac Scythicus mos. Exercitum non, ut aliae
gentes, liberorum, sed maiorem partem servitiorum habent, quorum vulgus nulli manumittendi potestate per-
missa ac per hoc omnibus servis nascentibus in dies cres-
cit. Hos pari ac liberos suos cura et equitare et sagittare
6 magna industria docent. Locupletissimus ut quisque est,

---

3 Bactria, approximately today's Afghanistan, was ruled by a
Greek-Macedonian elite for two centuries after Alexander the
Great's conquest; very prosperous, it held several cities named
after him and issued fine coins portraying its kings. One,
Menander (later 2nd century), ruled much of northern India
and is commemorated in the Buddhist work *The Dialogues of*

pire of a thousand cities,[3] than for their success in distant
wars; and they were also constantly plagued by serious   9
wars with Scythians and other neighbors and hard pressed
in various perilous situations. Driven from Scythia during   10
civil discord they furtively occupied the deserts bordered
by Hyrcania, the Dahae, Arei, Sparni[4] and Margiani. They   11
then advanced their frontiers, at first with no obstruction
from their neighbors, and later even against their opposi-
tion, to the extent of occupying not only vast, low-lying
plains but even steep hills and towering mountain ranges.
This is why most of Parthia has extremes of either heat or   12
cold, for there is always snow on the mountains and heat
on the plains.

2. Government of their people after their defection
from the Macedonian Empire lay with kings. Next in im-   2
portance to the kings is a rank of councilors; from them
they draw generals in war and from them magistrates in
peace. Their language is midway between Scythian and   3
Medic, and is a mixture of both. They once had their own   4
mode of dress; with rising prosperity it became like that
of the Medes, transparent and loose. Their weaponry is
native Scythian. They have an army not, like other peo-   5
ples, of free men, but mostly of slaves, and since no man-
umission is allowed and all slave children are therefore
born to a lifetime of slavery, their number is daily increasing. On these they bestow as much care as on their own
children and take great pains to teach them horsemanship
and archery. Each man's wealth determines the number   6

King Milinda.   [4] Or "Apartani" with Ruehl (variant read-
ings *sparthanos* and *hyparthanos*).

ita plures in bella equites regi suo praebet. Denique Antonio bellum Parthis inferenti cum L milia equitum occur-
rerent, soli CCCC liberi fuere.

7   Comminus in acie proeliari aut obsessas expugnare urbes nesciunt. Pugnant aut procurrentibus equis aut terga
dantibus; saepe etiam fugam simulant, ut incautiores ad-
8 versum vulnera insequentes habeant. Signum his in proelio non tuba, sed tympano datur. Nec pugnare diu possunt;
ceterum intolerandi forent, si quanta his est impetus vis,
9 tanta et perseverantia esset. Plerumque in ipso ardore certaminis proelia deserunt ac paulo post pugnam ex fuga
repetunt, ut, cum maxime vicisse te putes, tunc tibi discri-
10 men subeundum sit. Munimentum ipsis equisque loricae
plumatae sunt, quae utrumque toto corpore tegunt. Auri
argentique nullus nisi in armis usus.

3. Vxores dulcedine variae libidinis singuli plures ha-
2 bent, nec ulla delicta adulterio gravius vindicant. Quamobrem feminis non convivia tantum virorum, verum etiam
3 conspectum interdicunt. Carne non nisi venatibus quae-
4 sita vescuntur. Equis omni tempore vectantur; illis bella,
illis convivia, illis publica ac privata officia obeunt; super
illos ire, consistere, mercari, colloqui. Hoc denique discrimen inter servos liberosque est, quod servi pedibus, liberi
5 non nisi equis incedunt. Sepultura vulgo aut avium aut
canum laniatus est; nuda demum ossa terra obruunt.

---

5 In 36 (cf. 42.5.3).

6 The proverbial "Parthian shot" derives from this practice of
firing while in apparent retreat.

7 The Greek and then Roman term for the mail-clad Parthian
cavalry was "cataphracts;" similar armor was used by some trans-

of horsemen he provides his king for war service. Indeed when Antony launched his war on the Parthians and faced fifty thousand cavalry, only four hundred of them were free men.[5]

Of hand-to-hand combat or besieging and storming 7 cities they know nothing. They fight with horses either charging or retreating; and they also often feign flight to put a pursuing enemy off guard against their weapons.[6] Their signal in battle is given not on a trumpet but a drum. 8 They cannot fight for long, either; but they would be irresistible if their stamina matched the violence of their attack. They usually quit battles right in the heat of the 9 fray and a little later renew the fight after retreating, so that it is just when you think you have won that you must face the critical moment. Armor for them and their horses 10 is corselets covered with scales that completely cover the bodies of both.[7] Gold and silver is used for nothing other than weapons.

3. For the pleasure of sexual variety, they have several wives, and no crimes do they punish more severely than adultery. So they forbid women not only to dine among 2 men but even to be seen by them. The only meat they eat 3 comes from hunting. They are constantly riding horses; on 4 them they go to war, to feasts, and to all private and public functions; and on them they travel, halt, conduct business and hold conversations. In fact, the only clear distinction between their slaves and free men is that slaves travel on foot and free men only on horses. Burial usually means the 5 corpse being torn apart by birds or dogs; when bare the

Danubian peoples fighting Rome, and the Romans in turn later adopted the style for some of their own horsed units.

6 In superstitionibus atque cura deorum praecipua omnibus
7 veneratio est. Ingenia genti tumida, seditiosa, fraudolenta,
procacia; quippe violentiam viris, mansuetudinem mulie-
8 ribus adsignant. Semper aut in externos aut in domesticos
motus inquieti, natura taciti, ad faciendum quam ad di-
cendum promptiores; proinde secunda adversaque silen-
9 tio tegunt. Principibus metu, non pudore parent. In libi-
10 dinem proiecti, in cibum parci. Fides dicti promissique
nulla, nisi quatenus expedit.

4. Post mortem Alexandri Magni cum inter successores eius Orientis regna dividerentur, nullo Macedonum
dignante Parthorum imperium Staganori, externo socio,
2 traditur. Postea diductis Macedonibus in bellum civile
cum ceteris superioris Asiae populis Eumenen secuti sunt,
3 quo victo ad Antigonum transierunt. Post hunc a Nicatore
Seleuco ac mox ab Antiocho et successoribus eius possessi,
a cuius pronepote Seleuco primum defecere primo Punico bello, L. Manlio Vulsone M. Atilio Regulo consulibus.
4 Huius defectionis inpunitatem illis duorum fratrum regum, Seleuci et Antiochi, discordia dedit, qui dum invicem eripere sibi regnum volunt, persequi defectores omi-
5 serunt. Eodem tempore etiam Theodotus, mille urbium
Bactrianarum praefectus, defecit regemque se appellari
iussit, quod exemplum secuti totius Orientis populi a
Macedonibus defecere.
6 Erat eo tempore Arsaces, vir sicut incertae originis, ita

---

8 The Parthians, like the Persians, were Zoroastrians.

9 So the text; his name was in fact Stasanor (see 13.4.23).

10 At Diod. Sic. 19.29, they appear in 317 fighting with Antigonus against Eumenes.   11 The year is 256.

bones are finally buried.[8] In religion and divine worship 6
they are all very observant. The temperament of the race 7
of is impetuous, truculent, devious and insolent; in men
they consider violence appropriate, in females meekness.
They are always impatient, whether with strangers or their 8
own people, but by nature are taciturn, more ready to act
than talk; so their successes and failures they cloak in silence. Leaders they follow from fear, not respect. In sexual 9
pleasures they are unrestrained, in food sparing. There is 10
no integrity in word and promise unless it serves their
interests.

4. After the death of Alexander the Great when the
Eastern kingdoms were being partitioned among the successors, since no Macedonian felt the Parthian Empire
worthy of him it was given to Staganor, a foreign ally.[9]
When the Macedonians were later divided in a civil war, 2
the Parthians along with the other peoples of Upper Asia
followed Eumenes, and after his defeat went over to Antigonus.[10] After him they were under the power of Seleu- 3
cus Nicator and later under Antiochus and his successors,
and it was against Antiochus' great-grandson Seleucus that
they first revolted during the first Punic War, in the consul-
ship of L. Manlius Vulso and M. Atilius Regulus.[11] They 4
gained impunity for this revolt through the wrangling of
the two royal brothers Seleucus and Antiochus, who in
trying to wrest the kingdom from each other failed to
pursue the defectors. At this same time Theodotus, gov- 5
ernor of a thousand Bactrian cities, also rebelled and demanded to be declared king, and following his example
peoples throughout the east defected from Macedonia.

There was at that time one Arsaces who, though of 6

7 virtutis expertae. Hic solitus latrociniis et rapto vivere
   accepta opinione Seleucum a Gallis in Asia victum, solutus
   regis metu, cum praedonum manu Parthos ingressus praefectum eorum Andragoran oppressit sublatoque eo impe-
8 rium gentis invasit. Non magno deinde post tempore
   Hyrcanorum quoque regnum occupavit, atque ita duarum
   civitatium imperio praeditus grandem exercitum parat
9 metu cum Seleuci et Theodoti, Bactrianorum regis. Sed
   cito morte Theodoti metu liberatus cum filio eius, et ipso
   Theodoto, foedus ac pacem fecit, nec multo post cum
   Seleuco rege ad defectores persequendos veniente con-
10 gressus victor fuit; quem diem Parthi exinde sollemnem
   velut initium libertatis observant.

   5. Revocato deinde Seleuco novis motibus in Asiam
   dato laxamento regnum Parthicum format, militem legit,
2 castella munit, civitates firmat; urbem quoque nomine
   Daram in monte Apaorteno condit, cuius loci ea condicio
   est, ut neque munitius quicquam esse neque amoenius
3 possit. Ita enim et praeruptis rupibus undique cingitur, ut
   tutela loci nullis defensoribus egeat, et soli circumiacentis
4 tanta ubertas, ut propriis opibus expleatur; fontium ac sil-
   varum ea copia est, ut et aquarum abundantia inrigetur et
5 venationum voluptatibus exornetur. Sic Arsaces quaesito
   simul constitutoque regno non minus memorabilis Parthis
   quam Persis Cyrus, Macedonibus Alexander, Romanis
6 Romulus matura senectute decedit, cuius memoriae hunc
   honorem Parthi tribuerunt, ut omnes exinde reges suos
7 Arsacis nomine nuncupent. Huius filius et successor regni,

---

[12] His regnal dates are circa 238 to 215.
[13] Seleucus II (246–225).

obscure lineage, was also of proven courage. He, a man   7
used to a life of robbery and banditry, had heard that Seleucus had been defeated by the Gauls in Asia, and now
having no fear of the king he entered Parthia with a band
of robbers, defeated their governor Andragoras, and after
removing him took over his people.[12] Not much later he   8
then also seized the kingdom of Hyrcania, and being thus
furnished with the power of two peoples he raised a large
army from fear of both Seleucus and Theodotus, king of
Bactria. But when he was quickly freed of that fear by   9
Theodotus' death, he made a peace treaty with his son,
who was also named Theodotus, and not long afterward
fought a battle with King Seleucus,[13] who was coming to
suppress the rebellion, and he emerged the victor; that   10
day the Parthians have since then observed as the start of
their liberty.

5. When Seleucus was then recalled to Asia by fresh
troubles, Arsaces, given this respite, settled the Parthian
Kingdom, levied troops, built fortresses, and strengthened
his cities; he also founded a city called Dara on Mount   2
Apaortenon, its features such that nothing could be either
more secure or more attractive. For it is so surrounded by   3
sheer cliffs on all sides as to need no defending troops, and
such is the fertility of the surrounding soil that it is full of
local produce; and springs and woodlands are so abundant   4
that it has a plentiful water supply and is also provided
with pleasures of the hunt. So after both acquiring and   5
settling the kingdom Arsaces died at an advanced age, no
less renowned a figure for the Parthians than Cyrus is for
the Persians, Alexander for the Macedonians, and Romulus for the Romans; and the Parthians so revered his mem-   6
ory that they called all their following kings Arsaces. His   7

Arsaces et ipse nomine, adversus Antiochum, Seleuci filium, centum milibus peditum et XX milibus equitum instructum mira virtute pugnavit; ad postremum in societa-
8 tem eius adsumptus est. Tertius Parthis rex Priapatius fuit,
sed et ipse Arsaces dictus. Nam sicut supra dictum est,
omnes reges suos hoc nomine, sicuti Romani Caesares
9 Augustosque, cognominavere. Hic actis in regno XV annis
decessit relictis duobus filiis, Mithridate et Phrahate. Quorum maior Phrahates, more gentis heres regni, Mardos,
validam gentem, bello domuit nec multo post decessit plu-
10 ribus filiis relictis, quibus praeteritis fratri potissimum
Mithridati, insignis virtutis viro, reliquit imperium, plus
regio quam patrio deberi nomini ratus potiusque patriae
quam liberis consulendum.

6. Eodem ferme tempore, sicut in Parthis Mithridates,
ita in Bactris Eucratides, magni uterque viri, regna ineunt.
2 Sed Parthorum fortuna felicior ad summum hoc duce
3 imperii fastigium eos perduxit. Bactriani autem per varia
bella iactati non regnum tantum, verum etiam libertatem
amiserunt, siquidem Sogdianorum et Arachotorum et
Drancarum et Areorum Indorumque bellis fatigati ad
postremum ab invalidioribus Parthis velut exsangues op-
4 pressi sunt. Multa tamen Eucratides bella magna virtute
gessit, quibus adtritus cum obsidionem Demetrii, regis
Indorum, pateretur, cum CCC militibus LX milia hostium

---

[14] He died circa 190 and was succeeded by Phriapitius, who
ruled until 176; Phraates I reigned circa 176 to 171, and Mithridates I reigned circa 170 to 139 (cf. Diod. Sic. 33.18).

[15] Eucratides I (ca. 171–145). His plentiful coinage includes
some of the finest portraits in classical iconography.

son and successor to the kingdom, also named Arsaces,[14] fought with remarkable courage against Antiochus, Seleucus' son, who was equipped with a force of one hundred thousand infantry and twenty thousand cavalry; and he was finally accepted as his ally. The third Parthian king was 8 Priapatius, but he was also himself called Arsaces; for, as noted above, the Parthians gave all their kings this name, just as the Romans have used the name Caesar and Augustus for theirs. This one died after a fifteen-year reign, 9 leaving two sons, Mithridates and Phraates. The elder, Phraates, who, after their custom became heir to the kingdom, defeated the powerful Mardi nation and died soon after, leaving several sons. but passing over these he in- 10 stead left the kingdom to his brother Mithridates, a man of great integrity, believing his regal obligations more important than his paternal and his country more than his children.

6. At about the same time, while Mithridates was entering his rule in Parthia, Eucratides was starting his in Bactria,[15] both of them great men. Parthian fortunes, 2 greater under this king, took them to the height of their power. The Bactrians, however, shaken by various wars, 3 lost not only their empire but even their freedom; for exhausted after wars with the Sogdians, Arachosians, Drancae, Arei, and Indians, they finally fell, virtually exhausted, under a weaker people, the Parthians. Eucratides did 4 however fight some wars with great valor, and though he was weakened by them and faced a siege by Demetrius, king of the Indians,[16] he, by repeated sorties with three

16 Demetrius I may have reigned circa 200 to 185, Demetrius II circa 180 to 165, but they may be one and the same person.

adsiduis eruptionibus vicit. Quinto itaque mense liberatus
5 Indiam in potestatem redegit. Vnde cum se reciperet, a
filio, quem socium regni fecerat, in itinere interficitur, qui
non dissimulato parricidio, velut hostem, non patrem in-
terfecisset, et per sanguinem eius currum egit et corpus
abici insepultum iussit.
6   Dum haec apud Bactros geruntur, interim inter Parthos et Medos bellum oritur. Cum varius utriusque populi
casus fuisset, ad Postremum victoria penes Parthos fuit.
7 His viribus auctus Mithridates Mediae Bacasin praeponit,
8 ipse in Hyrcaniam proficiscitur. Vnde reversus bellum
cum Elymaeorum rege gessit, quo victo hanc quoque gentem regno adiecit imperiumque Parthorum a monte Cau-
caso multis populis in dicionem redactis usque flumen
9 Euphraten protulit. Atque ita adversa valetudine adrep-
tus, non minor Arsace proavo, gloriosa senectute decedit.

hundred men defeated sixty thousand of his enemy. So freed from the siege in its fifth month he brought India under his power. While returning from there, he was killed 5 en route by his son, whom he had made his joint ruler and who, not hiding the parricide, and as if it were an enemy, not a father, that he had killed, even drove a chariot through his blood and ordered his corpse cast aside unburied.

As this was taking place in Bactria, a war meanwhile 6 arose between the Parthians and the Medes. Although both had intermittent success, victory finally went to the Parthians. Bolstered by this strength Mithridates ap- 7 pointed Bocasis governor of Media, and he himself left for Hyrcania. Returning from there he fought a war with the 8 king of the Elymaeans, and on defeating him also added this people to his realm and advanced the Parthian Empire from the Caucasus Mountains right to the River Euphrates, bringing many peoples under his sway. And so, 9 taken by an illness, he, no less great than his great-grandfather Arsaces, died at a gloriously advanced age.

LIBER XLII

1. Post necem Mithridatis, Parthorum regis, Phrahates filius rex statuitur, qui cum inferre bellum in ultionem temptati ab Antiocho Parthici regni Syriae statuisset, Scy-
2 tharum motibus ad sua defendenda revocatur. Namque Scythae in auxilium Parthorum adversus Antiochum, Syriae regem, mercede sollicitati cum confecto bello iam supervenissent et calumnia tardius lati auxilii mercede fraudarentur, dolentes tantum itineris frustra emensum, cum vel stipendium pro vexatione vel alium hostem dari sibi poscerent, superbo responso offensi fines Parthorum
3 vastare coeperunt. Igitur Phrahates, cum adversus eos proficisceretur, ad tutelam regni reliquit Himerum quendam pueritiae sibi flore conciliatum, qui tyrannica crudelitate oblitus et vitae praeteritae et vicarii officii Babylo-
4 nios multasque alias civitates inportune vexavit. Ipse autem Phrahates exercitum Graecorum, quem bello Antiochi captum superbe crudeliterque tractaverat, in bellum secum ducit, inmemor prorsus quod hostiles eorum animos nec captivitas minuerat et insuper iniuriarum in-

---

1 Phraates II ruled from 139 to 129. Cf. Diod. Sic. 34/35.15. For Antiochus' attack, see above, 38.10.

BOOK XLII

1. After the death of Mithridates, king of the Parthians, his son Phraates was made king,[1] and after deciding to make war on Syria to avenge the attack on the kingdom of Parthia by Antiochus, he was recalled to defend his own lands by an uprising among the Scythians. For the Scythians, 2 who had been bribed to come to assist the Parthians against Antiochus, king of Syria, arrived only when the battle was already over and were cheated of their pay on the pretext that they had come too late with their support; and aggrieved at having made such a long journey for nothing they demanded to be given either payment for their trouble or another enemy, and when offended by a disdainful reply they began to plunder the lands of the Parthians. Now when Phraates went out to face them, he 3 left protecting his kingdom a certain Himerus, who in the bloom of his youth had been his lover, and he, behaving with tyrannical cruelty and forgetting both the manner of his former life and that he was a mere deputy, severely maltreated the Babylonians and many other peoples. Phraates himself, however, led into battle an army of 4 Greeks that he had captured in the war against Antiochus and treated in an offensive and brutal manner, forgetting that their hostility toward him had not been diminished by captivity and that their humiliating mistreatment had fur-

5   dignitas exacerbaverat. Itaque cum inclinatam Parthorum aciem vidissent, arma ad hostes transtulere et diu cupitam captivitatis ultionem exercitus Parthici et ipsius Phrahatis regis cruenta caede exsecuti sunt.

        2. In huius locum Artabanus, patruus eius, rex substituitur. Scythae autem contenti victoria depopulata Parthia

2   in patriam revertuntur. Sed et Artabanus bello Tochariis
3   inlato in bracchio vulneratus statim decedit. Huic Mithridates filius succedit, cui res gestae Magni cognomen dedere; quippe claritatem parentum aemulatione virtutis
4   accensus animi magnitudine supergreditur. Multa igitur bella cum finitimis magna virtute gessit multosque popu-
5   los Parthico regno addidit. Sed et cum Scythis prospere
6   aliquotiens dimicavit ultorque iniuriae parentum fuit. Ad postremum Artoadisti, Armeniorum regi, bellum intulit.
7   Sed quoniam in Armeniam transitum facimus, origo
8   eius paulo altius repetenda est. Neque enim silentio regnum tantum praeteriri fas est cum fines post Parthiam
9   omnium regnorum magnitudinem superent, siquidem Armenia a Cappadocia usque mare Caspium undecies centum milia patet, sed in latitudinem milia passuum sep-
10   tingenta porrigitur. Condita est autem ab Armenio, Iasonis Thessali comite, quem cum perditum propter insignem periculosamque regno suo virtutem Pelias rex cuperet, denuntiata militia in Colchos abire iubet pellemque arietis memorabilem gentibus reportare, sperans interitum viri aut ex periculis tam longae navigationis aut

---

    2 Artabanus I (ca. 128–124); Mithridates II (ca. 124–88).

    3 Justin's name for Artavasdes, who died circa 120. His son was Tigranes I (120–95), and grandson Tigranes II (95–ca. 55).

ther sharpened it. So when they saw the Parthian line give 5
way they defected to the enemy and took long-desired
revenge for their captivity by a bloody massacre of the
Parthian army and King Phraates himself.

2. In his place Artabanus,[2] his uncle, was made king.
The Scythians, satisfied with their victory, pillaged Parthia
and went home. But after making war on the Tocharii and 2
receiving a wound to his arm Artabanus also immediately
died. His son Mithridates succeeded him, whose achieve- 3
ments brought him the title "the Great"; for burning with
ambition to emulate the fame of his ancestors he surpassed them in greatness of spirit. So he fought many wars 4
with his neighbors with great courage and added many
peoples to the Parthian Empire. But he also had several 5
successful campaigns against the Scythians and avenged
the injury inflicted on his ancestors. Finally he made war 6
on Artoadistes, king of the Armenians.[3]

But since we are now making a transition to Armenia, 7
its origins need a little more examination. For it is not right 8
for such a great kingdom to be passed over in silence when
its lands exceed all kingdoms after Parthia, since Armenia, 9
from Cappadocia to the Caspian Sea, stretches eleven
hundred miles, but in breadth seven hundred miles. It was 10
founded by Armenius, a companion of Jason the Thessalian, whom King Pelias wanted killed because his remarkable courage threatened his rule; he ordered Jason to
take on a military expedition to Colchis[4] and bring back
the world-famous ram's fleece, hoping for his death either
in the perils he would face such a long sea journey or in a

---

[4] Colchis is approximately modern Georgia.

11 ex bello tam profundae barbariae. Igitur Iason divulgata opinione tam gloriosae expeditionis, cum ad eum certatim principes iuventutis totius ferme orbis concurrerent, exercitum fortissimorum virorum, qui Argonautae cognomi-

12 nati sunt, conparavit. Quem cum magnis rebus gestis incolumem reduxisset, rursum a Peliae filiis Thessalia magna vi pulsus cum ingenti multitudine, quae ad famam virtutis eius ex omnibus gentibus cotidie confluebat, comite Medea uxore, quam repudiatam miseratione exilii rursum receperat, et Medo, privigno ab Aegeo, rege Atheniensium, genito, Colchos repetivit socerumque Aeetam regno pulsum restituit.

3. Magna deinde bella cum finitimis gessit captasque civitates partim regno soceri ad abolendam superioris militiae iniuriam, qua filiam eius Medeam abduxerat et filium Aegialeum interfecerat, adiunxit, partim populis,

2 quos secum adduxerat, adsignavit primusque humanorum post Herculem et Liberum, qui reges Orientis fuisse tra-

3 duntur, eam caeli plagam domuisse dicitur. Populis quibusdam Erygium et Amphistratum, aurigas Castoris et

4 Pollucis, duces adsignavit. Cum Albanis foedus percussit, qui Herculem ex Italia ab Albano monte, cum Geryone extincto armenta eius per Italiam duceret, secuti dicuntur, quique memores Italicae originis exercitum Cn. Pompei

5 bello Mithridatico fratres salutavere. Itaque Iasoni totus ferme Oriens ut conditori divinos honores templaque constituit, quae Parmenion, dux Alexandri Magni, post multos

---

5 This is Seel's emendation; the manuscripts read, among other variants, *frigium/phrygium*.

6 Mithridates of Pontus.

war with barbarians so far inland. So after Jason spread the 11
news of such a glorious venture, and the finest young men
from almost all over the world came rushing to join him,
he brought together an army of truly brave men who were
called "the Argonauts." When he brought it safely home 12
after his great adventures, he was again driven from Thessaly with great violence by the sons of Pelias, and with a
large crowd that came daily flooding to him from all races
at reports of his valor he again made for Colchis, accompanied by his wife Medea (whom he had divorced but
taken back from pity over her exile), and also by his stepson Medus, whom Medea had borne to King Aegeus of
Athens, and he restored his father-in-law Aeëtes to the
throne from which he had been deposed.

3. He then fought serious wars with neighboring peoples and added cities that he captured to his father-in-law's
kingdom as compensation for the wrong done him on his
earlier expedition, when he had taken his daughter Medea
and killed his son Aegialeus, and others he assigned to
peoples that he had brought with him, and he is consid- 2
ered the first human after Hercules and Liber, who were
reputedly kings of the East, to have conquered that part
of the world. To some peoples he assigned Erygius[5] and 3
Amphistratus, the charioteers of Castor and Pollux, as
their leaders. He struck an alliance with the Albani, who 4
are said to have followed Hercules from Mount Albanus
in Italy when he was taking his cattle through Italy after
killing Geryon, and during the Mithridatic[6] war these
people, remembering their Italian origin, greeted Pompey's army as their brothers. Thus almost the entire East 5
accorded divine honors and temples to Jason as their
founder, which years later Parmenion, Alexander the

annos dirui iussit, ne cuiusquam nomen in Oriente ve-
6 nerabilius quam Alexandri esset. Post mortem Iasonis
Medus aemulus virtutis eius in honorem matris Mediam
urbem condidit regnumque ex nomine suo Medorum constituit, sub cuius maiestate Orientis postea imperium fuit.
7 Albanis vicinae Amazones sunt, quarum reginam Thales-
trim concubitum Alexandri petisse multi auctores prodidere.
8   Armenius quoque, et ipse Thessalus, unus de numero
ducum Iasonis, recollecta multitudine, quae amisso Ia-
9 sone rege passim vagabatur, Armeniam condit, a cuius
montibus Tigris fluvius modicis primo incrementis nasci-
tur; interiecto deinde aliquanto spatio sub terras mergitur,
atque ita post quinque et XX milia passuum grande iam
flumen in regione Sophene emergit ac sic in paludes Eu-
phratis recipitur.

4. Igitur Mithridates, rex Parthorum, post bellum Armeniae propter crudelitatem a senatu Parthico regno pel-
2 litur. Frater eius Orodes, cum regnum vacans occupasset,
Babyloniam, quo Mithridates confugerat, diu obsidet et
3 fame coactos in deditionem oppidanos conpellit. Mithridates autem fiducia cognationis ultro se in potestatem
4 Orodis tradit. Sed Orodes plus hostem quam fratrem cogi-
tans in conspectu suo trucidari iussit. Post haec bellum
cum Romanis gessit Crassumque imperatorem cum filio

---

7 See 12.3.5.

8 There is evident confusion. Justin (Trogus?) mistakes Mithridates II (d. ca. 88) for his descendant Mithridates III. The actual
succession after Mithridates II runs Gotarzes I (ca. 90–ca. 80),
Orodes I (ca. 80–78), Sinatruces (ca. 77–70), all brothers; then

Great's general, ordered destroyed so no one's name should be more venerated in the East than Alexander's. After the death of Jason, Medus, his father's equal in valor, founded the city of Media in honor of his mother and established the kingdom of the Medes, who were named after him; and it was with this kingdom that rule of the East subsequently lay. The Albani have as neighbors the Amazons, whose queen Thalestris requested sexual relations with Alexander, as many authors have recorded.[7]

Armenius, too, himself also a Thessalian and one of Jason's officers, founded Armenia by reassembling a crowd wandering aimlessly after King Jason's death. In its mountains rises the River Tigris, which is quite small at its headwaters; then after some distance it plunges underground, and twenty-five miles ahead it reemerges in the region of Sophene as a huge river and like that enters the marshes of the Euphrates.

4. Now Mithridates, king of the Parthians, was driven from the kingdom by the Parthian senate after the Armenian war, because of his cruelty.[8] His brother Orodes, after taking over the vacant kingdom, maintained a long siege of Babylon, where Mithridates had sought refuge, and he starved the townspeople into surrender. Mithridates, however, confident in their kinship, then willingly put himself in Orodes' hands. But Orodes seeing him more as an enemy than a brother had him savagely murdered in his sight. After that he fought a war with the Romans and wiped out their general Crassus along with his son and the

Phraates III (ca. 70–58), murdered by his sons Mithridates III (ca. 58/57) and Orodes II (ca. 58–39). The last-named defeated Crassus at Carrhae in 53 (*MRR* 2.230).

5 et omni exercitu Romano delevit. Huius filius Pacorus missus ad persequendas Romani belli reliquias magnis rebus in Syria gestis in Parthiam patri suspectus revocatur, quo absente exercitus Parthorum relictus in Syria a Cassio,

6 quaestore Crassi, cum omnibus ducibus trucidatur. His ita gestis non magno post tempore Romanis inter Caesarem Pompeiumque civile bellum oritur, in quo Parthi Pompeianarum partium fuere et propter amicitiam cum Pompeio bello Mithridatico iunctam et propter Crassi necem, cuius filium in partibus Caesaris esse audierant, quem ultorem patris victore Caesare futurum non deliberabant.

7 Itaque victis partibus Pompeianis et Cassio et Bruto auxilia adversus Augustum et Antonium misere, et post belli finem rursus Pacoro duce inita cum Labieno societate Syriam et Asiam vastavere castraque Ventidi, qui post Cassium absente Pacoro exercitum Parthicum fuderat, magna

8 mole adgrediuntur. Sed ille simulato timore diu continuit se et insultare Parthos aliquantisper passus est. Ad postremum in securos laetosque partem legionum emisit, qua-

9 rum impetu fusi Parthi in diversa abiere. Pacorus cum fugientes suos abduxisse secum legiones Romanas putaret, castra Ventidi, veluti sine defensoribus, adgreditur.

10 Tum Ventidius reliqua parte legionum emissa universam

---

9 *MRR* 2.229, 237, 242 (the latter in the year 51).
10 Cass. Dio 42.2.5 insists on Parthian hatred for Pompey. Caesar was planning a Parthian campaign at the time of his death. Crassus' elder son and namesake served under Caesar in the Gallic and civil wars.   11 For what follows through to 36, see the account in Cass. Dio 48–49. For P. Ventidius Bassus, see *MRR* 2.388, 393. Pacorus died in 38.

whole Roman army. His son Pacorus was sent to clear up 5
what remained of the Roman war but after great success
in Syria he was recalled to Parthia when he became suspected by his father, and in his absence the Parthian army
that was left in Syria was massacred by Cassius, the
quaestor of Crassus, with all its officers.[9] Not much later 6
than this a civil war between Caesar and Pompey arose
among the Romans, in which the Parthians took the Pompeian side both because of their accord with Pompey in
the Mithridatic War and also because of the killing of
Crassus, whose son they had heard had sided with Caesar,
and they had no doubt that he would avenge his father if
Caesar prevailed.[10] So when the Pompeian side was de- 7
feated they sent to both Cassius and Brutus auxiliary
troops against Augustus and Antonius,[11] and at the end of
the war when Pacorus was again their leader they made
an alliance with Labienus,[12] ravaged Syria and Asia and
launched a massive attack on the camp of Ventidius who,
like Cassius before him, had routed the Parthian army in
Pacorus' absence. But he, simulating fear, long held back 8
and allowed the Parthians to scoff at him for some time.
Finally, while they were confident and jubilant, he sent
some of his legions out against them, and scattered by
their charge the Parthians made off in various directions.
Since Pacorus thought that his men had in their flight 9
drawn the Roman legions off with them, he attacked Ventidius' camp, assuming it to be without defenders. Then 10
Ventidius sent out the rest of his legions and killed the

[12] Q. Labienus, a follower of Brutus and Cassius, defected to
the Parthians after the Republican defeat at Philippi.

Parthorum manum cum rege ipso Pacoro interficit; nec
11 ullo bello Parthi umquam maius vulnus acceperunt. Haec
cum in Parthia nuntiata essent. Orodes, pater Pacori, qui
paulo ante vastatam Syriam, occupatam Asiam a Parthis
audierat victoremque Pacorum Romanorum gloriabatur,
repente filii morte et exercitus clade audita ex dolore in
12 furorem vertitur. Multis diebus non adloqui quemquam,
non cibum sumere, non vocem mittere, ita ut etiam mutus
13 factus videretur. Post multos deinde dies, ubi dolor vocem
laxaverat, nihil aliud quam Pacorum vocabat; Pacorus illi
videri, Pacorus audiri videbatur, cum illo loqui, cum illo
consistere; interdum quasi amissum flebiliter dolebat.
14 Post longum deinde luctum alia sollicitudo miserandum
senem invadit, quem ex numero XXX filiorum in locum
15 Pacori regem destinet. Multae paelices, ex quibus gene-
rata tanta iuventus erat, pro suis quaeque sollicitae ani-
16 mum senis obsidebant. Sed fatum Parthiae fecit, in qua
iam quasi sollemne est reges parricidas haberi, ut scelera-
tissimus omnium, et ipse Phrahates nomine, rex statuere-
tur.

5. Itaque statim, quasi nollet mori, patrem interfecit;
fratres quoque omnes XXX trucidat. Sed nec in filiis ces-
2 sant parricidia. Nam cum infestos sibi optimates propter
adsidua scelera videret, ne esset qui nominari rex posset,
3 adultum filium interfici iubet. Huic Antonius propter auxilium adversus se et Caesarem latum bellum cum sedecim
validissimis legionibus intulit, sed graviter multis proeliis

---

13 Phraates IV reigned until 2 BC, when he in turn was murdered by Phraates V.

entire band of Parthians together with their prince Pacorus himself; and in no other war did the Parthians ever receive a greater blow. When this was reported in Parthia, 11 Orodes, the father of Pacorus, who a little earlier had been hearing of Syria devastated and Asia seized by the Parthians and was lauding Pacorus' victory over the Romans, now suddenly heard that his son was dead, and his army destroyed—and his grief turned to frenzy. For many days 12 he would speak to no one, take no food, utter not a word, to the point of even appearing to be struck dumb. Then 13 many days later, when grief had loosened his tongue, he would be calling out nothing but "Pacorus"; he thought he saw Pacorus, heard Pacorus, thought he was talking with him, standing with him; and sometimes he would tearfully mourn for him as lost. Then after a long period of grieving 14 another concern overtook the pitiful old man, which of his thirty sons to make heir to the throne in Pacorus' place. The numerous concubines by whom he had fathered so 15 many sons were, from concern for their own children, trying to catch the old man's attention. But Parthia's des- 16 tiny, where having parricidal kings is almost the rule, saw that the most wicked of all of them, also himself named Phraates, would be made king.[13]

5. So he immediately killed his father, as if he was unwilling to die; and he also slaughtered all his thirty brothers. Nor did the murders end with the sons. For when he 2 saw himself hated by the nobles because of his ongoing atrocities, he, so no one else should be appointed king, gave orders for his adult son to be killed. Since he brought 3 aid against him and Caesar, Antonius attacked him with sixteen very strong legions, but after heavy losses in many

4   vexatus a Parthia refugit. Qua victoria insolentior Phrahates redditus, cum multa crudeliter consuleret, in exi-
5   lium a populo suo pellitur. Itaque cum magno tempore
finitimas civitates, ad postremum Scythas precibus fatigas-
set, Scytharum maxime auxilio in regnum restituitur.
6   Hoc absente regem Parthi Tiridaten quendam consti-
tuerant, qui audito adventu Scytharum cum magna amicorum manu ad Caesarem in Hispania bellum tunc temporis gerentem profugit, obsidem Caesari minimum
Phrahatis filium ferens, quem neglegentius custoditum
7   rapuerat. Quo cognito Phrahates legatos statim ad Caesarem mittit, servum suum Tiridaten et filium remitti sibi
8   postulat. Caesar et legatione Phrahatis audita et Tiridatis
postulatis cognitis (nam et ipse restitui in regnum deside-
rabat, iuris Romanorum futuram Parthiam adfirmans, si
eius regnum muneris eorum fuisset) neque Tiridaten de-
diturum se Parthis dixit, neque adversus Parthos Tiridati
9   auxilia daturum. Ne tamen per omnia nihil a Caesare ob-
tentum videretur, et Phrahati filium sine pretio remisit et
Tiridati, quoad manere apud Romanos vellet, opulentum
10   sumptum praeberi iussit. Post haec finito Hispaniensi
bello, cum in Syriam ad conponendum Orientis statum
venisset, metum Phrahati incussit, ne bellum Parthiae vel-
11   let inferre. Itaque tota Parthia captivi ex Crassiano sive

---

14 In the year 36; *MRR* 2.400.

15 He lasted from about 30 to 25. See Cass. Dio 51.18.2ff.
Caesar is, of course, Augustus.

16 Cass. Dio 53.33 under the year 23; Augustus, *Res gestae* 32.

battles he fled from Parthia.[14] Following this victory 4
Phraates became more overbearing, and while he was contemplating many other brutal acts he was driven into exile
by his own people. And so after long importuning neigh- 5
boring states with entreaties for help, and finally turning
to the Scythians, he was, mostly with the help of the Scythians, restored to the throne.

During his absence the Parthians had appointed as 6
their king one Tiridates,[15] and he on hearing of the approach of the Scythians fled with a large band of his friends
to Caesar, who was then fighting a war in Spain, bringing
to Caesar as a hostage Phraates' youngest son, whom he
had seized when insecurely guarded. Learning of this, 7
Phraates immediately sent legates to Caesar to demand
the return of "his slave Tiridates" and the son.[16] Caesar 8
listened to Phraates' legation and also took note of Tiridates' demands (for he too wanted him restored to the
throne, asserting that Parthia would be under the Romans'
jurisdiction if the throne were his as a gift from them), and
then said he would neither surrender Tiridates to the Parthians nor assist Tiridates against the Parthians. But for it 9
not to seem that throughout all this nothing had been
gained from Caesar, he both restored the son to Phraates
without ransom and also ordered Tiridates be provided
with a life of luxury as long as he wished to remain with
the Romans. After this, when the Spanish war ended and 10
Caesar came to Syria to arrange the East settlement, he
struck fear into Phraates that he might want to make war
on Parthia. And so throughout Parthia captives from 11

Antoni exercitu recollecti signaque cum his militaria Augusto remissa. Sed et filii nepotesque Phrahatis obsides Augusto dati, plusque Caesar magnitudine nominis sui fecit, quam armis facere alius imperator potuisset.

Crassus' as well as Antonius' army were rounded up and sent back to Augustus with the military standards.[17] But the children and grandchildren of Phraates were also given to Augustus as hostages, and by the greatness of his name Caesar gained more than another general could have by force of arms.

12

[17] In 20; Cass. Dio 54.8; Augustus, *Res gestae* 29.2. The negotiations and handovers were carried out by Augustus' stepson and later successor Tiberius. The hostages, for whom see *Res gestae* 32.2, came to Rome around 10 BC.

LIBER XLIII

1. Parthicis orientalibusque ac totius propemodum orbis
rebus explicitis ad initia Romanae urbis Trogus veluti post
longam peregrinationem domum revertitur, ingrati civis
officium existimans, si, cum omnium gentium res gestas
2 inlustraverit, de sola tantum patria taceat. Breviter igitur
initia Romani imperii perstringit, ut nec modum propositi
operis excedat nec utique originem urbis, quae est caput
totius orbis, silentio praetermittat.
3   Italiae cultores primi Aborigines fuere, quorum rex
Saturnus tantae iustitiae fuisse dicitur, ut neque servierit
quisquam sub illo neque quicquam privatae rei habuerit,
sed omnia communia et indivisa omnibus fuerint, veluti
4 unum cunctis patrimonium esset. Ob cuius exempli memoriam cautum est, ut Saturnalibus exaequato omnium
iure passim in conviviis servi cum dominis recumbant.
5 Itaque Italia regis nomine Saturnia appellata, et mons in

---

1 Rome's origins were of great interest in the Augustan period,
an interest evident above all in Virgil's *Aeneid*. Two other contem-
poraries wrote histories still extant that begin with legendary
origins and the kingship, Livy and Dionysius of Halicarnassus.
There is, of course, no reason why Trogus should use a Greek
source for this section, and there was Roman historical writing to

BOOK XLIII

1. With the history of Parthia, the East and almost the whole world accounted for, Trogus now returns home to the beginnings of the city of Rome as if from a long trip abroad, thinking himself an ungrateful citizen if, after he had illuminated every other nation's history, he remained silent only about his own country. He therefore touches 2 briefly on the beginnings of the Roman Empire, in such a way as not to exceed the scope of his projected work but also certainly not pass over in silence the origin of a city that is the capital of the whole world.

Italy's first inhabitants were the Aborigines,[1] whose 3 king Saturnus is said to have been someone so just that under him there was neither slavery nor private ownership of property, but everybody shared all things together, undivided, as if it were one family estate. In memory of his 4 example, it was decreed that at the Saturnalia slaves everywhere, with all enjoying equality, could recline with their masters. So Italy was called Saturnia after the name 5 of its king, and the hill on which he lived, Saturnius, on

draw upon, going back especially to Cato's *Origines*. It is not to be expected that there would be complete agreement between versions. The word "aborigines" simply means "original inhabitants," from the Latin *ab origine*, "from the beginning."

quo habitabat Saturnius, in quo nunc veluti ab Iove pulso
6 sedibus suis Saturno Capitolium est. Post hunc tertio loco
regnasse Faunum ferunt, sub quo Euander ab Arcadiae
urbe Pallanteo in Italiam cum mediocri turba popularium
venit, cui Faunus et agros et montem, quem ille postea
7 Palatium appellavit, benigne adsignavit. In huius radici-
bus templum Lycaeo, quem Graeci Pana, Romani Luper-
cum appellant, constituit; ipsum dei simulacrum nudum
caprina pelle amictum est, quo habitu nunc Romae Lu-
8 percalibus decurritur. Fauno uxor fuit nomine Fatua, quae
adsidue divino spiritu inpleta veluti per furorem futura
praemonebat. Vnde adhuc, qui inspirari solent, fatuari
9 dicuntur. Ex filia Fauni et Hercule, qui eodem tempore
extincto Geryone armenta, victoriae praemia, per Italiam
ducebat, stupro conceptus Latinus procreatur.
10 Quo tenente regnum Aeneas ab Ilio Troia a Graecis
expugnata in Italiam venit statimque bello exceptus, cum
in aciem exercitum eduxisset, ad conloquium vocatus tantam admirationem sui Latino praebuit, ut et in societatem
regni reciperetur et Lavinia in matrimonium ei data gener
11 adsciceretur. Post haec commune utriusque bellum adversus Turnum, regem Rutulorum, propter fraudatas La-
viniae fuit nuptias, in quo et Turnus et Latinus interiere.
12 Igitur cum Aeneas iure victoriae utroque populo potiretur,

---

2 In historical times the Capitol was the site of the temple of
Jupiter Optimus Maximus.   3 The second has been omitted;
he was Picus, father of Faunus (Verg. *Aen.* 7.48).

4 The Lupercalia remain mysterious. There seems to be connection with wolves (the Latin for wolf is *lupus*). Cf. *OCD* s.v. See
K. K. Vé, "La cité et la sauvagerie: le rite des Lupercales," *Dialogues d'Histoire ancienne* 44.2 (2018): 139–90.

which—with Saturnus as it were evicted from his home by
Jupiter—the Capitol now stands.[2] In third place after him   6
they say[3] Faunus reigned, under whom Evander came into
Italy with a small group of his countrymen from the Arca-
dian city of Pallanteum, and to him Faunus kindly assigned land and a hill, which he later named the Palatium.
At its foot Evander erected a temple to Lycaeus, whom   7
the Greeks call Pan and the Romans Lupercus;[4] the statue
of the god is itself naked and cloaked with a goat skin, the
clothing in which the race in Rome at the Lupercalia is
now run. Faunus had a wife called Fatua who, always pos-   8
sessed by a holy spirit, would as if in a frenzy foretell the
future. Thus *fatuari* is still the word used of those divinely
inspired.[5] From the daughter of Faunus and from Hercu-   9
les Latinus was born, conceived through rape at the time
that Hercules was leading cattle, his victory prize, through
Italy after he killed Geryon.

While he was king,[6] Aeneas came to Italy from Ilium   10
after Troy was stormed by the Greeks and immediately
faced war; but when he led his army into battle and was
invited to parley he so impressed Latinus that he was welcomed to share his kingdom, given his daughter Lavinia
in marriage, and adopted as his son-in-law. After this there   11
was a joint war against Turnus, king of the Rutulians, because he was cheated of marriage to Lavinia, and in this
both Turnus and Latinus were killed. So when by right of   12
victory Aeneas had power over both peoples, he founded

[5] Etymological speculation is common among Roman anti-
quarians, and this one is unique; the verb occurs nowhere else in
this sense.

[6] That is, Latinus.

13 urbem ex nomine uxoris Lavinium condidit. Bellum deinde adversus Mezentium, Etruscorum regem, gessit, in quo cum ipse occidisset, in locum eius Ascanius filius successit, qui Lavinio relicto Longam Albam condidit, quae CCC annis caput regni fuit.

2. Post multos deinde huius urbis reges ad postremum
2 Numitor et Amulius regno potiti sunt. Sed Amulius cum vi aetate potiorem Numitorem oppressisset, filiam eius Ream in perpetuam virginitatem, ne quis vindex regni virilis sexus ex gente Numitoris oriretur, demersit, addita iniuriae specie honoris, ut non damnata, sed sacerdos
3 electa videretur. Igitur clausa in luco Marti sacro duos pueros, incertum stupro an ex Marte conceptos, enixa est.
4 Quo cognito Amulius multiplicato metu proventu duorum pueros exponi iubet et puellam vinculis onerat, ex quorum
5 iniuria decessit. Sed Fortuna origini Romanae prospiciens pueros lupae alendos obtulit, quae amissis catulis distenta ubera exinanire cupiens nutricem se infantibus praebuit.
6 Cum saepius ad parvulos veluti ad catulos reverteretur, rem Faustulus pastor animadvertit subtractosque ferae
7 inter greges pecorum agresti vita nutrivit. Martios pueros fuisse, sive quod in luco Martis enixi sunt sive quod a lupa, quae in tutela Martis est, nutriti, veluti manifestis argumentis creditum. Nomina pueris alteri Remo, alteri Ro-
8 mulo fuere. Adultis inter pastores de virtute cotidiana
9 certamina et vires et pernicitatem auxere. Igitur cum latrones a rapina pecorum industrie frequenterque submoverent, Remus ab isdem latronibus captus et velut ipse

the city of Lavinium, named after his wife. He then fought 13
a war against Mezentius, king of the Etruscans, in which
he himself was killed, and his son Ascanius succeeded him,
left Lavinium and founded Alba Longa, which for three
hundred years remained the capital of the kingdom.

2. Then, after many kings of this city, Numitor and
Amulius finally acquired the kingdom. But although Nu- 2
mitor had the advantage of age Amulius overthrew him
and forced his daughter Rea into lifelong virginity so no
male claimant to the throne should come from Numitor's
line, and he cloaked his injustice with a specious honor,
making it appear that she was not punished but chosen as
priestess. So she was shut away in a grove sacred to Mars 3
and gave birth to two boys, and it was uncertain whether
the conception came from illicit sex or from Mars. On 4
learning of it Amulius, his fear increased by the twin birth,
ordered the boys exposed and put the girl in chains, an
indignity from which she died. But Fortune, overseeing 5
Rome's beginnings, gave the boys to a she-wolf for suck-
ling, and she, having lost her cubs and eager to empty her
distended teats, offered herself to the infants as their
nurse. Since she was often returning to the babies as if to 6
her cubs, the herdsman Faustulus noticed it and taking
them from the animal brought them up in a rustic life
amid his herds. The boys, either from being born in the 7
grove of Mars or being suckled by a wolf, which is under
Mars' protection, were from these apparently clear indica-
tions believed to be sons of Mars. One of the boys' names
was Remus, the other Romulus. As adults among the 8
herdsmen daily contests increased their strength and agil-
ity. Now when they were keenly and frequently keeping 9
bandits from stealing their livestock, Remus was captured

279

esset, quod in aliis prohibebat, regi offertur; crimini datur
quasi greges Numitoris infestare solitus esset. Tunc a rege
10 Numitori in ultionem traditur. Sed Numitor adulescentia
iuvenis permotus et in suspitionem expositi nepotis ad-
ductus, cum eum nunc liniamentorum filiae similitudo,
nunc aetas expositionis temporibus congruens anxium
tenerent, repente Faustulus cum Romulo supervenit; a
quo origine cognita puerorum facta conspiratione et adulescentes in ultionem maternae necis et Numitor in vindictam erepti regni armantur.

3. Occiso Amulio regnum Numitori restituitur et urbs
2 Romana ab adulescentibus conditur. Tunc et senatus centum seniorum, qui patres dicti sunt, constituitur; tunc et
vicinis conubia pastorum dedignantibus virgines Sabinae
rapiuntur, finitimisque populis armis subiectis primo Italiae et mox orbis imperium quaesitum.

3 Per ea tempora adhuc reges hastas pro diademate
habebant, quas Graeci "sceptra" dixere. Nam et ab origine
rerum pro diis inmortalibus veteres hastas coluere, ob
cuius religionis memoriam adhuc deorum simulacris has-
tae adduntur.

4 Temporibus Tarquinii regis ex Asia Phocaeensium
iuventus ostio Tiberis invecta amicitiam cum Romanis
iunxit; inde in ultimos Galliae sinus navibus profecta Massiliam inter Ligures et feras gentes Gallorum condidit,
magnasque res, sive dum armis se adversus Gallicam feri-

---

7 The traditional date was around 754/3.

8 Tarquinius Priscus, who was held to have reigned from 616
to 578. Massilia (Marseilles) was founded around 600. Cf. 37.1.1.

by those same bandits and brought to the king, accused of himself doing what he was trying to prevent others from doing; and he was charged with regularly plundering Numitor's herds. Then he was by the king handed over to Numitor for punishment. Numitor, however, was touched 10 by the boy's youth and led to wonder whether he was his exposed grandson, since there was both a resemblance in features to his daughter, and his age also matched the time of the exposure, when suddenly Faustulus arrived with Romulus. By him the boys' origin was revealed, and hatching a conspiracy the young men took up arms to avenge their mother's death and Numitor to reclaim the throne that had been taken from him.

3. After Amulius was killed, the kingdom was restored to Numitor and the city of Rome was founded by the young men.[7] Then too, a senate of a hundred older men 2 who were called "fathers" was established; and then since their neighbors disdained marriage with shepherds, Sabine maidens were seized, neighboring peoples crushed in war, and Roman rule established, first over Italy and soon over the world.

In those days the kings still had spears, which the 3 Greeks called "scepters," instead of a diadem. For even from their beginnings the Romans worshipped old spears as representing the immortal gods, and in memory of this veneration the gods' statues are still furnished with spears.

In King Tarquin's time[8] some young Phocaeans sailing 4 from Asia into the mouth of the Tiber made an alliance with the Romans; and setting off from there in their ships into the most remote inlets of Gaul they founded Massilia between the Ligurians and fierce Gallic peoples; and they achieved great success, whether defending themselves

281

tatem tuentur sive dum ultro lacessunt, a quibus fuerant antea lacessiti, gesserunt.

5   Namque Phocaeenses exiguitate ac macie terrae coacti studiosius mare quam terras exercuere: piscando mercandoque, plerumque etiam latrocinio maris, quod illis tem-

6 poribus gloriae habebatur, vitam tolerabant. Itaque in ultimam Oceani oram procedere ausi in sinum Gallicum ostio

7 Rhodani amnis devenere, cuius loci amoenitate capti, reversi domum referentes quae viderant, plures sollicita-

8 vere. Duces classis Simos et Protis fuere. Itaque regem Segobrigiorum, Nannum nomine, in cuius finibus urbem condere gestiebant, amicitiam petentes conveniunt.

9   Forte eo die rex occupatus in apparatu nuptiarum Gyptis filiae erat, quam more gentis electo inter epulas genero

10 nuptum tradere illic parabat. Itaque cum ad nuptias invitati omnes proci essent, rogantur etiam Graeci hospites ad

11 convivium. Introducta deinde virgo cum iuberetur a patre aquam porrigere ei, quem virum eligeret, tunc omissis omnibus ad Graecos conversa aquam Proti porrigit, qui factus ex hospite gener locum condendae urbis a socero

12 accepit. Condita igitur Massilia est prope ostia Rhodani

13 amnis in remoto sinu, velut in angulo maris. Sed Ligures incrementis urbis invidentes Graecos adsiduis bellis fatigabant, qui pericula propulsando in tantum enituerunt, ut victis hostibus in captivis agris multas colonias constituerint.

    4. Ab his igitur Galli et usum vitae cultioris deposita ac

against barbarous Gauls or attacking those by whom they had earlier been attacked themselves.

For the Phocaeans, being confined to sparse and barren lands, applied themselves more to the sea than the land; it was by fishing and trading, and often even by piracy, which in those days was thought honorable, that they survived. So, boldly venturing to the farthest shores of the ocean, they reached the Gallic gulf at the mouth of the River Rhône, and captivated by the area's beauty they on their return recounted what they had seen and so induced others to come. The fleet commanders were Simos and Protis. So they met the king of the Segobrigii, whose name was Nannus, in whose lands they wished to build their city, to seek an accord.

By chance the king was that day busy arranging the wedding of his daughter Gyptis, and following his people's practice he was preparing to give her in marriage on the spot to a son-in-law chosen at the wedding feast. Now since all the suitors had been invited to the ceremony, the Greek visitors were also asked to the banquet. The girl was then brought in and, told by her father to offer water to the man of her choice, she passed by all the others, and turning to the Greeks handed the water to Protis; and he, becoming a son-in-law rather than visitor, received from his father-in-law a site for founding a city. So Massilia was founded in a remote bay near the mouth of the Rhône River, almost in a corner of the sea. The Ligurians, however, with a jealous eye on the city's growth, kept harassing the Greeks with persistent wars, but so brilliant were these in countering the threats that they defeated their enemies and founded many colonies in territory they captured.

4. So from these the Gauls learned a more civilized way

mansuefacta barbaria et agrorum cultus et urbes moeni-
2 bus cingere didicerunt. Tunc et legibus, non armis vivere,
tunc et vitem putare, tunc olivam serere consuerunt,
adeoque magnus et hominibus et rebus inpositus est nitor,
ut non Graecia in Galliam emigrasse, sed Gallia in Grae-
3 ciam translata videretur. Mortuo rege Nanno Segobrigiorum, a quo locus acceptus condendae urbis fuerat, cum
regno filius eius Comanus successisset, adfirmante quodam regulo, quandoque Massiliam exitio finitimis populis
futuram, opprimendamque in ipso ortu, ne mox validior
4 ipsum obrueret. Subnectit et illam fabulam: canem ali-
quando partu gravidam locum a pastore precario petisse,
in quo pareret, quo obtento iterato petisse, ut sibi educare
eodem in loco catulos liceret; ad postremum adultis catulis fultam domestico praesidio proprietatem loci sibi vin-
5 dicasse. Non aliter Massilienses, qui nunc inquilini vide-
6 antur, dominos quandoque regionum futuros. His incitatus
rex insidias Massiliensibus struit. Itaque sollemni Flora-
liorum die multos fortes ac strenuos viros hospitii iure in
urbem misit, plures sirpeis latentes frondibusque super-
7 tectos induci vehiculis iubet, ipse cum exercitu in proximis
montibus delitescit, ut, cum nocte a praedictis apertae
portae forent, tempestive ad insidias adesset urbemque
8 somno ac vino sepultam armatis invaderet. Sed has insi-

---

9 There is a lacuna in the text at this point, since the sentence
lacks a main clause; but the sense is clear enough.

10 The phrase *urbemque somno ac vino sepultam* ("a city
buried in sleep and wine") virtually reproduces Verg. *Aen.* 2.265,
urbem somno vinoque sepultam, itself a variant on Enn. *Ann.* 8.14
FRL, nunc hostes vino domiti somnoque sepulti.

of life, abandoning and softening their barbarous behavior, and also how to practice agriculture and surround their cities with walls. They then also became accustomed to living with laws, not weapons, and then also to cultivating the vine and planting the olive tree; and so brilliantly successful were their society and affairs that it did not seem as if Greece had migrated to Gaul, but that Gaul had been moved into Greece. When King Nannus of the Segobrigii died, the man from whom they had received the site for their city, and he was succeeded by his son Comanus, some minor king told him that Massilia would one day be the ruin of her neighboring peoples and needed to be crushed right at birth so she not overwhelm him later when she was stronger.[9] He also added the following story: a pregnant bitch once begged a shepherd for a spot to give birth, and when granted it she further asked she be allowed to raise the pups in the same place; and finally, when the pups were grown and she could rely on her family's support, she claimed title to the place for herself. No differently, he said, would the people of Massilia, who now seemed mere squatters, would one day be masters the country. Aroused by this the king set a trap for the Massilians. On the holy day of the Floralia festival he under the guise of hospitality sent large numbers of brave, powerful warriors into the city and ordered more brought in on wagons, hidden under baskets and covered with branches; he himself hid with his army in the nearby mountains so that when the gates were opened at night by the above mentioned men, he could arrive at the right moment for an assault and with his army fall upon a city buried in sleep and wine.[10] But this ambush was divulged

dias mulier quaedam regis cognata prodidit, quae adulte-
rare cum Graeco adulescente adsolita in amplexu iuvenis
miserata formae eius insidias aperuit periculumque decli-
9 nare iubet. Ille rem statim ad magistratus defert; atque ita
patefactis insidiis cuncti Ligures conprehenduntur laten-
10 tesque de sirpeis protrahuntur. Quibus omnibus interfectis insidianti regi insidiae tenduntur. Caesa cum ipso
11 rege hostium septem milia. Exinde Massilienses festis
diebus portas claudere, vigilias agere, stationes in muris
observare, peregrinos recognoscere, curas habere, ac veluti bellum habeant, sic urbem pacis temporibus custo-
12 dire. Adeo illic bene instituta non temporum necessitate,
sed recte faciendi consuetudine servantur.

    5. Post haec magna illis cum Liguribus, magna cum
Gallis fuere bella, quae res et urbis gloriam auxit et virtutem Graecorum multiplicata victoria celebrem inter fini-
2 timos reddidit. Karthaginiensium quoque exercitus, cum
bellum captis piscatorum navibus ortum esset, saepe fude-
3 runt pacemque victis dederunt, cum Hispanis amicitiam
iunxerunt, cum Romanis prope ab initio conditae urbis
foedus summa fide custodierunt auxiliisque in omnibus
bellis industrie socios iuverunt. Quae res illis et virium
fiduciam auxit et pacem ab hostibus praestitit.
4   Cum igitur Massilia et fama rerum gestarum et abundantia opum et virium gloria virente floreret, repente finitimi populi ad nomen Massiliensium delendum velut ad

---

11 For example, in 154; *MRR* 1.154.

by a certain female relative of the king, who was having an affair with a young Greek, and while in the boy's arms, she, being touched by his charms, revealed the plot and told him to avoid the danger. He immediately reported it to the 9 magistrates; and so when the plot came to light, all the Ligurians were arrested and the men in hiding dragged from the wickerwork. When these had all been killed a 10 trap was laid for the king who was laying his own. Seven thousand men were cut down together with the king himself. Since then Massiliots have closed their gates on feast 11 days, kept watch, posted lookouts on their walls, challenged foreigners, maintained security, and as if they were at war kept the city secure in times of peace. So far are 12 good institutions preserved there, not only in critical times but with consistently prudent behavior.

5. After this they faced great wars with the Ligurians[11] and great wars with the Gauls, which both increased their city's fame and, after a number of victories, made Greek valor famous among their neighbors. Carthaginian armies 2 were also frequently routed by them when war had broken out over the seizure of fishing boats, and after defeating them they left them in peace; with the Spaniards they 3 established friendly relations, and with the Romans they maintained with complete integrity the treaty they had made almost at the foundation of their city, and they actively supported allies in all their wars. This both increased their confidence in their strength and brought peace with their enemies.

Now while Massilia flourished and her exploits were 4 famous, her wealth abundant and her strength renowned, suddenly the peoples around her came together to wipe out the Massilian name, as if to extinguish a fire menacing

5   commune extinguendum incendium concurrunt. Dux
consensu omnium Catumandus regulus eligitur. Qui cum
magno exercitu lectissimorum virorum urbem hostium
obsideret, per quietem specie torvae mulieris, quae se
deam dicebat, exterritus ultro pacem cum Massiliensibus

6   fecit, petitoque ut intrare illi urbem et deos eorum ado-
rare liceret, cum in arcem Minervae venisset, conspecto
in porticibus simulacro deae, quam per quietem viderat,
repente exclamat illam esse, quae se nocte exterruisset,

7   illam, quae recedere ab obsidione iussisset. Gratulatusque
Massiliensibus, quod animadverteret eos ad curam deorum inmortalium pertinere, torque aureo donata dea in
perpetuum amicitiam cum Massiliensibus iunxit.

8   Parta pace et securitate fundata revertentes a Delphis
Massiliensium legati, quo missi munera Apollini tulerant,
audiverunt urbem Romanam a Gallis captam incensam-

9   que. Quam rem domi nuntiatam publico funere Massilienses prosecuti sunt aurumque et argentum publicum
privatumque contulerunt ad explendum pondus Gallis, a

10   quibus redemptam pacem cognoverant. Ob quod meri-
tum et immunitas illis decreta et locus spectaculorum in
senatu datus et foedus aequo iure percussum.

11   In postremo libro Trogus: maiores suos a Vocontiis originem ducere; avum suum Trogum Pompeium Sertoriano

---

12 In 387; see 6.6.5, 20.5.4, 24.4.3, 28.2.4, 38.4.8.

13 That is, from Gallia Narbonensis (see the Introduction).
Pompey fought against Sertorius in Spain in the years 76 to 72.
On Pompey and Mithridates, see 37.1.8. Those granted citizenship took their Roman name from their patron, hence "Trogus"
becomes "Pompeius."

everyone. By common consent Catumandus was chosen 5
their leader. He, while he was besieging an enemy city
with a large army of elite soldiers, was terrified in his sleep
by a dream of a fierce-looking woman, who said she was a
goddess, and he readily made peace with the Massilians;
and then on asking permission to enter the city and wor- 6
ship their gods he came to the acropolis of Minerva and
caught sight of the goddess's statue in the portico—the
woman he had seen in his dream—and he immediately
cried out that she was the one who had frightened him in
the night, the one who had ordered him to raise the siege.
He then congratulated the Massiliots on the protection 7
that he saw the immortal gods afforded them, and after
presenting the goddess with a golden necklace he made a
permanent peace treaty with the Massiliots.

After peace and security had been established some 8
delegates returning from Delphi, where they had been
sent with gifts for Apollo, heard that the city of Rome had
been captured and burned by the Gauls.[12] When that news 9
was brought home it was received with public mourning
by the Massiliots and they contributed gold and silver
from public and private sources to make up the total
weight demanded by the Gauls, from whom they had
learned that the Romans had bought peace. For this good 10
deed they were decreed exemption from taxation and also
given seats among the senators for public shows, and an
agreement of equal rights was concluded.

In his last book Trogus says that his ancestors were of 11
Vocontian origin,[13] his grandfather, Pompeius Trogus, re-

12 bello civitatem a Cn. Pompeio percepisse, patruum Mi-
    thridatico bello turmas equitum sub eodem Pompeio
    duxisse; patrem quoque sub C. Caesare militasse epistu-
    larumque et legationum, simul et anuli curam habuisse.

ceived Roman citizenship from Gnaeus Pompeius in the war with Sertorius, his uncle had been a cavalry squadron 12 leader under the same Pompeius in the Mithridatic war, and his father had also served under Gaius Caesar and been responsible for his correspondence, diplomatic missions, and official seal.

LIBER XLIV

1. Hispania sicuti Europae terminos claudit, ita et huius
2 operis finis futura est. Hanc veteres ab Hibero amne primum Hiberiam, postea ab Hispalo Hispaniam cognomi-
3 naverunt. Haec inter Africam et Galliam posita Oceani
freto et Pyrenaeis montibus clauditur. Sicut minor utraque
4 terra, ita utraque fertilior. Nam neque ut Africa violento
sole torretur, neque ut Gallia adsiduis ventis fatigatur, sed
media inter utramque hinc temperato calore, inde felici-
bus et tempestivis imbribus in omnia frugum genera fe-
cunda est, adeo ut non ipsis tantum incolis, verum etiam
Italiae urbique Romanae cunctarum rerum abundantia
5 sufficiat. Hinc enim non frumenti tantum magna copia est,
verum et vini, mellis oleique. Nec ferri solum materia
6 praecipua, sed et equorum pernices greges. Sed nec sum-
mae tantum terrae laudanda bona, verum et abstrusorum
metallorum felices divitiae. Iam lini spartique vis ingens,
7 minii certe nulla feracior terra. In hac cursus amnium non
torrentes rapidique, ut noceant, sed lenes et vineis cam-

---

1 The mythical founder of Seville (Hispalus).

2 This is odd, as in section 6 wealth of metals is mentioned,
and at 3.8, below, the same words as here recur.

292

BOOK XLIV

1. As Spain marks the bounds of Europe, so will it also be the end of this work. The ancients first named it Hiberia after the River Hiberus, and later Hispania after Hispalus.[1] Lying between Africa and Gaul it is bounded by the waters of the Ocean and the Pyrenees Mountains. While smaller than both countries, it is also more fertile than both. For it is neither baked by intense sun like Africa, nor buffeted by incessant winds like Gaul; but lying between both and having a temperate climate on one hand and seasonal rains on the other it is rich in all manner of crops, so much that its abundant production of foodstuffs suffices not only for its own people but also for Italy and the city of Rome. For from it come large quantities not only of wheat, but also of wine, honey and oil; and there are not just exceptional iron deposits,[2] but also herds of swift horses. But it is not only its produce above ground that merits praise, but so also does its great wealth of hidden metals. There is flax and Spanish broom in abundance,[3] and in cinnabar certainly no land is richer. Here rivers are not so violent or fast-flowing as to be dangerous, but move

[3] Ruehl wished to transpose these words to the end of the first sentence in section 5 so as to keep the mentions of crops and metals separate.

pisque inrigui, aestuariis quoque Oceani adfatim piscosi, plerique etiam divites auro, quod in balucibus vehunt.
8 Vno tantum Pyrenaei montis dorso adhaeret Galliae, reli-
9 quis partibus undique in orbem mari cingitur. Forma terrae prope quadrata, nisi quod artantibus freti litoribus in Pyrenaeum coit. Porro Pyrenaei montis spatium sexcenta
10 milia passuum efficit. Salubritas caeli per omnem Hispaniam aequalis, quia aeris spiritus nulla paludium gravi nebula inficitur. Huc accedunt et marinae aurae undique versus adsidui flatus, quibus omnem provinciam penetrantibus eventilato terrestri spiritu praecipua hominibus sanitas redditur.

2. Corpora hominum ad inediam laboremque, animi ad mortem parati. Dura omnibus et adstricta parsimonia.
2 Bellum quam otium malunt; si extraneus deest, domi hos-
3 tem quaerunt. Saepe tormentis pro silentio rerum creditarum inmortui; adeo illis fortior taciturnitatis cura quam
4 vitae. Celebratur etiam bello Punico servi illius patientia, qui ultus dominum inter tormenta risu exultavit sere-
5 naque laetitia crudelitatem torquentium vicit. Velocitas genti pernix, inquies animus: plurimis militares equi et
6 arma sanguine ipsorum cariora. Nullus in festos dies epularum apparatus. Aqua calida lavari post secundum Punicum bellum a Romanis didicere.

---

⁴ This generalization is at odds with the claim in section 4 that Spain lacks the "incessant winds" that buffet Gaul.

⁵ The liege man (not a slave) of a Spanish noble executed by Hannibal's brother-in-law Hasdrubal, who then assassinated Hasdrubal in revenge in 221, and seemed to laugh when being tortured to death (Livy 21.2.6; cf. 5.5 below).

gently, irrigating vineyards and plains, and at their estuaries they are also well provided with fish, and most are also rich in gold, which they carry along as gold dust. Only at the Pyrenees Mountain range does it touch Gaul; everywhere else it is surrounded by the sea. The shape of the country is roughly square, except for a narrowing at the Pyrenees where the shoreline compresses it. In fact, the Pyrenees Mountain range runs for six hundred miles. The climate is uniformly healthy throughout Spain because the air is nowhere infested with noxious marsh vapors. In addition, there are also sea breezes continuously blowing everywhere,[4] penetrating the whole province and driving off the odors that rise from the land so that people are granted especially good health.

2. Their men's physique prepares them for hunger and hard work, their spirit is ready to face death. All maintain strict, rigorous frugality. They prefer war to peace; if they lack a foreign enemy, they look for one at home. They have often died under torture to keep secrets entrusted to them; so much more important to them is confidentiality than life. There is even a famous story of the fortitude of that slave in the Punic War who, after avenging his master, broke into laughter under torture and with serene cheerfulness triumphed over his torturers' cruelty.[5] They are a nimble, agile race, with a restless spirit; for most of them warhorses and weapons are more precious than their own blood. There is no banqueting on holidays. Bathing in hot water they learned from the Romans after the second Punic War.

7   In tanta saeculorum serie nullus illis dux magnus praeter Viriatum fuit, qui annis decem Romanos varia victoria
fatigavit; adeo feris propiora quam hominibus ingenia
gerunt. Quem ipsum non iudicio populi electum, sed ut
cavendi scientem declinandorumque periculorum peri-
8   tum secuti sunt. Cuius ea virtus continentiaque fuit, ut,
cum consulares exercitus frequenter vicerit, tantis rebus
gestis non armorum, non vestis cultum, non denique victum mutaverit, sed in eo habitu, quo primum bellare coepit, perseveraverit, ut quivis gregarius miles ipso imperatore opulentior videretur.

3. In Lusitanis iuxta fluvium Tagum vento equas fetus
concipere multi auctores prodidere. Quae fabulae ex
equarum fecunditate et gregum multitudine natae sunt,
qui tanti in Gallaecia ac Lusitania et tam pernices visuntur,
2   ut non inmerito vento ipso concepti videantur. Gallaeci
autem Graecam sibi originem adserunt; siquidem post
finem Troiani belli Teucrum morte Aiacis fratris invisum
patri Telamoni, cum non reciperetur in regnum, Cyprum
concessisse atque ibi urbem nomine antiquae patriae Sala-
minam condidisse; inde accepta opinione paternae mortis
3   patriam repetisse, sed cum ab Eurysace, Aiacis filio, ac-
cessu prohiberetur, Hispaniae litoribus adpulsum loca, ubi
nunc est Karthago Nova, occupasse; inde Gallaeciam
transisse et positis sedibus genti nomen dedisse.
4   Gallaeciae autem portio Amphilochi dicuntur. Regio
cum aeris ac plumbi uberrima, tum et minio, quod etiam

---

⁶ See Diod. Sic. 33; App. *Hisp.* 56–75; and *MRR* 1 under the
years from 147 until the victory of Q. Servilius Caepio in 138.
Viriatus was leader of the Lusitani in western Iberia.

In the many ages of their history they had no great 7
leader except Viriatus, who harassed the Romans for ten
years with mixed success;[6] so much closer is their character to wild animals than human beings. He was himself not
formally elected by vote of his people; they followed him
for his skill in taking precautions and avoiding dangerous
situations. Such was his integrity and restraint that, al- 8
though he often defeated consular armies, he did not
change the style of his arms, his dress, or even his diet, but
continued in the same fashion as when he first started
fighting wars, so that any ordinary soldier appeared richer
than the general himself.

3. In Lusitania close to the River Tagus, mares are
impregnated by the wind according to many authors. Such
stories arise from the fertility of its mares and the large
number of its herds of horses, which in Gallaecia and Lusitania are apparently so numerous and so swift that they
might well seem conceived by the wind itself. The Gallae- 2
cians actually claim Greek ancestry; for at the end of the
Trojan War, Teucer, they say, being hated by his father
Telamon for his brother Ajax's death and not welcomed
back to his kingdom, left for Cyprus and there founded a
city called Salamis after his old fatherland; then on receiving news of his father's death he went back to his fatherland; but when he was prevented from putting in there by 3
Eurysaces, Ajax's son, he landed on the coast of Spain and
occupied the region where New Carthage stands today;
and from there he moved on to Gallaecia and settling
there gave his name to its people.

Part of Gallaecia is actually inhabited by people called 4
Amphilochians. It is a region very rich in copper and lead
but also in cinnabar, which has even given a river in the

5 vicino flumini nomen dedit. Auro quoque ditissima, adeo
6 ut etiam aratro frequenter glebas aureas excidant. In huius
gentis finibus sacer mons est, quem ferro violari nefas
habetur; sed si quando fulgure terra proscissa est, quod in
his locis adsidua res est, detectum aurum velut dei munus
7 colligere permittitur. Feminae res domesticas agrorumque
8 culturas administrant, ipsi armis et rapinis serviunt. Praecipua his quidem ferri materia, sed aqua ipso ferro violen-
tior; quippe temperamento eius ferrum acrius redditur,
nec ullum apud eos telum probatur, quod non aut Birbili
9 fluvio aut Chalybe tinguatur. Vnde etiam Chalybes fluvii
huius finitimi appellati ferroque ceteris praestare dicuntur.

4. Saltus vero Tartessiorum, in quibus Titanas bellum
adversus deos gessisse proditur, incoluere Curetes, quorum rex vetustissimus Gargoris mellis colligendi usum
2 primus invenit. Huic cum ex filiae stupro nepos provenis-
set, pudore flagitii variis generibus extingui parvulum voluit; sed per omnes casus Fortuna quadam servatus ad
postremum ad regnum tot periculorum miseratione per-
3 venit. Primum omnium cum eum exponi iussisset et post
dies ad corpus expositi requirendum misisset, inventus est

---

7 The Minius, modern Minho; the Latin for red lead (cinnabar) is *minium*.

8 That is, the men.

9 The Birbilis (in Roman times more often called the Salo) was
today's Jalón, a tributary of the Ebro; it flows past Martial the
epigrammatist's hometown Bilbilis (near Catalayud). The Chalybs
and its resident ironworking Chalybes, however, lay in northeastern Asia Minor (Xen. *Anab.* 4.7.15, 5.5.1; Strabo 12.548C; et al.);
Trogus must have imported this mistaken mention from some

area its name.[7] It is also very rich in gold, so rich that they 5
often even plow up clods of gold. In this people's territory 6
is a holy mountain, violating which with iron implements
is considered sacrilege; but whenever the soil is split by
lightning, a common phenomenon in the area, and gold is
unearthed, gathering it is permitted as it appears god
given. Women take care of domestic matters and farming 7
the land and they themselves[8] take charge of war and plundering. They have iron of especially high quality, but their 8
water is more destructive than iron itself; for when mixed
with it iron is sharpened, and among them no weapon has
approval that has not been dipped in either the River Birbilis or the Chalybs. Hence people living along this river 9
are also called Chalybes and are said to have better iron
than anyone else.[9]

4. Now the woodlands of the Tartessii, in which the
Titans are said to have made war on the gods, were inhabited by the Curetes whose earliest king Gargoris origi-
nated honey gathering.[10] When a grandson was born from 2
his daughter's illicit sex, he from shame over her conduct
tried in various ways to have him killed; but when by some
good fortune he survived all his trials the grandfather felt
sorry for all the dangers he had faced, and he finally succeeded to the throne. After he first of all ordered him 3
exposed and then some days later sent someone to look for
the exposed child's corpse, he was found to have been

other source—perhaps because the Caucasus region, near the
Chalybes, also had a territory called Iberia.

[10] Tartessus, seemingly the Biblical Tarshish, lay in southwest
Spain in the Rio Tinto region, famous even then for its silver and
iron.

4   vario ferarum lacte nutritus Deinde relatum domum tramite angusto, per quem armenta commeare consueverant, proici iubet, crudelis prorsus, qui proculcari nepotem,

5   quam simplici morte interfici maluit. Ibi quoque cum inviolatus esset nec alimentis egeret, canibus primo ieiunis et multorum dierum abstinentia cruciatis, mox etiam sui-

6   bus obiecit. Itaque cum non solum non noceretur, verum etiam quarundam uberibus aleretur, ad ultimum in Ocea-

7   num abici iussit. Tum plane manifesto quodam numine inter furentes aestus ac reciprocantes undas, velut nave,

8   non fluctu veheretur, leni salo in litore exponitur, nec multo post cerva adfuit, quae ubera parvulo offerret. Inde denique conversatione nutricis eximia puero pernicitas fuit; interque cervorum greges diu montes saltusque haud

9   inferior velocitate peragravit. Ad postremum laqueo captus regi dono datus est. Tunc et liniamentorum similitudine et notis corporis, quae inustae parvulo fuerant, nepos

10   agnitus. Admiratione deinde tot casuum periculorumque ab eodem successor regni destinatur.

11   Nomen illi inpositum Habidis, qui ut regnum accepit, tantae magnitudinis fuit, ut non frustra deorum maiestate tot periculis ereptus videretur. Quippe et barbarum populum legibus vinxit et boves primus aratro domari frumentaque sulco quaerere docuit et ex agresti cibo mitiora vesci odio eorum, quae ipse passus fuerat, homines coegit.

nourished by various kinds of animal milk. Then when he   4
was brought home, he ordered him thrown on a narrow
pathway on which cattle would come and go, a truly heartless man who preferred to have his grandson trampled
underfoot rather than die a simple death. When there, too,   5
he was unharmed and not without nourishment, he first
threw him before starving dogs that had been tormented
by being kept many days without food, and soon after that
even before pigs. So when he was not only unharmed but   6
also fed at the teats of some animals, he finally ordered
him thrown into the ocean. Then, quite clearly with some   7
divine help, he was transported amid surging waves and
ebbing and flowing waters as if on a ship, not a tide, and
set ashore by a gentle swell, and not much later a hind   8
appeared to offer her udders to the infant. Then eventually, by associating with his "nurse," the boy achieved remarkable swiftness; and among herds of deer he long traversed hills and forests with no less speed than they did.
Finally caught in a trap he was given to the king as a gift.   9
Then both from his familiar features and marks that had
been branded on his body as an infant, he was recognized
as his grandson. Then from wonder at so many mischances   10
and dangers he was designated by him as successor to the
kingdom.

He was given the name Habis, and when he accepted   11
the kingdom, his greatness was such that it seemed not in
vain that he had been snatched from so many dangers by
the gods' majesty. For he compelled a barbarous people
to live by laws, and he was also the first to teach them to
break in oxen for plowing and to grow grain through planting; and from revulsion with foods that he had himself
earlier experienced he forced men to leave a primitive diet

12 Huius casus fabulosi viderentur, ni et Romanorum conditores lupa nutriti et Cyrus, rex Persarum, cane alitus pro-
13 deretur. Ab hoc et ministeria servilia populo interdicta et
14 plebs in septem urbes divisa. Mortuo Habide regnum per
multa saecula ab successoribus eius retentum.

In alia parte Hispaniae et quae ex insulis constat, regnum penes Geryonem fuit. In hac tanta pabuli laetitia est,
ut, nisi abstinentia interpellata sagina fuerit, pecora rum-
15 pantur. Inde denique armenta Geryonis, quae illis temporibus solae opes habebantur, tantae famae fuere, ut
16 Herculem ex Asia praedae magnitudine inlexerint. Porro
Geryonem ipsum non triplicis naturae, ut fabulis proditur,
fuisse ferunt, sed tres fratres tantae concordiae extitisse,
ut uno animo omnes regi viderentur, nec bellum Herculi
sua sponte intulisse, sed cum armenta sua rapi vidissent,
amissa bello repetisse.

5. Post regna deinde Hispaniae primi Karthaginienses
2 imperium provinciae occupavere. Nam cum Gaditani a
Tyro, unde et Karthaginiensibus origo est, sacra Herculis
per quietem iussi in Hispaniam transtulissent urbemque
ibi condidissent, invidentibus incrementis novae urbis finitimis Hispaniae populis ac propterea Gaditanos bello
lacessentibus auxilium consanguineis Karthaginienses mi-
3 sere. Ibi felici expeditione et Gaditanos ab iniuria vindicaverunt et maiore iniuria partem provinciae imperio suo

---

11 See 1.4. Compare also the tales of the cast-out babies Moses, Oedipus, and (King) Arthur; a widespread founder-myth.

12 In fact, the word used is "province," reflecting the status of
Spain in the Roman Empire. For the founding of Carthage, see
18.3ff. "Gades" is Cadiz.

for one more refined. His adventures might seem mythical 12
but for reports that Rome's founders were suckled by a
wolf and that Cyrus, the king of the Persians, was, nourished by a dog.[11] By him the people were forbidden servile 13
occupations and the population was divided into seven
cities. On Habis' death the realm for many generations 14
remained with his successors.

In another part of Spain and one that was made up of
islands, regal power lay with Geryon. In it pasture is so
lush that without limit placed on their feeding animals
would burst. Thus the cattle of Geryon (cattle at the time 15
being thought the only form of wealth) were so famous
that they enticed Hercules from Asia by the size of the
plunder. Geryon himself was not triple bodied, as found 16
in mythology, they say, but there were three brothers living in such harmony that they all seemed guided by one
mind, and they did not of their own will make war on
Hercules but on seeing their cattle being stolen, had tried
to recover by war what they had lost.

5. After the Spanish dynasties the Carthaginians were
the first to take over the country.[12] For when the Gadita- 2
nians brought the cult of Hercules to Spain from Tyre,
which was also the Carthaginians' country of origin, having been so instructed in a dream, and there founded a
city, the neighboring Spanish peoples, envying the new
city's progress, made war on them, and the Carthaginians
sent their cousins help. There in a successful campaign 3
they both defended the people of Gades against aggression and also with even greater aggression annexed part of

4 adiecerunt. Postea quoque hortantibus primae expeditionis auspiciis Hamilcarem imperatorem cum manu magna
ad occupandam provinciam misere, qui magnis rebus gestis, dum fortunam inconsultius sequitur, in insidias deduc-
5 tus occiditur. In huius locum gener ipsius Asdrubal mittitur, qui et ipse a servo Hispani cuiusdam, ulciscente
6 domini iniustam necem, interfectus est. Et maior utroque
Hannibal imperator, Hamilcaris filius, succedit, siquidem
utriusque res gestas supergressus universam Hispaniam
domuit. Inde Romanis inlato bello Italiam per annos sede-
7 cim variis cladibus fatigavit, cum interea Romani missis in
Hispaniam Scipionibus primo Poenos provincia expule-
runt, postea cum ipsis Hispanis gravia bella gesserunt.
8 Nec prius perdomitae provinciae iugum Hispani accipere
potuerunt, quam Caesar Augustus perdomito orbe victri-
cia ad eos arma transtulit populumque barbarum ac ferum
legibus ad cultiorem vitae usum traductum in formam
provinciae redegit.

---

13 Gades claimed to have been founded in 1101 BC, almost
three centuries before Carthage; though a fable, it belies the
claim that to help the early city Carthage sent forces. In fact, there
is no evidence of Carthaginian rule in Spain before Hamilcar
Barca's time.

14 Hamilcar Barca. He, Hasdrubal, and Hannibal can be followed through Polyb. 1–3 and Rome's war with Hannibal through
Livy 21–30. The brothers P. and Cn. Cornelius Scipio went out to
Spain in 218 and remained there until their deaths in 211, to be
succeeded in 210 by the son of the former, the future Africanus,
who expelled the Carthaginians in 206.

the country to their empire.[13] Later, too, encouraged by   4
the success of their first expedition, they sent their general
Hamilcar[14] with a large force to seize the country, but
recklessly following up his good fortune after some great
success he was drawn into an ambush and killed. As his   5
replacement his own son-in-law Hasdrubal was sent out,
and he was also himself killed, by a certain Spaniard's slave
who was avenging the unjust execution of his master. And   6
a general greater than both succeeded him, Hannibal, son
of Hamilcar, since he surpassed both men's exploits and
conquered all Spain. Then bringing war on the Romans
he exhausted Italy with various defeats over sixteen years,
while in the meantime the Romans, sending the Scipios to   7
Spain, first drove the Carthaginians from the province and
then fought bitter wars with the Spaniards themselves.
But the Spaniards could not accept the yoke of their prov-   8
ince's subjection until Caesar Augustus,[15] having conquered the world, turned on them his victorious arms, and
bringing a wild, barbarous people to a more civilized way
of life under the rule of law reduced them to a regular
province.

[15] As Augustus himself noted at *Res gestae* 26.2. There was
campaigning in Spain from 27 to 19.

TROGI HISTORIARUM
PHILIPPICARUM
PROLOGI

1. Primo volumine continentur haec: Imperium Assyriorum a Nino rege usque ad Sardanapallum post quem
translatum est per Arbacem ad Medos, usque ad ultimum
regem Astyagem ; is a nepote suo Cyro pulsus regno, et
Persae regno potiti. ut Croeso Lydiae regi bellum intulit
Cyrus victumque cepit; hic in excessu dicti Aeolicarum et
Ionicarum urbium situs originesque Lydorum et in Italia
Tuscorum. post Cyrum filius Cambyses Aegyptum domuit; repetitae Aegypti origines urbium. extincto Cam-
byse Darius occisis magis regnum Persicum accepit cap-
taque Babylone bella Scythica molitus est.

2. Secundo volumine continentur haec: Scythiae et
Ponti situs originesque Scythiae usque ad bellum, quo est
inde pulsus Darius qui post hanc fugam Graeciae bellum
intulit per Datim et Tisaphernem, quod soli Athenienses
sustinuere. hic origines Athenarum repetitae et reges usque ad Pisistrati tyrannidem, qua extincta Marathone vi-

PROLOGUES TO THE
PHILIPPIC HISTORY
OF TROGUS

1. In the first volume the following is found: The empire of the Assyrians from King Ninus down to Sardanapallus, after whom sovereignty was transferred by Arbaces to the Medes, where it remained until their last king, Astyages. Astyages was driven from the throne by his grandson, Cyrus, and the Persians took power. Then an account of Cyrus' attack on King Croesus of Lydia, whom he defeated and captured. Here there is a digression on the geography of the Aeolic and Ionian cities and the origins of the Lydians, and, in Italy, of the Etruscans. After Cyrus, his son Cambyses conquered Egypt. Then one returns to the Egyptian cities' beginnings. After Cambyses' death, Darius killed the seers, acquired the throne of Persia, captured Babylon, and worked on Scythian wars.

2. In the second volume the following is found: The geography of Scythia and Pontus, and the early history of Scythia up to the war in which Darius was driven from there; after this rout he, using Datis and Tissaphernes, launched a war on Greece that only the Athenians could resist. Then comes the early history of Athens and an account of its kings down to the tyranny of Pisistratus, and after eliminating this, the Athenians defeated the Persians

307

cere Persas. ut mortuo Dario filius eius Xerxes bellum
Graeciae intulit: ac repetitae origines Thessaliae; expulsoque Graecia Xerxe bellum ab Atheniensibus translatum
in Asiam usque ad Xerxis interitum.

3. Tertio volumine continentur haec: ut mortuo Xerxe
filius Artaxerxes ultus interfectorem patris Artabanum
bellum cum defectore Aegypti habuit, primoque dux eius
Achaemenes victus est, iterum per Bagabaxum Aegyptus
recepta. ut Graecis cum rege pacificatis bella inter ipsos
orta sint. inde repetitae Peloponnensium origines: ut ab
Herculis posteris Dorico populo sit occupata. Deinde
bella Argolica et Messania, coalitique Sicyone et Corinthio
tyranni. Bellum Crisaeum et quod Athenienses primo
cum Boeotis, dein cum Peloponnesiis gesserunt.

4. Quarto volumine continentur res Siculae, ab ultima
origine usque ad deletam Syracusis Atheniensium classem.

5. Quinto volumine continentur haec: bellum inter
Athenienses et Lacedaemonios, quod Deceleicum voca-
tur, usque ad captas Athenas. ut expulsi sunt Athenis XXX
tyranni. bellum quod Lacedaemonii in Asia cum Artaxerxe
gesserunt propter Cyrum adiutum. hinc repetitum in excessu Cyri cum fratre bellum et Graecorum, qui sub eo
militaverunt.

6. Sexto volumine continentur haec: bellum Lacedaemoniorum gestum in Asia cum Persicis praefectis, ducibus
belli Dercylide et Agesilao, usque ad proelium navale factum Cnido : quo victis illis Athenienses repetiere impe-

at Marathon. Then how after Darius' death his son Xerxes made war on Greece; one goes back to the origins of Thessaly; after Xerxes was driven from Greece, war was transported into Asia up until Xerxes' death.

3. In the third volume the following is found: After Xerxes' death, his son Artaxerxes' vengeance on his father's murderer, Artabanus, and his war with the man responsible for the secession of Egypt; how, at first, his general Achaemenes was defeated, and how Egypt was retaken by Bagabaxus. How, after the Greeks made peace with the king, wars arose among themselves. Then one goes back to the beginnings of the Peloponnesians, how their country was occupied by Hercules' descendants, a Dorian people. Next the Argolic and Messanian wars and the alliance between the tyrants of Sicyon and Corinth. The war of Crisa and the one the Athenians fought first with the Boeotians and afterward with the Peloponnesians.

4. In the fourth volume the following is found: Sicilian history from its first beginnings down to the destruction of the Athenian fleet at Syracuse.

5. In the fifth volume the following is found: The war between the Athenians and the Spartans, called the Deceleian War, up to the capture of Athens. How the Thirty Tyrants were driven from Athens. The war that the Spartans waged with Artaxerxes in Asia because of the help given to Cyrus. Then a digression on the history of the war fought with his brother by Cyrus and the Greeks who served under him.

6. In the sixth volume the following is found: The war fought with the Persian satraps in Asia by the Spartans, led by Dercylides and Agesilaus, down to the naval battle at Cnidus, in which the Spartans were defeated, and the

rium. dein bellum Corinthiacum et bellum Boeotium, quo
Leuctris et Mantineae victi Spartani amisere imperium. in
Thessalia deinde Iasonis et post illum Alexandri Pheraei
coalitum atque extinctum imperium. tum sociale bellum
gestum adversus Athenienses a Chiis et Rhodiis et Byzan-
tiis. transitus hinc ad res Macedonicas.

7. Septimo volumine continentur origines Macedonicas regesque a conditore gentis Carano usque ad magnum
Philippum; ipsius Philippi res gestae usque ad captam
urbem Mothonen. additae in excessu Illyriorum et Paeo-
num origines.

8. Octavo volumine contingentur res gestae Philippi
Magni post captam urbem Mothonen, a principio belli
Phocensis, quod sacrum vocant, usque ad finem eius,
interiectumque huic bellum, quod Philippus cum Chalci-
dicis urbibus gessit, quarum clarissimam delevit Olyn-
thon. ut Illyrici reges ab eo victi sunt, et Thracia atque
Thessalia subactae, et rex Epiro datus Alexander erepto
Arybba, et frustra Perinthos oppugnata.

9. Nono volumine continentur haec: ut Philippus a
Perintho summotus. Byzantii origines, a cuius obsidione
summotus Philippus Scythiae bellum intulit. repetitae
inde Scythicae res ab his temporibus, in quibus illa prius
finierant, usque ad Philippi bellum, quod cum Athea Scythiae rege gessit. unde reversus Graeciae bellum intulit
victisque Chaeroneae, cum bella Persica moliretur prae-

Athenians regained their empire. Then the Corinthian War and the Boeotian War, in which the Spartans, defeated at Leuctra and Mantinea, lost their empire. Then, in Thessaly, the rule of Jason, and after him, of Alexander of Pherae, and its dissolution. Then the social war fought against the Athenians by the people of Chios, Rhodes, and Byzantium. At this point there is a transition to Macedonian history.

7. In the seventh volume the following is found: the early history of Macedonia and its kings, from its race's founder Caranus down to Philip the Great; and the exploits of Philip himself to the capture of the city of Mothone. In a digression there is also the early history of the Illyrians and the Paeonians.

8. In the eighth volume the following is found: Philip the Great's exploits after the capture of the city of Mothone, from the start of the Phocian War, which they call the Sacred War, to its end; and inserted into this is the war that Philip fought with the cities of Chalcidice, the most famous of which, Olynthus, he destroyed. How the Illyrian kings were defeated by him, Thrace and Thessaly conquered, and Alexander made king in Epirus after deposing Arybbas, and his unsuccessful attack on Perinthus.

9. In the ninth volume the following is found: How Philip was driven from Perinthus. The beginnings of Byzantium, the siege of which Philip was forced to abandon before his attack on Scythia. Then the history of Scythia is traced from the period at which the earlier account had broken off, right down to the war that Philip fought with Atheas, king of Scythia. Returning from there Philip invaded Greece and defeated the Greeks at Chaeronea, but while he was preparing for hostilities against Persia and

missa classe cum ducibus, a Pausania, occupatis angustiis nuptiarum filiae, occisus est, priusquam bella Persica inchoaret. repetitas res inde Persicae ab Dario Notho, cui successit filius Artaxerxes cognomine Mnemon, qui post fratrem Cyrum victum pulsaque Cnido per Conona classe Lacedaemoniorum bellum cum Euagora rege Cyprio gessit: originesque Cypri repetit.

10. Decimo volumine continentur Persicae res. ut Artaxerxes Mnemon pacificatus cum Euagora rege Cyprio bellum Aegyptium in urbe Ace conpararit, ipse in Cadusis victus, defectores in Asia purpuratos suos persecutus, primum Dotamen praefectum.—Paphlagonon origo repetita—, deinde praefectum Hellesponti Ariobarzanen, deinde in Syria praefectum Armeniae Oronten, omnibusque victis decesserit filio successore Ocho. is deinde occisis optimatibus Sidon accepit. Aegypto bellum ter intulit. ut post mortem Ochi regnarit Arses, deinde Darius, qui cum Alexandro Macedonum rege bello conflixit.

11. Undecimo volumine continentur res gestae Alexandri Magni usque ad interitum regis Persarum Darii, dictaeque in excessu origines et reges Cariae.

12. Duodecimo volumine continentur Alexandri magni bella a Bactriana et Indica usque ad interitum eius, dictaeque in excessu res a praefecto eius Antipatro in Graecia

had sent ahead a fleet with his generals aboard, he was assassinated by Pausanias (who caught him in a narrow passage at his daughter's wedding) before he could commence his Persian campaign. Persian history is then retraced to Darius Nothus, who was succeeded by his son, Artaxerxes, nicknamed Mnemon, who, defeating his brother Cyrus, and using Conon to rout the Spartan fleet at Cnidus, waged war with Evagoras, king of Cyprus. Then the author returns to Cyprus' beginnings.

10. In the tenth volume the following is found: Persian history. How Artaxerxes Mnemon, on making peace with Evagoras, king of Cyprus, prepared for war with Egypt in the city of Acre, how he was himself defeated among the Cadusi and punished his officials who were defecting in Asia, starting with Dotames, satrap of Paphlagonia. There is the early history of the Paphlagonians; then there is Artaxerxes' punishment of the satrap of the Hellespont, Ariobarzanes, and then, in Syria, of the satrap of Armenia, Orontes, and after vanquishing all these, Artaxerxes died, to be succeeded by his son, Ochus. This man then executed the nobles and captured Sidon; he made war on Egypt three times. After Ochus' death, Arses was king, and then Darius, who clashed with Alexander, king of the Macedonians.

11. In the eleventh volume the following is found: the history of Alexander the Great down to the death of Darius, king of Persia, with a digression on the origins and kings of Caria.

12. In the twelfth volume the following is found: Alexander the Great's Bactrian and Indian campaigns down to the time of his death, with digressions on the activities of his general Antipater in Greece, and those of the Spartan

gestae, et ab Archidamo, rege Lacedaemoniorum, Molos-
soque Alexandro in Italia, quorum ibi est uterque cum
exercitu deletus. additae his origines Italicae, Apulorum,
Lucanorum, Samnitium, Sabinorum, et ut Zopyrion in
Ponto cum exercitu periit.

13. Tertio decimo volumine continentur haec: ut mortuo Alexandro optimates castrorum eius provinciarum imperia sint partiti; ut veterani, qui ab eodem lecti erant in
colonias, moliti relictis illis in Graeciam redire a Pithone
sint deleti. bellum Lamiacum, quod Antipater in Graecia
gessit. bellum quo Perdiccas regem Ariarathem occidit;
occisus est. bellum quo Eumenes Neoptolemum et Cra-
teron occidit. additae in excessu origines regesque Quire-
narum.

14. Quarto decimo volumine continentur haec: bellum
inter Antigonum et Eumenen gestum: quem ut Cappadocia expulit Antigonus, sic Phrygia minore Arridaeum et
Cliton victos in Hellesponto nauali bello. repetitum rursus
bellum ab Eumene per Argyraspidas; quo victus ab Antigono interiit. ut in Macedonia Cassander victo Polyper-
chonte receptaque a Nicanore Munychia matrem Alexandri Olympiada Pydnae obsessam interfecit.

15. Quinto decimo volumine continentur haec: ut Demetrius Antigoni filius Gazae victus est ab Ptolomaeo. ut
Cassander in Macedonia filium Alexandri regis interfecit,
ac alterum Polyperchon. ut Cypro Ptolomaeum vicit
classe Demetrius idemque ab obsidione Rhodi summotus
est. repetita in excessu origo Rhodiorum. unde digressus

---

[1] That is, of Cyrene, as in Justin's text.

king Archidamus and Alexander the Molossian in Italy, where both were destroyed with their armies. Additional information is given on the beginnings in Italy of the Apulians, Lucanians, Samnites, and Sabines, and on how Zopyrion perished with his army in the Pontus.

13. In the thirteenth volume the following is found: How on Alexander's death his chief officers distributed governorships of provinces among themselves, and how veterans chosen by him to man the colonies left them and tried to return to Greece but were wiped out by Pithon. The Lamian War, which Antipater fought in Greece. The war in which Perdiccas killed King Ariarathes, and how Perdiccas was killed. The war in which Eumenes killed Neoptolemus and Crateros. There is also a digression on the origins and kings of the Quirenae.[1]

14. In the fourteenth volume the following is found: the war fought between Antigonus and Eumenes; Antigonus' expulsion of Eumenes from Cappadocia and of Arridaeus and Clitos from Lesser Phrygia, after defeat in a naval battle in the Hellespont. The war was restarted by Eumenes, using the Argyraspids, but he died after being defeated by Antigonus. How, in Macedonia, Cassander, after defeating Polyperchon and recovering Munychia from the defector Nicanor, besieged Alexander's mother Olympias at Pydna and killed her.

15. In the fifteenth volume the following is found: how Demetrius, son of Antigonus, was defeated at Gaza by Ptolemy. How in Macedonia Cassander killed King Alexander's son and Polyperchon killed the other. How Demetrius defeated Ptolemy with his fleet off Cyprus but was also forced to raise the siege of Rhodes. The early history of the Rhodians is traced in a digression; leaving there

Demetrius liberavit a Cassandro Graeciam. dein pater eius Antigonus bellum cum Lysimacho et Seleuco habuit, repetitaeque Seleuci res et regis Indiae Sandrocotti. ut victus bello Antigonus interiit reliquiaeque imperii sunt a filio collectae. Cleonymi deinde Spartani res gestae Corcyrae et Illyrico et in Italia, cui ablata Corcyra. rex Cassander interiit.

16. Sexto decimo volumine continentur haec: ut mortuo Cassandro ortisque inter filios eius certaminibus Demetrius adiutor alteri adhibitus occiso eo Macedoniae regnum tenuit: quo mox evictus a Pyrro Epiri rege, translatis in Asiam bellis captus a Seleuce decessit. ut Ptolomaeus nuncupato successore filio Philadelpho decessit. ut Lysimachus in Ponto captus ac missus a Dromichaete rursus in Asia civitates, quae sub Demetrio fuerant, et in Ponto Heracleam occuparit. Repetitae inde Bithyniae et Heracleoticae origines, tyrannique Heracleae Clearchus et Satyrus et Dionysius, quorum filiis interfectis Lysimachus occupavit urbem.

17. Septimo decimo volumine continentur haec: ut Lysimachus occiso filio Agathocle per novercam Arsinoen bellum cum rege Seleuco habuit, quo victus interiit: ultimumque certamen conmilitonum Alexandri fuit. ut Seleucus amissis in Cappadocia cum Diodoro copiis interfectus est ab Ptolomaeo fratre Arsinoes uxoris Lysimachi, in cuius vicem Ptolomaeus cognomine Ceraunus creatus ab exercitu rex Macedoniam occupauvit; bella cum Antiocho

Demetrius liberated Greece from Cassander. Then his father Antigonus waged war with Lysimachus and Seleucus. The history of Seleucus and of the Indian king Sandrocottus is taken up again. How Antigonus died after defeat in battle and the remnants of his empire were brought together by his son. Next come the exploits of the Spartan Cleonymus in Corcyra, Illyricum and Italy, and his loss of Corcyra. Then the death of King Cassander.

16. In the sixteenth volume the following is found: how, after Cassander died and disagreements arose among his sons, Demetrius, called to the support of one of them, killed him and assumed the throne of Macedonia; but, soon deposed by Pyrrhus, king of Epirus, he transferred the theater of war to Asia and died after being captured by Seleucus. How Ptolemy died after designating his son Philadelphus as his successor. How Lysimachus, captured in Pontus and released by Dromichaetes, again seized control of city-states in Asia that had been under Demetrius, and also of Heraclea in Pontus. One then goes back to the early history of Bithynia and Heraclea, and the tyrants of Heraclea: Clearchus, Satyrus and Dionysius, whose sons Lysimachus put to death and then took over the city.

17. In the seventeenth volume the following is found: how Lysimachus had his son Agathocles murdered by his stepmother Arsinoë, and then fought a war with King Seleucus in which he was defeated and lost his life; and that was the last fight between Alexander's comrades. How Seleucus, having lost his troops along with Diodorus, in Cappadocia, was killed by Ptolemy, brother of Lysimachus' wife, Arsinoë, and how Ptolemy, surnamed Ceraunus, made king in his place by the army, seized Macedonia;

et Pyrro conposuit, datis Pyrro auxiliis, quibus iret contra
Romanos defensum Tarentum. inde repetitae origines regum Epiroticorum usque ad Pyrrum, ipsiusque Pyrri res
gestae priusquam in Italiam traiecit.

18. Octavo decimo volumine continentur res a Pyrro
Epirota in Italia gestae contra Romanos, postque id bellum transitus eius in Siciliam adversus Carthaginenses.
inde origines Phoenicum et Sidonos et Veliae Carthagi-
nisque res gestae in excessu dictae.

19. Undevicensimo volumine continentur res Carthaginensium in Africa per Sabellum Annonem gestae et in
Sicilia, cum Selinuntem et Agragantum et Camerinam et
Gelam ceperunt; quo bello Dionysius Syracusanus Siciliae
regnum occupavit. bellum quod cum eo Poeni per Himil-
conem gesserunt, qui obsidione Syracusarum exercitum
et classem amisit.

20. Vicensimo volumine continentur res gestae Dionysii Siculi patris. ut pulsis Poenis Italica bella sit molitus.
inde repetitae origines Venetorum et Graecorum et Gallorum, qui Italiam incolunt. deductisque Dionysii rebus
ad interitum eius dictae quas Anno magnus in Africa gessit.

21. Uno et vicensimo volumine continentur haec: ut in
Sicilia Dionysius filius a patre amisso tractarit imperium.
per Dionysius eiectus bellum cum Siculis gessit, donec
amissis liberis et fratribus Corinthum ⟨stetit⟩ ; statim ⟨a

---

[2] "Sabellus," a conjecture by Ruehl adopted by Seel, means
"Sabine," which makes no sense: Hanno is Carthaginian. The
MSS reading *per Rubellum Annorum* may conceal a mention of
many (?) "years" (*per bellum multorum annorum?*) or some other
Punic name.

he brought the wars with Antiochus and Pyrrhus to an end, giving Pyrrhus aid to go to the defense of Tarentum against the Romans. Then one goes back to the early history of the Epirot kings down to the time of Pyrrhus, and the achievements of Pyrrhus himself before he crossed to Italy.

18. In the eighteenth volume the following is found: the exploits of Pyrrhus of Epirus against the Romans in Italy, and his expedition to Sicily after this war to face the Carthaginians. There follows a digression on the early years of the Phoenicians, Sidon, and Velia, and on the history of Carthage.

19. In the nineteenth volume the following is found: Carthaginian operations in Africa under Sabellus Anno,[2] and in Sicily, when they captured Selinus, Acragas, Camerina and Gela. In this war Dionysius the Syracusan seized control of Sicily. There is an account of the war that the Carthaginians fought against him under Himilco, who in besieging Syracuse lost his army and his fleet.

20. In the twentieth volume the following is found: the achievements of the elder Dionysius of Sicily. How, after defeating the Carthaginians, he undertook wars in Italy. Then one goes back to the origins of the Veneti, the Greeks and the Gauls that live in Italy. After an account of Dionysius' career up to his death, the exploits of Hanno the Great in Africa are recounted.

21. In the twenty-first volume the following is found: how, in Sicily, Dionysius the younger managed an empire after his father had died. Driven out by Dion, Dionysius battled with the Sicilians until, after losing his children and his brothers, he retired to Corinth. How Sicily was

Tim>oleonte Carthaginensium bello sit liberata Sicilia mortuoque Sosistrato iterum facta seditione arcessitique a bello Carthaginenses obsederunt Syracusas quo bello Agathocles nanctus imperium est.

22. Secundo et vicensimo uolumine continentur haec: res gestae Agathoclis: ut a Poenis nanctus imperium bellum cum ipsis gessit, primum in Sicilia; dehinc victus traiecit in Africam, ubi possessa provincia Ophellam regem Cyrenarum interfecit. ut rursus in Siciliam reversus, occupata totius insulae dominatione, cum revertisset in Africam, amissis copiis solus inde profugit in Siciliam, belloque ibi repetitus et cum Poenis pacem conposuit et dissidentes a se Siculos subiecit.

23. Tertio et vicensimo volumine continentur haec: ut Agathocles domita Sicilia bellum in Italia Bruttiis intulit. repetitae inde Bruttiorum origines. omnibus subactis rex seditione filii exheredati ac nepotis oppressus interiit. inter peregrinos deinde milites eius et Siculos bellum motum, quae causa Pyrrum, regem Epiri, in Siciliam adduxit. bella quae Pyrrus cum Poenis et Mamertinis ibi gessit et a Sicilia reuersus in Italiam victusque proelio a Romanis revertit Epirum.

24. Quarto et vicensimo volumine continentur haec: bellum quod inter Antigonum Gonatam et Antiochum Seleuci filium in Asia gestum est. bellum, quod Ptolo-

---

3 Sosistratus was an oligarchic leader at Syracuse between 330 and 316, at odds with Agathocles and then other enemies; he was murdered at a banquet in Acragas in 314 by a supposed ally, Acrotatus of Sparta.

4 The Mamertini, who called themselves after the Oscan war-

delivered from war with Carthage by Timoleon, and how, on Sosistratus' death,[3] there was a second revolt, and the Carthaginians were called in, who then blockaded Syracuse. In this war Agathocles came to power.

22. In the twenty-second volume the following is found. The history of Agathocles; how he gained power through the Carthaginians and later waged war against them, in Sicily first of all; then, defeated by them, he crossed to Africa, seized the province and killed Ophellas, king of Cyrene. Returning to Sicily again and taking over the whole island, he then returned to Africa, lost his troops, fled from there, alone, to Sicily and there, under attack again, he both made peace with the Carthaginians and brought under his power the Sicilians who had revolted from him.

23. In the twenty-third volume the following is found. How Agathocles, after subduing Sicily, made war on the Bruttii in Italy. Then one goes back to the origins of the Bruttii. After crushing all his foes, the king died in a conspiracy hatched by his son (whom he had disinherited) and his grandson. War then broke out between his foreign troops and the native Sicilians, and this brought Pyrrhus, king of Epirus, to Sicily, where he went to war with the Carthaginians and the Mamertini.[4] Returning to Sicily from Italy, Pyrrhus was defeated in battle by the Romans, and he returned to Epirus.

24. In the twenty-fourth volume the following is found. The war fought in Asia between Antigonus Gonatas and Antiochus, son of Seleucus. The war fought in Macedonia

god Mamers (Mars), were Italian mercenaries who after Agathocles' death seized Messana and plundered surrounding regions.

maeus Ceraunus in Macedonia cum Monio Illyrio et Ptolomaeo Lysimachi filio habuit, utque Arsinoen sororem suam imperio Macedonicarum urbium exuit, ipse cum Belgio Gallorum duce congressus interiit. repetitae inde Gallorum origines qui Illyricum occuparunt; atque ut ingressi Graeciam Brenno duce Delphis victi deletique sint.

25. Quinto et vicensimo volumine continentur haec: ut Antigonus Gallos delevit, deinde cum Apollodoro, Cassandreae tyranno, bellum habuit. ut Galli transierunt in Asiam bellumque cum rege Antiocho et Bithunia gesserunt: quas regiones Tyleni occuparunt. ut Pyrrus ex Italia reversus regno Macedoniae Antigonum exuerit, Lacedaemona obsederit, Argis interierit; filiusque eius Alexander Illyricum cum rege Mitylo bellum habuerit.

26. Sexto et vicensimo volumine continentur haec: quibus in urbibus Graeciae dominationem Antigonus Gonatas constituerit. ut defectores Gallos Megaris delevit regemque Lacedaemonium Area Corinthi interfecit, dehinc cum fratris sui Crateri filio Alexandro bellum habuerit. ut princeps Achaiae Aratus Sicuonem et Corinthum et Megara occuparit. ut in Syria rex Antiochus cognomine Soter altero filio occiso, altero rege nuncupato Antiocho decesserit. ut in Asia filius Ptolomaei regis socio Timarcho desciverit a patre. ut frater Antigoni Demetrius occupato Cyrenis regno interiit. ut mortuo rege Antiocho filius eius Seleucus Callinicus regnum acceperit.

27. Septimo et vicensimo volumine continentur haec:

by Ptolemy Ceraunus against Monunius the Illyrian and Ptolemy, son of Lysimachus, and how Ptolemy stripped his sister Arsinoë of her rule over the Macedonian cities and how he himself died in a clash with Belgius, leader of the Gauls. Then one returns to the early history of the Gauls who seized Illyricum; and after that they entered Greece under Brennus' leadership and were defeated and wiped out at Delphi.

25. In the twenty-fifth volume the following is found. How Antigonus wiped out the Gauls, then the war he fought with Apollodorus, tyrant of Cassandrea. How the Gauls crossed into Asia and made war on King Antiochus and Bithynia, regions that the Tyleni occupied. How on his return from Italy, Pyrrhus took the kingdom of Macedonia from Antigonus, blockaded Lacedaemon and died at Argos, and how his son Alexander went to war in Illyria with King Mitylus.

26. In the twenty-sixth volume the following is found. The Greek cities in which Antigonus Gonatas established his hegemony. How he wiped out the mutinous Gauls at Megara and killed the Lacedaemonian king, Areus, at Corinth; and then the war he fought with his brother Craterus' son Alexander. How the leader of Achaea, Aratus, seized Sicyon, Corinth and Megara. How in Syria King Antiochus, surnamed Soter, died after killing one of his sons and appointing the other, Antiochus, as heir to the throne. How in Asia King Ptolemy's son became an ally of Timarchus and rebelled against his father. How Antigonus' brother Demetrius died after assuming the rule of Cyrene; how, on the death of King Antiochus, his son Seleucus Callinicus ascended the throne.

27. In the twenty-seventh volume the following is

Seleuci bellum in Syria aduersus Ptolomaeum Tryphonem: item in Asia adversus fratrem suum Antiochum Hieracem, quo bello Ancurae victus est a Gallis: utque Galli Pergamo victi ab Attalo Zielan Bithunum occiderint. ut Ptolomaeus Adaeum denuo captum interfecerit, et Antigonus Andro proelio navali Sophrona vicerit. ut a Callinico fusus in Mesopotamia Antiochus insidiantem sibi effugit Ariamenen, dein postea custodes Tryphonis; quo a Gallis occiso Seleucus quoque frater eius decessit, maioremque filiorum eius Apaturius occidit.

28. Octavo et vicensimo volumine continentur haec: ut mortuo rege Epiri Alexandro Laodamiam Epirotae occiderint. dictique in excessu Basternici motus. ut rex Macedoniae Demetrius sit a Dardanis fusus: quo mortuo tutelam filii eius Philippi suscepit Antigonus, qui Thessaliam in Asia Cariam subiecit et adiutis Achaeis contra regem Spartanum Cleomenem cepit Lacedaemona: amissoque regno Cleomenes Spartanus confugit Alexandriam atque ibi interiit. dictum in excessu bellum Illyricum quod Romani gessere cum Teuta.

29. Undetricensimo volumine continentur haec: res gestae Philippi regis adversus Dardanos et Aetolos. repetitaeque inde Creticae origines; post cuius insulae societatem Philippus cum Illyriis et Dardanis et rursus Aetolis bello congressus est adiuvantibus Aetolos Romanis: quo finito intulit Attalo bellum.

30. Tricensimo volumine continentur haec: ut mortuo

found: Seleucus' war in Syria against Ptolemaeus Trypho, and again in Asia against his own brother Antiochus Hierax, a war in which he was defeated by the Gauls at Ancyra; and how the Gauls, defeated by Attalus at Pergamum, killed Zielas of Bithynia. How Ptolemy captured Adaeus for the second time and put him to death, and how Antigonus defeated Sophron in a naval battle at Andros. How Antiochus, put to flight in Mesopotamia by Callinicus, escaped the clutches of Ariamenes, who was plotting against him, and later escaped from Trypho's guards; and after he was killed by the Gauls, his brother Seleucus also died, and Apaturius killed the elder of Seleucus' sons.

28. In the twenty-eighth volume the following is found: How on the death of Alexander, king of Epirus, the people of Epirus killed Laodamia. There is a digression on upheavals among the Basterni. How King Demetrius of Macedon was defeated by the Dardani; and how on his death, the guardianship of his son, Philip, was taken up by Antigonus, who reduced Thessaly and Caria in Asia and, assisting the Achaeans against the Spartan king Cleomenes, captured Sparta. On losing his throne, the Spartan Cleomenes fled to Alexandria and there died. In a digression there is an account of the Illyrian War that the Romans fought with Teuta.

29. In the twenty-ninth volume the following is found: The exploits of King Philip against the Dardani and the Aetolians, and then one returns to the early history of Crete. After forming an alliance with this island, Philip clashed with the Illyrians, the Dardani and then again with the Aetolians, who received assistance from the Romans. When that ended, Philip attacked Attalus.

30. In the thirtieth volume the following is found: How,

Ptolomaeo Tryphone filius eius Philopator Antiochum
regem vicit Raphiae, ipse amore Agathocleae corruptus
decessit relicto filio pupillo, in quem cum Philippo rege
Macedonum consensit Antiochus. Philippi deinde gesta in
Asia, cum movisset Attalo bella: a quibus reversus bellum
habuit cum ducibus Romanis Sulpicio et Flaminino, a quibus victus; pax. transitus deinde ad res Antiochi, qui post
regnum acceptum persecutus defectores in Mediam Mo-
lonem, in Asiam Achaeum, quem obsedit Sardibus, pacata
superiore Asia Bactris tenus in bella Romana descendit.

31. Uno et tricensimo volumine continentur haec: bellum, quod cum Lacedaemonio Nabide Titus Flamininus
et Philopoemen dux Achaeorum gessit. item bellum, quod
cum Antiocho in Achaia per Acilium consulem, et in Asia
per Scipionem gestum est, denique Hannibalis ad regem
a Carthagine fuga. bellum cum Aetolis gestum per eundem Acilium, qui Antiochum Graecia expulerat.

32. Secundo et tricensimo volumine continentur haec:
defectio ab Achaeis Lacedaemoniorum et Messeniorum,
qua Philopoemen interiit. Romanorum in Asia duce Manlio adversus Gallos bellum. regis Philippi propter ablatas
sibi civitates alienatus in Romanos animus, et ob hoc alter
filiorum Demetrius occisus, concitatique ab eo Basternae
transire conati in Italiam. inde in excessu dictae res Illyri-
cae: ut Galli, qni occuparant Illyricum, rursus redierunt in
Galliam: originesque Pannoniorum et incrementa Daco-

---

[5] Gnaeus Manlius Vulso, consul 189; this war, and the loot
Manlius gained, were strongly criticized at Rome.

on the death of Ptolemy Trypho, his son Philopator defeated King Antiochus at Raphia, and how Philopator himself died, ruined by love for Agathoclea and leaving a son who was still a minor (against whom Antiochus conspired with Philip, king of Macedon). Then come Philip's exploits in Asia after he started wars with Attalus and, returning from there, he fought with the Roman generals, Sulpicius and Flamininus, by whom he was defeated. Peace followed. Then a transition to the history of Antiochus who, after taking the throne, pursued the rebels, Molon into Media and Achaeus into Asia. Achaeus he besieged in Sardis and then, after subduing Upper Asia as far as Bactria, he went into his Roman wars.

31. In the thirty-first volume the following is found: The war that Titus Flamininus and Philopoemen, the leader of the Achaeans, fought with the Lacedaemonian Nabis. Also the war fought with Antiochus in Achaea under the consul Acilius, and in Asia under Scipio, and finally Hannibal's flight to the king from Carthage. Then the war with the Aetolians prosecuted by the same Acilius who had driven Antiochus from Greece.

32. In the thirty-second volume the following is found: The Spartans' and Messenians' defection from the Achaeans, during which Philopoemen was killed. Then the war of the Romans against the Gauls in Asia, conducted by the Romans under Manlius' leadership.[5] King Philip's anger with the Romans over cities taken from him and the killing of one of his sons, Demetrius, over this, and his incitement of the Basternae, who attempted to cross to Italy. Then a digression on Illyria, on how the Gauls who had seized Illyricum returned to Gaul again; and on the beginnings of Pannonia and the progress of the Dacians thanks to

327

rum per Burobusten regem. in Asia bellum ab rege Eu-
mene gestum adversus Gallum Ortiagontem, Pharnacem
Ponticum et Prusian, adivuante Prusian Hannibale Poeno.
res gestae Hannibalis post victum Antiochum et mors.
Mortuo Seleuco filio Magni Antiochi successit regno frater
Antiochus.

33. Tertio et tricensimo volumine continentur haec: ut
cum Perse Philippi filio, rege Macedonum, Romani bellum gesserint: quo capto deleta est Epiros. Achaicae civitates ab unitate corporis deductae, inter Achaeos et Lacedaemonios certamine orto. bellum rursus in Macedonia
gestum a Romanis cum Pseudophilippo.

34. Quarto et tricensimo volumine continentur haec:
bellum Achaicum, quod Romani per Metellum et Mum-
mium gessere, quo diruta est Corinthos. bellum regis
Eumenis cum Gallograecis et in Pisidia cum Selegensibus.
res quas gessit Syrias rex Antiochus, et rex Aegypti Ptolomaeus [repetitae inde origines rerum Cappadocium] Epiphanes. ut mortuo Ptolomaeo relicti ab eo filii duo Philometor et Euergetes primum cum Antiocho habuere
bellum, quod per Romanos finitum est, deinde inter se,
quo maior est expulsus, restitutoque Romani inter fratres
regna diviserunt. ut mortuo Antiocho rege Syriae Demetrius cognomine Soter, qui Romae fuerat obses, clam fugit
occupataque Syria bellum cum Timarcho Medorum rege

---

6 Burebista (the usual spelling) was king of Dacia in the mid-
first century BC, more than a century after the other events in
Book 32.

7 "Pseudo-Philip" was one Andriscus, who claimed to be the
son of Perseus, and so the rightful king of Macedonia. He seized

King Burobustes.[6] The war fought in Asia by King Eumenes against the Gaul Ortiagontes, Pharnaces of Pontus, and Prusias, in which the Carthaginian Hannibal aided Prusias. Then Hannibal's exploits after the defeat of Antiochus, and his death. When Seleucus, son of Antiochus the Great, died, his brother Antiochus succeeded to the throne.

33. In the thirty-third volume the following is found: The war the Romans fought with Perseus, son of Philip, king of Macedon, on whose capture Epiros was destroyed. The collapse of the unity of the Achaean city-states through antagonism arising between the Achaeans and Spartans. Then recommencement of the war in Macedonia by the Romans against Pseudo-Philip.[7]

34. In the thirty-fourth volume the following is found: The Achaean War, which the Romans fought under the leadership of Metellus and Mummius, and in which Corinth was destroyed. King Eumenes' war with the Gallograeci and, in Pisidia, with the Selegenses. The exploits of King Antiochus of Syria and King Ptolemy Epiphanes of Egypt. How, on the death of Ptolemy, the two sons left by him, Philometor and Euergetes, first fought a war against Antiochus (one finished by the Romans), and then fought one between themselves, in which the elder was driven out, and when he was restored the Romans divided the kingdom between the two brothers. How, on the death of Antiochus, king of Syria, Demetrius, surnamed Soter, who had been a hostage in Rome, fled surreptitiously and seizing Syria made war on Timarchus, king of the Medes,

the country in 149 with some popular support but was defeated and captured in 148 by Metellus.

habuit Ariarathe rege Cappadocum. repetitae inde origines regum Cappadocum. ut habita inter Ariarathen et Orophernem regni certamina. ut mortuo rege Asiae Eumene suffectus Attalus bellum cum Selegensibus habuit et cum rege Prusia.

35. Quinto et tricensimo volumine continentur haec: bellum piraticum inter Cretas et Rhodios; seditio Cnidiorum aduersus Ceramenses. ut adversus Demetrium Sotera subornatus est Alexander tamquam genitus Epiphane Antiocho, quo bello victus Demetrius. invisum stultitia Alexandrum bello vicit adiuvante Ptolomaeo Philometore, qui eo bello interiit. ut deinde orta Demetrio bella sint cum Diodoto Tryphone expulsusque a Tryphone regno Syriae Demetrius. repetit inde superioris Asiae motus factos per Araetheum et Arsacen Parthum.

36. Sexto et tricensimo volumine continentur haec: ut Trypho pulso Syria Demetrio captoque a Parthis bellum gessit cum fratre eius Antiocho cognomine Sidete. ut Antiochus interfecto Hyrcano Iudaeos subegit. repetita inde in excessu origo Iudaeorum. ut rex Asiae Attalus Caenos Thracas subegit successoremque imperii Attalum Philometora reliquit. Mortuo denique Philometore regno Asiae occupato bellum cum Romanis gessit, quo captus est.

37. Septimo et tricensimo volumine continentur haec: repetitis regum Ponticorum originibus, ut ‹ad› ultimum

---

8 Ceramus stood on the Ceramic Gulf, Asia Minor, opposite the peninsula of Cnidus.

9 Philometor (Mother-loving) was a title taken by Attalus III of Pergamum, who died in 133 BC.

and Ariarathes, king of Cappadocia. Then one returns to Cappadocia's early history. How there were quarrels over the throne between Ariarathes and Orophernes. How, on the death of Eumenes, king of Asia, Attalus replaced him and fought a war with the Selegenses and King Prusias.

35. In the thirty-fifth volume the following is found: The pirate war between the peoples of Crete and Rhodes; and the rebellion of the people of Cnidus against the Ceramians.[8] How Alexander was induced to challenge Demetrius Soter, claiming to be the son of Antiochus Epiphanes, this leading to war in which Demetrius was defeated and died. How then Demetrius, the eldest of his sons, defeated Alexander, who had become hated because of his stupidity, with the help of Ptolemy Philometor, who died in that war. How wars then arose between Demetrius and Diodotus Trypho, resulting in Demetrius being driven from the throne of Syria by Trypho. The author then goes back to the upheavals in Upper Asia caused by Araetheus and the Parthian Arsaces.

36. In the thirty-sixth volume the following is found: How after Demetrius had been driven from Syria and taken prisoner by the Parthians, Trypho made war on Antiochus, surnamed Sidetes, Demetrius' brother. How Antiochus killed Hyrcanus and crushed the Jews. Then a digression on the beginnings of the Jews. How Attalus king of Asia conquered the Thracian Caeni and left Attalus Philometor as successor to his empire. Finally, on King Philometor's death,[9] his brother Aristonicus seized the kingdom of Asia and fought a war with the Romans in which he was captured.

37. In the thirty-seventh volume the following is found: After a return to the early history of the Pontic kings, the

Mithridaten Eupatora series imperii deducta sit, atque ut
ingressus ille regnum subegit Pontum et Paphlagoniam,
priusquam in bella Romana descendit. dictaeque in excessu regum Bosporanorum et Colchorum origines et res
gestae.

38. Octavo et tricensimo volumine continentur haec:
ut Mithridates Eupator occiso Ariarathe Cappadociam
occuparit victoque Nicomede et Maltino Bithyniam. ut
mortuo Ptolomaeo Philometore frater eius Physcon accepto regno Aegypti seditiones populi, deinde bellum cum
uxore sua Cleopatra et cum rege Syriae Demetrio habuit.
inde repetitum, ut Demetrius captus sit a Parthis et frater
eius victo in Syria Tryphone bellum Parthis intulerit, qui
cum exercitu suo deletus est.

39. Nono et tricensimo volumine continentur haec: ut
extincto a Parthis Antiocho Sidete frater eius Demetrius
dimissus regnum Syriae recepit suborvatoque in bellum
adversus eum Alexandro Zabineo interiit: filiusque eius
Antiochus Grypos victo Zabinaeo regnum occupavit: dehinc cum fratre suo Antiocho Cyziceno bellum in Syria
Ciliciaque gessit. ut Alexandria mortuo rege Ptolomaeo
Physcone filius eius Ptolomaeus Lathyros accepto regno
expulsus est a matre Cyprum et in Syria bello petitus ab
eadem, suffecto in locum eius fratre Alexandro, donec
occisa per Alexandrum matre recepit Aegypti regnum. ut
post Lathyrum filius Alexandri regnarit expulsoque eo suffectus sit Ptolomaeus Nothus. ut Syriam Iudaei et Arabes

succession of power in Pontus down to its last king, Mith-ridates Eupator; and then how, on assuming the throne, Mithridates subdued Pontus and Paphlagonia before entering his wars with Rome. There is a digression on the beginnings and exploits of the kings of the Bosphorus and Colchis.

38. In the thirty-eighth volume the following is found: how Mithridates Eupator killed Ariarathes and seized Cappadocia, and after defeating Nicomedes and Maltinus, Bithynia. How, on the death of Ptolemy Philometor, his brother Physcon on acceding to the throne of Egypt, first faced rebellions among his people, then war with his sister Cleopatra and with the king of Syria, Demetrius. Then a glance back to Demetrius' capture by the Parthians and how his brother, after defeating Trypho in Syria, made war on the Parthians, and was wiped out with his army.

39. In the thirty-ninth volume the following is found: How, after Antiochus Sidetes was killed by the Parthians, his brother Demetrius was released and recovered the throne of Syria, but died when Alexander Zabinaeus was bribed into making war on him; and his son Antiochus Grypos then defeated Zabinaeus, seized the throne, and thereafter fought a war in Syria and Cilicia with his brother Antiochus Cyzicenus. How, on King Ptolemy Physcon's death in Alexandria, his son Ptolemy Lathyrus came the throne but was driven out to Cyprus by his mother, and how in Syria he was attacked by her, after she had put his brother Alexander on the throne, until eventually the mother was killed by Alexander, and he recovered the throne of Egypt. How after Lathyrus Alexander's son reigned, and on his expulsion was replaced by Ptolemy Nothus. How Jews and Arabs plagued Syria with maraud-

terrestribus latrociniis infestarint, mari Cilices piraticum
bellum mouerint, quod in Cilicia Romani per Marcum
Antonium gesserunt. ut in Syria Heracleo post mortem
regis occuparit imperium.

40. Quadragensimo volumine continentur haec: ut
mortuo Grypo rege Cyzicenus cum filiis eius bello congressus interiit, hi deinde a filio Cyziceni Eusebe; extinc-
taque regum Antiochorum domo Tigranes Armenius Syriam occupavit, quo mox victo Romani abstulere eam. ut
Alexandriam post interitum Ptolomaei Lathyri substituti
sint eius filii: alteri data Cypros, cui P. Clodii rogatione
Romani abstulerunt eam; alter seditione flagitatus Alexandriae Romam profugit belloque per Gabinium gesto recepit imperium: quo mortuo successit filius, qui cum sorore
Cleopatra certamine insumpto et Pompeium magnum
interfecit et bellum cum Caesare Alexandriae gessit. Ut
successit eius regno soror Cleopatra, quae inligato in amo-
rem suum M. Antonio belli Actiaci fine extinxit regnum
Ptolomaeorum.

41. Uno et quadragensimo volumine continentur res
Parthicae et Bactrianae: in Parthicis ut est constitutum
imperium per Arsacem regem. successores deinde eius
Artabanus et Tigranes cognomine Deus, a quo subacta est

---

10 Heracleo was a favorite of Antiochus VIII Grypos and had
him murdered in 96 in hopes of becoming king of Syria, but was
prevented by the dead king's brother, who briefly became ruler
as Seleucus VI.

11 Publius Clodius Pulcher, the aristocratic populist and bitter
enemy of Cicero, was tribune in 58 and carried a law to annex
Cyprus, intending to seize its royal treasury for the Roman voters'

ing on land, and the Cilicians started a pirate war at sea, one that the Romans fought in Cilicia under Marcus Antonius. How Heracleo seized power in Syria after the death of the king.[10]

40. In the fortieth volume the following is found: How, on King Grypos' death, Cyzicenus died in armed conflict with the man's sons, and how these were then wiped out by Eusebes, son of Cyzicenus; and how, when war broke out again and the royal house of the Antiochi was wiped out, the Armenian Tigranes seized Syria but was soon defeated and the Romans took it from him. How, at Alexandria, after Ptolemy Lathyrus' death, his sons replaced him; one of them was given Cyprus, which the Romans took from him on the proposal of P. Clodius;[11] the other when his arrest was demanded during an uprising in Alexandria, fled to Rome, and he later recovered his throne through a war fought by Gabinius. On his death he was succeeded by his son who, now in rivalry with his sister, Cleopatra, murdered Pompey the Great and also went to war with Caesar at Alexandria. How his sister, Cleopatra, succeeded him on the throne, how she embroiled M. Antonius in a love affair, and how, with the end of the battle of Actium, she wiped out the rule of the Ptolemies.

41. In the forty-first volume the following is found: Parthian and Bactrian history. How in Parthia their empire was founded by King Arsaces. Then come his successors Artabanus and Tigranes, surnamed Theos,[12] by whom

---

benefit. The humiliated king committed suicide. The other son of Lathyrus was Ptolemy XII Auletes (Flute player), whose daughter was the memorable Cleopatra VII.

[12] "God," a common title among Hellenistic kings.

Media et Mesopotamia. dictusque in excessu Arabiae situs. in Bactrianis autem rebus ut a Diodoto rege constitutum imperium est: deinde quo repugnante Scythicae gentes, Saraucae et Asiani, Bactra occupavere et Sogdianos. Indicae quoque res additae, gestae per Apollodotum et Menandrum, reges eorum.

42. Secundo et quadragensimo uolumine continentur Parthicae res: ut praefectus Parthis a Phrate Himerus Mesenis bellum intulit et in Babylonios et Seleucenses saevit : utque Phrati successit rex Mithridates cognomine Magnus, qui Armeniis bellum intulit. inde repetitae origines Armeniorum et situs. ut varia conplurium regum in Parthis successione imperium accepit Orodes, qui Crassum delevit et Syriam per filium Pacorum occupavit. illi successit Phrates, qui et cum Antonio bellum habuit et cum Tiridate. additae his res Scythicae. reges Tocharorum Asiani interitusque Saraucarum.

43. Tertio et quadragensimo volumine continentur origines priscorum Latinorum, situs urbis Romae et res usque ad Priscum Tarquinium. origines deinde Liguriae et Massiliensium res gestae.

44. Quarto et quadragensimo volumine continentur res Hispaniae et Punicae.

Media and Mesopotamia were brought into subjection. In a digression, the Arabian geography. In Bactrian history, how the empire was founded by King Diodotus; then, during his reign, the Scythian tribes, the Saraucae and the Asiani conquered Bactra and Sogdiana. Indian history is also added, the achievements of the Indian kings Apollodotus and Menander.

42. In the forty-second volume the following is found: Parthian history. How, when made governor of Parthia by Phrates, Himerus made war on the Meseni and brutally treated the Babylonians and Seleucians; and how Phrates was succeeded by King Mithridates, surnamed The Great, who made war on the Armenians. There follows a review of the beginnings of Armenia and its geography. How, after a succession of several different kings in Parthia, Orodes came to the throne, the man who destroyed Crassus and through his son Pacorus seized control of Syria. He was succeeded by Phrates, who went to war with both Antonius and Tiridates. A section on Scythian history is added. The Asian kings of the Tochari, and the end of the Saraucae.

43. In the forty-third volume the following is found: The origins of the ancient Latins, the topography of the city of Rome and its history down to Tarquinius Priscus. Then the beginnings of Liguria and the history of Massilia.

44. In the forty-fourth volume the following is found: The history of Spain and Carthage.

INDEX TO THE *EPITOME*

Romans are listed according to family name; elements of nomenclature given in parentheses do not appear in the text of Justin.

heroes of assist Hercules
against the Amazons, 2.4.19;
Pausanias aims for monarchic
power in, 2.15.14; internal
war in, 3.2.1; treasury of,
3.6.4; seized by the Athenians, 4.3.5; combined council of, 8.1.4; end of independence of, 9.3.11; Philip, not
king, but general of, 9.4.2;
council of selected by Philip,
9.5.2; cities of summoned to
Corinth by Alexander, 11.2.5;
Antipater made governor of,
13.4.5; Polyperchon made
governor of, 13.6.9; is under
Cassander's control, 15.1.5;
attacked by the Gauls, 24.4.6,
24.6.1; makes war on Philip
V, 30.3.7; independence of
restored, 31.3.2; cities of
complain about Philip in
Rome, 32.2.3

Greeks: take Troy, 43.1.10; favor
Croesus, 1.7.9; defeat Xerxes,
2.15.20; are old enemies of
the Persians, 11.9.4; army of
against Mardonius, 2.14.4;
ten thousand of return from
the Persians, 5.11.10f.; ordered by Artaxerxes to cease
hostilities, 6.6.1; desert Alexander, 11.2.9f.; in Alexander's
army, 11.9.4; refined teach-
ings of, 2.2.14, 11.11.12; hold
Italy, 20.1.3ff., 20.2.1f.; fawn
upon Philip, 8.4.7; accept
Philip and his son Alexander
as "general," 9.4.2, 11.2.5;

rush to arms against Alexander, 12.1.6; sign of conceding
victory among, 6.6.10

Grinus, 13.7.2

Grypos. *See* Antiochus VIII
Grypos

Gygaea, 7.4.5

Gyges (king of Lydia), 1.7.17ff.

Gylippus, 4.4.7ff., 4.5.9

Gyptis, 43.3.9ff.

Habis, 44.4.11ff.

Haemus, Mount, 7.4.1

Halicarnassus, 2.12.23

Hamilcar (father of Hannibal),
general in Spain, 44.5.4,
44.5.6

Hamilcar (son of Gisgo; 314–
309), 22.3.6ff.; lays siege to
Syracuse, 22.4.1; dies, 22.7.1,
22.8.2

Hamilcar (son of Mago),
19.1.1ff.; killed in Sicily along
with his army (480/79), 4.2.7,
19.2.1; sons of, 19.2.1

Hamilcar (surnamed "Roda-
nus"; ca. 330), 21.6.1ff.

Hamilcar (uncle of Bomilcar),
22.7.10; fights in Sicily (314),
22.2; condemned by his own
people, dies opportunely,
22.3.2ff.

Hammon: attempt on temple of
by Cambyses, 1.9.3; visited by
Alexander, 11.11.2ff.; Alexander wishes to be buried in the
temple of, 12.15.7; Alexander's body escorted to the
temple of, 13.4.6

INDEX TO THE *EPITOME*

Ninias (son of Ninus and Semi-
ramis), 1.1.10, 1.2.10f.
Ninus (first king of the Assyri-
ans), 1.1, 2.3.18
Nola, people of, 20.1.13
Nomius, 13.7.7
Numidians, 19.2.4, 22.8.10,
33.1.2, 38.6.5
Numitor, 43.2f.
Nysa, 12.7.6

Ocean: Indian, 12.10.1, 12.10.4,
12.13.1; in the West, 43.3.6,
44.1.3
Ochus, 10.1.1, 10.3.1ff.
Cn. Octavius (praetor 168),
33.2.5
Oenanthe, 30.2.3f.
Olympias (daughter of Neoptolemus, king of the Molos-
sians), 7.6.10, 17.3.14; descended from the Aeacids,
12.16.3; wife of Philip, 7.6.10;
repudiated by Philip, 9.5.9,
11.11.3ff.; goes away to Epirus, 9.7.5ff.; believed to have
been aware of his murder,
9.7; kills Philip's widow,
Cleopatra, 9.7.12; mother of
Alexander and Cleopatra,
9.5.9, 12.16.2, 13.6.4; makes
accusations against Antipater
to Alexander, 12.14.3; favor-
ably disposed toward Perdiccas, 13.6.4; lives in Macedonia, 13.6.12; sent for by
Polyperchon, 14.5.1; comes
from Epirus to Macedonia,
14.5.9; has Arridaeus and Eu-

rydice killed, 14.5.10; be-
sieged and killed by Cas-
sander, 14.6.1ff., 15.1.3; her
brother, 8.6.5; her sister,
7.6.11; her name, 9.7.13
Olympias (daughter of Pyrrhus),
28.1.1ff., 28.3.1f.
Olympic festival, 13.5.3
Olympic games, 7.2.14, 12.16.6
Olympus, Mount, 7.4.1
Olynthians, attacked by the
Macedonians, 7.4.6
Olynthus: captured by Mardo-
nius, 2.14.1; attacked by
Philip, 8.3.10f.
Onomarchus (general of the
Phocians), 8.1.14
Ophelias, 22.7.4f.
Orchomenians (enemies of the
Thebans), 11.3.8
Orestes, 17.3.7
Orithyia (queen of the Ama-
zons), 2.4.17, 2.4.20ff.
Orodes (king of the Parthians),
42.4.2ff., 42.4.11ff.
Oroles, 32.3.16
Oropastes, 1.9.9
Oropherynes, 35.1.2f.
Orpheus, 11.7.14
Ostia, 34.3.8
Oxyartes, 13.4.21

Pacorus, 42.4.5, 42.7.9ff.
Paeonia, 7.1.5
Palatium, 43.1.6
Pallanteum, 43.1.6
Pamphylia, 13.4.15
Pan, 43.1.7
Panasagorus, 2.4.28

374

6.2.13, 12.7.11; worship only
one god, 1.10.5; custom of at
banquets, 7.3.3; under the
leadership of Cyrus, revolt
against the Medes and trans-
fer power over Asia to themselves, 1.6ff.; handed over to
Sybares' control, 1.7.1; wage
war with the Athenians, 2.9;
wage war with the Greeks,
2.11ff.; wage war with Alexander, Books 11–12; wage
war with the Scythians,
1.8.10, 37.3.2; wage war with
the Tyrians, 18.3.6; attacked
by Philip, 9.5.8; submissively
accept the Macedonian yoke
of enslavement, 11.14.7; in
Alexander's army, 12.12; allotted to Peucestes, 13.4.23; aid
the Syrians against the Parthians, 36.1.4
Perusia, 20.1.11
Peucestes, 13.4.23
Phalantus, 3.4.8ff.
Pharnabazus (satrap of Artaxerxes Mnemon), 6.1.2ff.
Pharnabazus (satrap of Darius
Nothus), 5.4.1
Pharnaces (Mithridates' grandfather), 38.6.2
Phasis, 2.2.1
Philip (Alexander's doctor),
11.8.5
Philip (Alexander's general),
upon Alexander's death, Par-
thians allotted to, 13.4.23
Philip (brother of Lysimachus),
15.3.12

Philip (father of Antigonus),
13.4.14
Philip (son of Antipater),
12.14.6ff.
Philip (son of Argeus; king of
Macedon), 7.2.5
Philip (son of Lysimachus),
24.3.5ff.
Philip (son of Perseus), 33.2.5
Philip II (son of Amyntas and
Eurydice), 7.5.1ff.; his brothers, 7.4.5, 8.3.11; hostage in
Thebes, 6.9.7, 7.5.2, 11.4.5;
hostage in Illyria, 7.5.1; becomes king, 7.5.9ff.; his ac-
complishments, 7.6, 8.1 ff.,
9.1ff.; his life, 9.8.1; his esti-
mation among the Greeks,
8.2.5ff.; put to flight by the
Scythians, 9.2, 9.3.1ff., 37.3.2,
38.7.3; victorious against the
Illyrians and in a race at
Olympia, 12.16.6; repudiates
Olympias and does not ac-
knowledge Alexander, 9.5.9,
11.11.4f.; promotes Cleopatra's relatives to high offices,
11.5.1; his troops, 9.5.6; his
death, 9.6.4; his natural abil-
ity, 7.6.1; his character,
9.8.4ff.; his sons, 9.8.2f.,
11.2.3; his daughter, 14.6.3
Philip IV (son and successor of
Cassander), 15.4.24; his
death, 16.1.1
Philip V (son of Demetrius;
king of Macedon), 28.3.9; his
age, 28.4.16, 29.1.2, 30.4.12;
wages war with the Dardani-

its borders touched by Vezosis, 1.1.6; its gulf conquered by the Amazons, 2.4.26; its governor Zopyrion, 12.2.16; occupied by Mithridates, 37.3.3

Pontus (sea), 2.1.19, 13.4.6

(C.) Popillius (Laenas; Roman ambassador to Antiochus IV), 34.3.1ff.

(M. Porcius) Cato (orator), 33.2.1; Pref. 5

M. (Porcius) Cato (son of previous), 33.2.1

Porus, 12.8

Praesidae, 12.8.9

Priam, 17.3.6

Priapatius, 41.5.8

Protarchus, 39.1.4

Protis, 43.3.8, 43.3.11

Prusias (king of Bithynia): receives Hannibal, 32.4.2, 32.4.5; wages war with Eumenes, 32.4.2ff.; replaced and killed by his son, 34.4

Ptolemy (Apion; king of Cyrene), 39.5.2

Ptolemy (general in Alexander's army): promoted from the ranks, 13.4.10; miraculously restored to health, 12.10.3; rejects Arridaeus' claim to the throne, 13.2.11; allotted Egypt and part of Africa and Arabia, 13.4.10; adds Cyrene to his empire, 13.6.20; how he ruled, 13.6.18ff.; has Perdiccas as his adversary, 13.6.13, 13.6.16; defeats De-

metrius at Gaza, 15.1.6; defeated by Demetrius, 15.2.6; given the title "King," 15.2.11; wages a final battle against Antigonus, 15.2.15ff., 15.4; allies himself with Lysimachus, 15.4.24; shifts the theater of war against Demetrius to Europe, 16.2.1; his kingdom, 15.1.5; dies after passing the crown on to his son, 16.2.7; his son, 15.2.7; his brother, 15.2.7

Ptolemy (grandson of Pyrrhus), 28.1.1, 28.3.1

Ptolemy (son of Lysimachus), 24.2.10

Ptolemy (son of Pyrrhus), 18.1.3; defeats Antigonus Gonatas in battle, 25.3.8; dies, 25.4.6ff.

Ptolemy Ceraunus (brother of Ptolemy II), 24.1.1; kills Seleucus, 17.2.4; marries his sister Arsinoë and plots to deprive her of her kingdom and kill her sons, 17.2.7, 24.2f.; aids Pyrrhus, 17.2.14f.; engages in various battles, 24.1; seizes Macedonia, 24.1.8; makes peace with Antiochus, 24.1.8; killed by Gauls, 24.3.10, 24.4.6ff.; his daughter, wife of Pyrrhus, 17.2.15, 24.1.8

Ptolemy II (Philadelphus), successor to his father, 16.2.7; reconciled with his brother Ceraunus, 17.2.9; offers gifts

seizes Macedonia, 25.3.6; his
actions in the Peloponnese,
25.4f.; his death and eulogy,
25.5.1ff.; his disposition,
17.2.12, 25.4.2f.; his wife, the
daughter of Ptolemy Ceraunus, 17.2.15, 24.1.8; his other
wife, daughter of Agathocles,
23.3.3; his sons, 18.1.3; his
daughter, 28.1.1
Pyrrhus II (grandson of the preceding; son of Alexander;
king of Epirus), 28.1.1; dies,
28.3.1
Pythagoras, 20.4

(T. Quinctius) Flamininus (consul 198): defeats Philip,
30.4.8ff.; defeats Nabis,
31.1.6f., 31.3.1

Raetians, 20.5.9
Raetus, 20.5.9
Rea, 43.2.2ff.
Remus, 43.2.7
Rhegium, 4.1.7; people of di-
vided, 4.3.1ff.; under the con-
trol of a tyrant, 21.3.2
Rhodes: taken by Alexander,
11.11.1; struck by an earth-
quake, 30.4.3
Rhodians: complain to Rome
about Philip, 30.3.5, 30.3.8
Rhône (river in Gaul), 43.3.6,
43.3.12
Riphaean Mountains, 2.2.1
Romans: their early history,
43.1ff.; descended from he-
roes of Ilium, 31.8.1; cen-

sured by the Aetolians,
28.2.8ff.; censured by Mithridates, 38.4ff.; their kings,
38.6.7; allies of the Massilians, 43.5.3ff.; helped by the
Massilians, 43.5.9; conquered
by Italian cities, 38.4.12; enter into treaty with Alexander
of Epirus, 12.2.12; are ulti-
mately world rulers, 41.1.1;
do not attack the Scythians,
2.3.5; safeguard the kingdom
of Egypt, 30.2.8, 30.3.3ff.,
31.1.2f.; give Asia to the allies, 31.8.9; demand the surrender of Hannibal, 32.4.3,
32.4.8; give the Jews their independence, 36.3.9; named
as heirs of Asia, 36.4.5; heirs
of Cyrene, 39.5.2; subjugate
Crete and Cilicia, 39.5.3; use
the names Caesar and Augustus, 41.5.8. *For wars see also*
Achaeans; Aetolians; Antiochus; Aristonicus; Hannibal;
Mithridates; Parthians; Perseus; Philip; Pyrrhus; Spaniards; Tarentines
Rome, 44.1.4; founded, 43.3.1,
18.6.9; as judged by Cineas,
18.2.10; captured by Gauls,
6.6.5, 20.5.4, 24.4.2, 28.2.4,
38.4.8, 43.5.8
Romulus (son of Rea and Mars;
grandson of Numitor),
43.2.3ff., 38.6.7; founds
Rome, 41.5.5, 43.2.4ff.
Roxane (wife of Alexander),
13.2.9; Alexander left while

19.2.7ff., 23.2.13; sends embassies to Leonidas' brother, 19.1.9; to Alexander, 12.13.1; to Pyrrhus, 18.2.4, 18.2.11; subject to Dionysius' rule, 20.1.1

Sicyon, 13.5.10

Sidon, 18.3.4f.; King Abdalonymus of, 11.10.8

Simos, 43.3.8

Sinai, Mount, 36.2.14

Siris, 20.2.4, 20.2.10

Sogdiana, twelve cities in founded by Alexander, 12.5.13

Sogdians: on the death of Alexander, allotted to Staganor, 13.4.23; at war with the Bactrians, 41.6.3

Soleus, 13.4.23

Solon, 2.7, 3.2.4

Sophene, 42.3.9

Sophites, 12.8.10

Sophocles, 3.6.12

Sosthenes, 24.5.12ff., 24.6.2

Spain: described, 44.1ff.; islands of, 44.4.14; named after Hispalus, 44.1.2; landed upon by Teucer, 44.3.3; sends embassies to Alexander, 12.13.1; seized by the Carthaginians, 44.5.1ff.; crushed by the Romans, 30.4.8; seized by the Romans, 44.5.7f.; Caesar at war in, 42.5.6ff.

Spaniards: characteristics of, 44.2.1ff.; form an alliance with the Massilians, 43.5.3; make war on the people of

Gades, 44.5.2; wage war against the Carthaginians, 44.5.3ff.; wage war against the Romans, 44.5.7f.; burning for war, 31.3.10

Spargos, 1.4.14

Sparni. *See* Arei

Sparta, pillaged by Athenians, 3.7.5. *See also* Lacedaemon

Spartans. *See* Lacedaemonians

Spina, 20.1.11

Staganor: allotted the Sogdians, 13.4.23; given the Parthian kingdom, 41.4.1

Stasanor, 13.4.22

Statira, 12.10.9

Strato, 18.3.9ff.

Sudracae, 12.9.3

Sulla, 37.1.8

Sun: Persian god to whom horses are sacred, 1.10.5; priestess of, 10.2.4

Suniatus, 20.5.12

Susa, 11.14.9

Susiana, people of, 13.4.14

Sybares, 1.6.2ff., 1.7.1

Sybaris, people of, 20.2.3

Syphax, 38.6.5

Syracusans: oppress the people of Catana, 4.3.4, 4.4.1; construct a fleet, 4.3.5; seek assistance from the Spartans against the Athenians, 4.4.6; defeat the Athenians, 4.5.6; help the Spartans, 5.4.5; wage war with Dionysius the younger, 21.2.4ff.; drive the latter from the city, 21.2.8; drive him out a second time,

INDEX TO THE *PROLOGUES*